Pay, Pack, and Follow

THE STORY OF MY LIFE

by Inglis Fletcher

ILLUSTRATED WITH PHOTOGRAPHS

Henry Holt and Company, New York

82858–0119
Printed in the United States of America

FOR MY HUSBAND
JOHN GEORGE FLETCHER
who shared these adventures
with me.

Foreword

When Mr. Harry Shaw first approached me with the suggestion that I write my autobiography, I said No, emphatically, I could not do it. I did not know anything about that type of writing and didn't intend to learn. He was wise and let the matter drop, until he saw me again. By this time, I had thought it over and wasn't quite so adamant in my refusal. After all, other people had written autobiographies, people no better known than I. Perhaps . . .

And so, eventually, I started.

As the years unfolded from my typewriter, I began to see them in new perspective. The eighteen-eighties and -nineties and the early nineteen hundreds were years of pleasant living in an atmosphere which retained a degree of elegance carried over from Victorian and Edwardian days. We had horses and carriages. Ladies served tea in the afternoon and dressed in imposing "tea gowns" that swept the floor. They wore silks and satins and black lace over colored silk petticoats. Men dressed in frock coats or cutaways in the afternoon and wore high silk or bowler hats. In the evening, they changed to tails and crushed opera toppers.

On New Year's Day the men called at house after house where the ladies were receiving.

Young girls made their debuts at home, standing in line with their mothers at receptions. Young folk went to picnics in "drags" and had coaching parties, or drove about in smart traps. They went to dances in family carriages with their mothers, meeting their escorts at the ballroom. They carried tasseled dance programs, which their escorts filled in with the names of their partners. They danced polkas, schottisches, the two-step, and waltz; sometimes at a "German," they had square or figure dances and occasionally a minuet.

All of this living is gone. Our clothes are streamlined; we hurry about in cars. Going steady, dancing only with one's escort has taken the place of the dance program. Is the new way a gain or a loss? I do not know. I know only that it is different.

Perhaps the stories from my happy childhood will interest people today. Perhaps some of my readers may find appeal in the life my husband and I led in mining camps, where, far from civilization, we made our own entertainment, riding horseback from morning to night, visiting other mines in the West. Still others, perhaps, may enjoy the stories which tell of my research and writing.

So, I have written my autobiography, not the whole story of happenings over the years, but about the people, the places, and the events that led to my development as a writer. From an imaginative child to an historical novelist is a long journey. I hope it will prove not uninteresting, the trail that I followed from Alton, Illinois, through "Pay, Pack, and Follow," to my present writing life at Bandon Plantation.

Bandon Plantation   Inglis Fletcher

PART ONE

Our friends in San Francisco were horrified when, in 1944, I told them that my husband and I were leaving California and moving to North Carolina. "Whoever heard of such a thing!" they exclaimed. "Whoever heard of anyone's giving up California for a place like North Carolina? Why, you will be out of everything!"

"Marines go from El Toro Base to Edenton Base," I ventured.

"Oh, Marines! They don't count; they have to go where they are ordered. But just to go because you want to, under your own steam! Well, it just isn't done. You will be out of the world!"

"I can't imagine your living on a plantation fifteen miles from the nearest town. It isn't normal. I can't think of you anywhere but in your flat in San Francisco, overlooking that magnificent view of the Golden Gate Bridge, Mount Tamalpais, and all of San Francisco Bay."

I answered, "If I live by choice in any city again, it will be San Francisco; but I must go to the source of the Colonial history I am writing about."

Similar opinions were voiced by friends in southern California.

3

Particularly vocal were those who belonged to the P.E.N. Club. "No writers in North Carolina! You know how it is here in Hollywood; we have literary people from all over the world. You will miss our meetings."

Only my sister Jean and her husband, Lloyd Chenoweth, understood why we had made such a drastic decision. They approved of the move. They realized that I had begun to write my Carolina Series of novels after finishing two books with an African background. They understood that when the first Carolina book, *Raleigh's Eden*, led us to Edenton to verify background material, we had been delighted with the "little town on Queen Anne's Creek."

Our decision came about through a telegram from Edenton which arrived soon after we had completed the restoration of an old house in Santa Ana; a Colonial house more than a hundred and fifty years old and sixty-three acres of land were for sale at an incredibly low figure. After some deep and prayerful thinking, we decided to buy Bandon Plantation, Chowan County, fifteen miles north of Edenton.

We had sold most of our furniture but kept a few choice antiques. We made arrangements to ship these pieces, some china, rugs, pictures, and a few "thousand" books, and then we were off, driving across country to our new home.

And in a real sense it *was* home. North Carolina had been the home of my mother's people; my grandfather had been born in Tyrrell County, on the opposite side of Albemarle Sound from Edenton. His father and his father's father, all the way back to 1684, had lived on Albemarle Sound near the mouth of the Scuppernong River. An early Chapman forebear, Richard, had had a shipyard on the sound. (Another Richard Chapman had had a shipyard near Appledore, in Devon, in the days of Queen Elizabeth.)

The move from the West Coast to North Carolina was thus a true homecoming for me. I felt that perhaps there was some truth in the belief that the land always calls to its own.

4

My husband, John Fletcher, liked Carolina country and its people, and since he had retired from mining and from the Standard Oil Company a few years before, he was free to accompany me to the home of my ancestors. John, or Jack as we always call him, was born in Evanston, Illinois. His people were Canadians, one generation away from Scotland. He had no roots in California and was eager for the new venture. Although we were both in our fifties, we were like young people in our excitement as we drove across this vast America.

On the way, we made a game of guessing what Bandon Plantation was like. We recalled an empty house, neglected and sad in its aloneness, set in a grove of oaks, maples, and pines. Both of us vividly remembered from previous visits long streamers of Spanish moss that hung dejectedly from the trees. We remembered, also, the sandy lane that led from the road to the house and continued to the broad sweep of sandy beach and river.

The Chowan River was broad as it passed our place, about two miles wide, a quiet stream of deep water that grew from two Virginia rivers, the Meherrin and the Blackwater, and emptied into Albemarle Sound some twelve miles below the plantation. All this we remembered well. And by consulting the sketch plan that had been sent to us, we found that we had a half mile of river frontage.

All the way across the continent in late September, 1944, we discussed the house and grounds. Finally, we crossed the Roanoke River and the long pocosin (green swamp) on Highway 17 and saw the sign, Chowan County. An hour later we turned into the sandy lane that led to the entrance of Bandon.

Autumn had spread its foliage over the land: brilliant yellows and reds of the sourwood, the gold of sycamores, and the deep red of oaks. The heavy green of pines and junipers made a pattern as gay as an oriental rug.

As we turned into Bandon, a sorry prospect met our eyes. Nothing is sadder than a neglected house which the decades have passed over. Winds and rains had left their mark; the paling fence had tumbled down, a gate was off its hinges. Spanish moss trailing from the trees made me think of a company of widows in black weeds moving along the path.

The house had apparently once been painted yellow but had long since lost its brightness. Strips of iron from the red-painted roof hung over the side. Spikeweeds, grown to four and five feet, covered what had once been a lawn.

The house was two stories high with one-story wings at each end, half hiding tall brick chimneys. As we walked around the house, we saw gallery rails swinging free of dangling posts. Steps had completely rotted away.

A two-story wing projected from the house at the rear, with six windows on each story. The view of the river was obscured by a long, rattletrap building connected with the back gallery by a covered bridge. This was a kitchen which had come into use when the old plantation kitchen a few feet away from the house had been discarded.

There were several dependencies, all in the same sorry state: the plantation schoolhouse, the kitchen, the smokehouse. A latticed summerhouse was half-tumbled down; a small glass structure set against the milkhouse was lying on the ground. The pump house was "modern," not more than fifty years old, but the pump and motor had been taken away. Large barns, stables, carriage house, and woodsheds looked forlorn and neglected.

Jack and I stared at each other. No words were needed and none were used. We walked about the premises. The old fields, garden plots, and orchard were smothered in a young growth of ailanthus trees, the product of seeds dropped by two seventy-foot giants at opposite corners of the yard.

My heart was sinking and Jack wore that dour Scotch look which his face assumes when he is disapproving. He walked away.

Suddenly through a gap in the trees I saw the sparkling Chowan River. I ran to the opening; there it lay, serene and quiet, reflecting the clear blue of the sky. Cypress trees, knee-deep in the water, grew at it's edge. Across the river on the opposite shore were miles and miles of pine trees.

Water birds flew across the surface of the river, white cranes and long-legged herons. An eagle soared lazily overhead. A mockingbird flew into a bush; two cardinals nestled in the gray moss that drooped from a primeval cedar. A rabbit scudded across an open space. A covey of quail scurried through the orchard into dense brush.

The quiet was profound. I thought to myself, This is the spot for writing a book.

When Jack returned from tramping about the place his face still held its grimness. His clothes were rumpled, his trousers a mass of cockleburs, sandspurs, and beggar's-lice.

"Let's go inside," he said. We had no key so we crawled in through a window from the north gallery and opened a door into a side hall. I was sorry not to come into the house through the front door, so that I could get the full effect at a glance, but we entered sideways, crablike.

The first thing that met my eye was a great swinging chandelier of colored glass which hung from the ceiling of the drawing room. It held a nest of swallows which flew out of the inverted bowl, dragging straw after them. The heart pine floor boards and the sills of the six windows were spotted with white bird droppings.

I heard a rumble from Jack. "There are a hundred and thirty-five broken windowpanes. I've been in every room and counted them. There are only three rooms without any fallen plaster, and someone has hammered dozens of nails into the beautiful woodwork of the dining room."

Through the mess and the dirt, I saw the beautiful reeded mantel and overdoor, the wood paneling, and the chair rail. Later, when architects visited us, we were told that this is a perfect Adam room in style and measurements.

The windows were traditional; each had nine panes of ten-by-twelve-inch hand-blown glass. The upstairs windows had nine

7

panes in the upper section and six in the lower. The doors were traditional Spirit doors, with the cross.

All woodwork, in fact all of the building, was heart pine and therefore somewhat impervious to termites and weather, but instead of being polished, the beautifully grained pine had been "marbelized" in hideously ugly shades of brown and yellow.

The halls and three of the rooms on each floor had at least one twenty-foot dimension. End wings were somewhat smaller but would be considered large by modern standards. The halls would make more than adequate living rooms. A "hidden stairway" went straight up from the side of the front door, under a lovely arch. Three other arches in the hall, all graceful, added beauty to the chaste lines of the room.

Eighteenth-century fireplaces stood in each room. Later, Mr. William Perry, architect for the Colonial Williamsburg restoration, told us that three of the mantels dated from 1740, whereas the others were built in 1790. He also told us that Bandon is one of the few Colonial houses in existence that has not been changed from original plans.

The condition of the upstairs was even more discouraging: fallen plaster, swallows' nests, and hundreds and hundreds of dirt dauber nests (the dirt dauber is a species of wasp). We could hear rats and squirrels scurrying between the walls. Almost every door had a corner gnawed off. Everywhere were dirt and plaster dust and the smell of a long closed and neglected house.

We had little to say as we drove on to Greenfield Plantation, where we were to stay with friends, the George Wood family. I could see beauty in the spacious rooms, but my heart sank when I thought of furniture. Aside from many hundreds of pounds of books, rugs, and pictures, I had saved only two pieces, an early English pier table of dark oak, Gothic style, and an enameled Chinese Chippendale tea table.

I was resolved to have only eighteenth-century furniture, but where to find it? My mind was wrestling with furniture when I heard Jack muttering to himself, "A hundred and thirty-five bro-

8

ken windowpanes! A hundred and thirty-five broken window-panes." I said nothing. I was determined not to express my fearful thoughts aloud.

The Woods were waiting for us. Their gracious hospitality, their warm, sincere welcome made us forget our gloom. We sat down to dinner, ten of us, family and friends. Ham from our host's own smokehouse, escalloped oysters, fresh vegetables from their own garden, hot biscuits with jelly, and chess pies for dessert soon removed our depression.

With bounteous food in empty stomachs our spirits rose. Everyone at the table was excited that we had returned to Albemarle, this time to stay. They welcomed with toasts the wanderers who had returned to the home of ancestors. Our arrival created some excitement, but there was more because Bandon was to be restored after long neglect.

We slept well that night, weary from driving and our emotions at seeing our own "home."

Our hospitable friends had the idea of giving a picnic at Bandon and inviting old Edenton associates. Five-foot spikeweeds, snakes in the cellars, and rats in the walls "made no mind." Fifty or more Edenton friends were invited, people whom we had met during previous summers spent in Edenton. The Woods and we drove out early the Sunday morning of the picnic with great baskets of food and beverages. Several colored servants did the heavy work. They cut a space in the weeds large enough for two long tables which soon held fried chicken and cold boiled smoked ham, stuffed eggs, pickles, and preserves. A fire in the great fireplace in the old plantation kitchen with its swinging crane embedded in the brick chimney was ideal for making a huge kettle of coffee.

By one o'clock the driveway was packed with cars, and people were tramping about on tours of discovery. Strangely, many Edentonians had not been to Bandon a single time during the eighteen years it was vacant. Others had driven down the lane to the beach at the old wharf but had not looked at the house. One

9

man told me that he had not been here since steamers used to run from Edenton to Franklin in Virginia, a run taken off many years ago.

People sat on the front stoop and talked about old times. They told about Parson Daniel Earle, who had come here to live in 1754, and about his boys' school in the old schoolhouse in the side yard. Someone spoke about the Parson's son-in-law, Charles Johnson, a Scot who had been a senator during Thomas Jefferson's administration. They believed that Jefferson's influence accounted for the hidden stairway. Jefferson was allergic to stairways.

They spoke of the great hospitality extended when the Johnson family lived at Bandon; of the duel of Dr. Daniel Johnson with an attorney from Hertford, at Bladensburg, Maryland. The doctor was brought home by steamer and landed at Bandon's wharf, and a company of guests had trooped down to meet the steamer only to find not the living man coming home, but his corpse. We learned more about the house and its previous occupants that one day than we have ever learned since.

Our guests tramped about the grounds and down to the river front, a pleasant spot with large shade trees and a sandy beach that extends far out before the water is over the heads of little children. It is the only safe beach in this part of the country; all summer long it is crowded with families.

After walking all about the house, viewing the fallen plaster and general devastation, one of our guests told us that he wouldn't give ten cents for the whole place (a statement that he retracted; a year later he offered twice what we had in the property).

A banker who had helped with the sale said: "It may have been a fine house one day but that day has passed. Besides, under these wartime conditions you won't find workmen to do the repairs. It may be two or three years before you can get a carpenter to work for you." I laughed at this gloomy prediction, but we found later that it had some truth in it.

We went home to Greenfield after watching the sunset on the

broad Chowan, a sight that stirred the heart—a golden river cutting its way between green swamps and high banks.

Arrived at Greenfield, Jack was unusually silent. That night he ran a high temperature. He insists that he had flu, but I have always thought that the house brought on the fever. He stayed in bed for days with his face to the wall, muttering something about broken windowpanes.

The Woods and I fruitlessly scoured the country for workmen. We did find one man who promised to mend the tin roof to keep out winter rain. As I was having a Coke at the drugstore, I boasted about the roofer's promise. A woman who overheard me said, "Mr. P—— talks mighty pretty but he won't come." She spoke the truth; a year later he had not arrived.

It was the same with the plumber. There were bathrooms in the house, but fixtures had been taken out years before. The plumber promised and promised, but it was almost two years before he came to put them in. (I was having a tea party at the time.)

When Jack finally got "off the bed," he started out with renewed vigor to find workmen. He had a little luck and many near misses. He himself would go out to the house and put in windowpanes, and by the time a well rigger had a pump on the back porch, Jack had three rooms almost habitable and we moved in.

Then, after many calls, he finally found a carpenter sitting by his fireside, swapping yarns with a friend. Mr. Hobbs was a delightful old man with a fund of stories about Bandon and the vicinity. He had built one hundred and twenty-five tenant and farm houses in the district. He knew everybody and everything that had gone on along the Virginia Road for decades. He was practically retired, but he promised that as soon as his nineteen-year-old son finished his job plowing for a farmer, they would come over and "hope" us. ("Hope" is Albemarle dialect for "help.") The first structures they built for us were two "little houses," as he called them: one for colored people, one for white.

There was a pump house, but without a motor; hence, no electricity or running water. The nearest power was more than a mile away. It was four years before we had a telephone or lights.

The first person who came to work when he said he would was the man who dug our well and put in a hand pump. Because he had the same name as that of some of my Carolina ancestors, I called him "Cousin." He had a little engine in the back of a Ford roadster; when he reached a certain stage in the operation, he would jump up and stand on the rig while the engine chugged away. I never understood the mechanics involved, but presently we had water.

Cousin was proud of his work. His incredibly blue eyes glowed with pride when he handed me the first glass of water from the new well. It was a symbolic act. He told me he thought it was gravely important to bring water to people. "What could they do without water?" I had never thought of that before. He was even more proud the day he gave me a report on the analysis of the water, a report that had come officially from Raleigh.

"The best water in the county, the very best. Coming as it does through that deep bed of sand, it is as pure as water can be."

That deep bed of sand is good for water, but not for growing things. Tobacco, cotton, and corn all need heavier soil. Peanuts were our best crop.

We didn't care really because we had bought Bandon for a home, not for farming. We had less than twenty acres of cleared land. All the rest was woodland, and eventually we planted many thousands of pine seedlings, some of them now nearly marketable.

In December, 1944, a few days before Christmas, we moved into Bandon. We had a little old wood stove in the kitchen and we put what furniture we had in the dining room except for beds in the master chamber.

Much ceiling plaster was down and split laths showed above our heads. I was certain I could see big rats running about and sat up parts of several nights expecting rodents to fall down on me. Jack got some heavy paper and tacked it over the holes; after that I slept peacefully.

We began to get things done more rapidly after we moved in, but the hospitable Woods continued to protest that we would die of cold in this great barn of a place.

We bought green slab wood from a sawmill for the fireplaces (we have eleven) and later we got some large oak wood. We had candles for light.

We had no cook, but I discovered a colored woman who came in to clean twice a week and do some cooking. I remember that the first time she made a lemon pie she inquired whether she should "put a ring on it." I was puzzled until it occurred to me that she meant meringue.

Soon I collected some kerosene lamps. After a long time we were able to buy a Delco generator and then we had lights. It was not until four years had passed that we had "real" electricity.

Our visitors began coming as soon as we started putting the house in order. On Sundays some twenty or thirty people would come to see how we were progressing. The Davises and the Mc-Mullans and the Congers knew every step we were taking and drove out from Edenton from time to time to encourage us. I am sure they shook their heads over our slow progress and wondered if we would ever make it habitable.

Only "K. B." (Mr. Davis, who had the drugstore as well as information about everything and had suggested to the agent that he offer to sell us the house) knew how long we had been trying to buy a place. He was confident that Bandon would be just right for us.

I learned later that Edenton people did not believe we would stick it out. A great bare house with only a few pieces of furniture was not conducive to pleasant living, especially for people from San Francisco. What they did not know was that we had lived many years in isolated mining camps, in tents and cabins, and that we were accustomed to "make do."

With green wood, great yawning fireplaces, and a tiny cook-stove, we really had a struggle, but we survived and spring came early, to our delight.

13

Jack finally replaced those broken windowpanes, all one hundred and thirty-five of them. Next we had some workmen take away the big kitchen behind the gallery that had shut off the view of the beautiful Chowan from our drawing room windows. They put the building on log rollers and trundled it down beyond the big barn. There, they set it up on piers beside the open stretch of land that lay between the house and River Road.

Later we added two wings to the long room and a kitchen at the back. We were really making progress. For we now had a house for a cook.

Jack plastered the bedroom ceiling; his rough work still remains. I could write a little essay on plaster, the kind we have in the old house. It is almost two inches thick and is held together with hog bristles. The laths on which it clings are of hand-split hickory bound with square iron nails.

The plaster is firm, tough, and heavy. Every once in awhile a great slab of it breaks off and falls to the floor. It sounds like an exploding bomb.

Now we are quite civilized at Bandon. River Road is paved and no longer a sandy path. We have electricity and a measure of heat. We live in comfortable quietude, but the river remains the same —beautiful, serene, almost undisturbed save during the spring run of herring. Then there is great activity; nets and boats and fishermen take over the river and it becomes a thoroughfare for a few weeks. Again it drops back into silence until the young folk take over in the summer and it becomes modern, with power boating, water skiing, swimming, gaiety, and laughter. But it returns to the old quiet in autumn. From Indian canoes on the river to water skiing is a long journey. Between these two lies the long line of history that has given me the background of eleven historical novels.

Since that first rustic picnic at Bandon among the spikeweed and the tall grass there have been many large groups which have breakfasted, lunched, and dined with us. I remember one meal for the Eastern North Carolina Press Association when, according to our cook Bessie, "we fed one hundred and fifty head." We prepared six big peanut-fed hams from our smokehouse, wooden tubs of salad, and large casseroles of my famous Bandon beans (a recipe from Mexico). These beans created a sensation. One newspaper editor confessed that he went back five times to the old kitchen (*circa* 1740) to refill his plate. I was importuned for the recipe, but I always refused. "When you want Bandon beans, come to Bandon," I told them. The beans were written up in half a dozen newspapers, poems were even written about them, but to date I have not divulged the secret.

Many clubs and groups and, occasionally, a busload of school children have been entertained here—the Historical and Literary Society of North Carolina, the North Carolina Society for the Preservation of Antiquities, the D.A.R., the Colonial Dames of America, the Colonial Dames of the Seventeenth Century, the Roanoke-Chowan Group.

The North Carolina Writers had a garden dinner at Bandon which stands out in my mind. The group met in Edenton for three days of the hottest weather I have ever experienced in North Carolina. It was so hot that a number of the men slept out on the Village Green in Edenton trying to catch a breath of air.

We had tables set up on the brick terrace in front of the schoolhouse and on the terrace in the garden. There were almost a hundred guests—writers, families, and friends. They came from as far west as Asheville; as far east as the Outer Banks; and from Virginia and South Carolina.

We had just finished dessert and were having coffee when a sudden, small hurricane came winding up the river. Thunder rolled; the western sky looked like daylight from the almost continuous flashes of lightning.

Everyone rushed for the house as great drops of rain began to fall. Colored servants dashed about gathering up dishes and silver, but they soon retreated to the old kitchen to sit out the storm.

There was a terrific flash of lightning, a blast of thunder, and the lights went out. We groped about for candles. Fortunately we had boxes of them; we had so recently lived by candlelight that we were well prepared.

I was reminded of a comment in Philip Fithian's *Journal* when he described a Christmas dinner before the Revolution at one of the great James River houses: "The dining room was brilliantly illuminated by eighteen candles." Something happens under candlelight, the rhythm of living is changed. Candle glow makes women lovelier, more seductive; men take on more masculinity. Perhaps we revert to times when the chief business of women was to be alluring . . . to men!

That night the storm had its effect not only on the looks of the guests but it added brilliancy to the conversation. We have had many meetings of the North Carolina Writers, at least one gathering every year, but never before or since have I heard them talk so well or so interestingly. I have been to many writers' meetings, in San Francisco, Hollywood, Atlanta, New York, Zurich, Venice, London, Edinburgh, and Glasgow. I have never heard better or more lively talk anywhere than in that candlelight.

I think it was the late Jimmie Street who set things going with a question about the responsibility of the writer to the public. Among those present were Burke Davis, who writes biographies of Southern leaders; his wife, Evangeline, the book critic; William Polk, the ranking political writer of the state who had just finished *Southern Accent* which many critics think the finest interpretation of the South yet written; Ovid Pierce, whose *The Plantation* shows another phase of Southern living, equally important; and Bernice Kelly Harris, noted for her characterization of Southern folk on farms and small villages. Her plays depicting the simple lives of plain people undergird the very foundation of our society.

Then there were Mebane Burgwin, who writes such fine juveniles; Frank Haynes, whose book length poems have a genuine impact on readers; Dr. Jacox, one of the Rockefeller scientists who spent thirty years in India; and David Sticks of *The Graveyard of the Atlantic*. I don't remember whether Jonathan Daniels was at that meeting in the storm. He was probably in Washington as

17

news secretary to President Truman; but a number of the staff of the Raleigh *News and Observer* were there: Margaret Smethurst, the columnist; Charlotte Hilton Green, who knows everything in the world about birds; and Paul Green, the North Carolina Pulitzer playwright.

Sometimes the thunder was so loud that we could not hear the speakers, but the noise deterred them for only a few seconds. I remember that the most lively discussion was based on a writer's integrity and his responsibility to the reader.

Jimmie Street was always vocal about the responsibility of the writer. He was a foe of slick and pretentious writing. He wrote about fundamentals, and his style was straightforward and true. I used to call him "God's Angry Man."

I have often thought that the old house added its share to the success of the evening. In its early days the walls of Bandon had echoed to the voices of men who stood in the top rank of our Founding Fathers: James Iredell, appointed to the Supreme Court by President George Washington; Joseph Hewes, signer of the Declaration of Independence and Secretary of Maritime Affairs (tantamount to our present-day Secretary of the Navy); Dr. Hugh Williamson, physician to General Greene's Southern Army and signer of the Constitution as one of the representatives of North Carolina.

The first Senator for North Carolina, Samuel Johnston of Hayes, later governor of the state, was a frequent visitor to Bandon when the house was owned by Parson Daniel Earle, who named the place for his home in Ireland.

Then there was Stephen Cabarrus, nephew of the great Spanish banker who lived in Paris and who was of such great help to Benjamin Franklin, who had often visited Bandon.

These were Edenton worthies of national importance; they were contemporaries and friends of the Scot, Charles Johnson, who inherited Bandon through Parson Earle's daughter. These Englishmen who came frequently to Bandon must have had many heated discussions before they decided to espouse the side of the revolutionists in the great civil war which we now call the Revolution.

I felt the spirit of those men brooding over us the night of the storm when we were discussing the duty of the writer to hold fast to his integrity. If the writer is not true to his ideals, to whom are we to look for leadership? I think everyone present felt something outside himself for each "spoke better than he could."

Walter Spearman of the Department of Journalism at the University of North Carolina; Richard Walser, professor of English, North Carolina State College; and Elizabeth Coker, the talented novelist who depicts the early history of her South Carolina, all entered into the discussion with zest.

Again I say I think Bandon itself entered into the discussion and dreamed of those days before the Revolution when great men gathered within its hospitable walls and talked of the problems that beset the young country.

Between the meeting of the North Carolina Writers and Edenton's great men of the Revolution stretch almost two hundred years. But the house had weathered all the years between and viewed each passing epoch of history with calmness and serenity.

I am sure we were closer that night to our founding fathers than at any other time until a meeting of the North Carolina chapter of the Society of the Cincinnati. It was then that we entertained descendants of the officers of General Washington's Army who met at the cantonment on the Hudson River in the year 1783 and formed the Society of the Cincinnati. The idea was based on the ancient Roman, Lucius Quinctius Cincinnatus, who twice left his farm to govern his people. When the wars were won, he returned to "his little fields."

These officers of General Washington's Army followed his example: sheathe the sword and set hands to the plow.

The meeting of The Cincinnati at Edenton was of particular interest to me and I was eager to entertain its members. My Revolutionary ancestor, Captain Andrew Inglis, was a charter member; he was present at the cantonment when the Constitution was drawn up. The plan was:

> In remembrance of the vast event, as the mutual friendships which have been formed under the pressure of common danger and in many instances by the blood of the parties, the officers of the American Army do hereby, in the most solemn manner, associate, constitute and confine themselves into one Society of Friends, to endure as long as they shall endure, or any of their eldest male posterity, and in failure thereof, the collabrant branches who may be judged worthy of becoming its supporters and members.
>
> The following principles shall be immutable and form the basis of the Society:
>
> An incessant attention to preserve inviolate, those exalted rights and liberties of human nature, for which they have fought and bled, and without which the high rank of a rational being is a curse instead of a blessing.
>
> An unalterable determination to Promote and Cherish, Between the Respective States that Union and National Honor so essentially necessary to their happiness, for the future dignity of the American Empire.
>
> In order to form funds with which may be respectable, and assist the unfortunate, each officer shall deliver to the treasurer of his State's Society, one month's pay, which shall remain forever to the use of the State Society; the interest only of which, if necessary, to be appropriated to the relief of the unfortunate.

It is not difficult to envisage the meeting of officers of Washington's Army seated about a fire on the shore of the Hudson on a moonlit night. This was a serious moment in their lives. Soon, like Cincinnatus, they would be returning to peacetime ways. They were sad to think of parting with the men who had been their close companions during the dreary years of war.

There were others they would miss; those gallant French officers who had come to their aid: the Marquis de Lafayette, the Count d'Estaing, the Count de Grasse, Viscount de Barras, and the Chevalier de Touche. Count de Rochambeau, the Commander in Chief, and the generals and colonels of the Army were all included in the Society. Baron von Steuben and General Knox waited on His Excellency, General George Washington, with a copy of the Constitution and requested him to honor the Society by placing his name at the head of the list.

This was the beginning; to this day, the body of the Constitution is a guide for the sons of these men. To me its admonitions show, as do many of our public documents, the character of the men who gave us our liberties—how far-sighted they were.

It was the descendants of these men whom we wanted to honor. Edenton was surely the most appropriate spot in North Carolina to hold the Society of the Cincinnati's spring meeting.

Plans were made: a dinner meeting at Greenfield; a luncheon at Bandon; a banquet at Hotel Joseph Hewes; and the wives' dinner at Belvedere, the 1725 plantation home of the Chenoweths, my sister Jean and her husband, Lloyd, who had followed us from California.

Edenton has had a reputation for hospitality since earliest Colonial days. Many young French officers had stayed there during the Revolution, guests of Stephen Cabarrus. They had extolled the beauty of the women and the excellence of the food. We wanted nothing less when the Cincinnati came.

An April day dawned in spring beauty. Yellow daffodils bloomed at the verge of our garden. Fruit trees were laden with blossoms. Young tender green leaves were bursting on maples and elms; the giant fernlike sprays of the ailanthus were silhouetted against a bright blue sky.

Our cook, Bessie, was in her element. She likes nothing so much as to serve "a whole passel" of guests. Her brother John, who fetched wood and tended fires, put on a white coat and directed traffic. Later he would serve drinks.

There was other colored help brought in for the occasion: John's wife, Elizabeth, and Bessie's sister, Dorothy. It was fitting for the whole Sessom family to serve the guests. Their family had been on Bandon since Colonial days, and they belonged to the land through the ancient right of residence.

Uncle Vanderbilt and Aunt Fanny had been invited to "set in the old kitchen," to give veracity to the scene. Down through the years they had taken to their rocking chairs by the huge brick fireplace. Now that age was upon them, they took their ease and watched the guests. I do not know what thoughts passed through their heads; perhaps they thought back to the time when there were five hundred slaves on Bandon. Then the kitchen was a beehive of activity with sweet potatoes roasting in the embers, shoulders of pork browning in the iron Dutch ovens, and golden cornbread baking in the brick oven. The quarters line, where the slaves lived, was only a step away. Children played in front of the cabins. At the close of the day banjos strummed and the Negroes sang the ancient songs of Africa.

But now the old couple rocked and watched the company with dimming, lackluster eyes. Much they had seen and many things remembered. Presently when the guests had departed, they would enjoy the food and perhaps a little tot of rum.

In the garden, Bessie and her helpers set up tables and chairs on the brick terraces that looked on the river. A committee of the D.A.R. came out to supervise the food and see that wineglasses were placed at each sitting. The Cincinnati has a ritual about drink. French wine, Grand Vin Chateau Ferrière, had been sent down from New York; it was a traditional wine for each meeting.

The spring air was soft; it smelled of pines and the fragrance of blossoms. The guests wandered about the old house and the gardens. They examined ancient documents that some of them had brought.

There were almost a hundred guests. The president was from Richmond. There were members from New York and New Jersey, Pennsylvania, Maryland, Virginia, South Carolina, and as far as Louisiana. It was a goodly company.

They ate their food with pleasure and they toasted the early members, those men who fought for the freedom we now enjoy.

What interested me most was that these men whose ancestors had fought in the Revolution were men of substance in their own communities. These inheritors who sat at our tables were themselves carrying on the principles that their ancestors had fought for. It occurred to me that those early men of Edenton who had helped to gain our freedom would have been pleased that day.

I felt a little emotional as I went up the out-of-doors stairway to the dormitory of Parson Earle's old schoolhouse. The president had asked me to talk about the old house and its history. As I stood a little above the seated company, I could look out on the great Chowan River that flowed so gently, holding Bandon in its embrace.

I talked of those first gentlemen adventurers who were brought from Devon, England, by the great naval hero, Sir Richard Grenville; many of the audience were cousins of Sir Richard and of Sir Walter Raleigh. In that first little group of one hundred and eight young men, many were cadets of the old county families of Devon and Cornwall, which had given greatness to Elizabethan England.

The first written word about the spot in which we live was in Richard Hakluyt's great book, *Principall Navigations, Voiages, and Discoveries of the English Nation.* After setting the scene, I went on with my speech:

It was two days before Easter, 1585, that the first English adventurers set foot on the soil of Bandon. Ralph Lane, Sir Walter Raleigh's governor of the colony on Roanoke, described the adventure of his little ships that sailed up the Chowan River for one hundred and twenty miles, seeking gold and pearls:

"In the evening wherefore, [I quoted] about three of the clocke we heard certain Savages call as we thought, Manteo, who was also with me in the boat, whereof we all being very glad, hoping of some friendly conference with them, and making him to answer them, they presently began a song, as we thought, in token of our welcome to them: but Manteo presently betook himself to his piece [gun], and told me that

23

they meant to fight with us which worde was not so soon spoken by him, and the light horsemen ready to put to shoare, but their lighted a volley of their arrowes amongst them in the boat but did no hurt (God be thanked) to any man. Immediately, the other boate lying ready with their shot to skoure the place for our hand weapons to land upon, which was presently done, although the land was very high and steepe, the savages forthwith quitted the shoare, and betooke themselves to flight: we landed and having faire and easily followed for a small time after them, who had wooded themselves we knew not where: the Sunne drawing then towards the setting, and being then assured that the next day if we would pursue them, though we might happen to meet with them, yet wee would be assured to meet with none of their victuall, which we then had good cause to think of; therefore choosing for the company a convenient ground in safetie to lodge in for the night, making a strong corps of guard, and putting out good Centinels, I determined the next morning before the rising of the Sunne to be going back againe, if possibly we might recover the mouth of the river, into the broad sound, which at my first motion I found my whole company ready to assent unto: for they were now come to their dogges porredge (a stew made of their dogs, since they had nothing else to eat) that they had bespoken for themselves if that befell them which did, and I before did mistrust we should hardly escape. The ende was, we came the next day by night 'to the Rivers mouth wherein foure or five miles of the same' having rowed in one day down the current, as much as in foure days we had done against the same: we lodged upon an island where we had nothing in the world to eate but pottage of Sassafras leaves, the like whereof for a meate was never used before as I thinke. The broad sound wee had to passe the next day all fresh and fasting; that day the winde blew so strongly, and the billow so great, that there was no possibilitie of passage without sinking of our boates. This was upon Easter eve, which was fasted very truely. Upon Easter Day in the morning the wind coming very calme, we entered the sound."

Thus it was [I resumed] that white men first set foot on the site of what was later to be known as Bandon Plantation.

Certainly it was either on the property or not far from it, where "the land was very high and steepe" and where the explorers were only a day's rowing to "within foure or five miles of the rivers mouth."

So at Bandon as at Roanoke Island, we belong to Elizabethan England. We come before Jamestown and before Plymouth Rock. We are proud of our ancient heritage.

After the guests had departed I went up to my bedroom to change for dinner. I paused to look out of my window at the sunset over the Chowan. The river was pure gold; the sun was sinking into a dark cloud bank. A heron flew low, and the call of night birds trembled over the still air. The musical voices of the Negroes rose softly. There was laughter as they worked clearing the tables.

My mind turned to the questions that had been asked after I had made my little talk about the Elizabethans who had first discovered the land where Bandon stands. The question that was asked more frequently than any other was not about the Elizabethan adventurers, nor the history of the house, nor the history of Edenton and its great men of the Revolution. It was one question repeated over and over: "How did you happen to write novels? What led to your interest in North Carolina and its history? Why? Why? Why?"

I knew the interest they expressed was not personal. It went beyond that. What makes a novelist, any novelist? Why does anyone turn to writing books?

There has always been immense curiosity about those who put pen to paper. I believe each person thinks, "I could have written a book as good as that one. My life would have been as interesting, as dramatic as the one depicted."

My mind turned inward. Why did I write? What impulse had caused me to turn to the quiet life of the writer? The creative impulse is deeply seated in some people, not in others. Why?

The force of the questions asked that day set me thinking. I knew the creative impulse had always been strong in me. Was there something in the subconscious that was bound to rise to the surface? The Hindus and the Arabs believe that one lives many lives before one reaches nirvana.

I remembered the sand-diviner who read my future as we sat in the sand near the great pyramids: "You have come a long way, Madam. You walk this earth for the last time. Your goal lies directly ahead."

I remembered also, the talk I had with Gertrude Atherton shortly after she had written her book about Greece. She said: "I go to the country about which I am going to write. I lie down on the earth in a quiet spot and I wait. I go again and again, until the earth speaks to me and the past arises in me and I become a part of the land and the people."

I resolved that night that sometime I would write about life as I had experienced it. Perhaps somewhere I would find the answer to why writers write.

To do this I knew I must begin at the beginning, for we are truly a part of the past. Each generation has given something of itself to us. We are as much a part of the past as we are of the future. Living is a continuous story, for no one stands alone. Like Biblical "begats," the life of everyone bears close connection to those who have gone before.

My returning to North Carolina was a call of the blood and the land where my people lived for long generations. The chapters which follow will not be a closely connected story of my life but an account of the places, the events, and the people who have knowingly or unknowingly moved me toward my goal. I am trying to write honestly about "the education of a novelist."

3

When I think back to my childhood my first remembrance is of a river and a wide doorway, with panes of colored glass as a border —varicolored glass that changed the mighty Mississippi from blue to green, to red, or amber. Watching the river on its way to its confluence with the Missouri, a few miles south, was a game to be played alone.

The Mississippi was a placid river flowing from the far north to the Gulf of Mexico; at spring freshet, however, it overflowed its banks and was held in check on the east by high bluffs. On the west it flooded bottom lands for miles, and left behind earth and silt and fertility. It was like the Nile, cutting the country in half and giving riches to the valley.

The Missouri was a wild river from its origin in the tumultuous West and through high mountains and broad prairie lands to its junction, in Missouri State, with the Mississippi. On its way through the western states, it brought yellow clay which dyed the water to an angry, turgid yellow. But at twilight it took on the glow of the setting sun; then it became the golden river of my childhood.

These two rivers served me in lieu of dolls and toys. I think now that the Mississippi, viewed through the colored glass of our doorway, was the source of a young and vivid imagination. Seen through blue glass, the stream was quiet; through green, it reminded me of springtime, the growing season. Yellow was an autumn color, but red was tumult and battle and death; and the Mississippi was a river where battles had been fought by Indians in their long canoes, by Spanish explorers, by French voyageurs, by the English, and, last, by Americans.

The long reaches of quiet rivers and far horizons beyond the flat green land were always before my eyes. They left their imprint on my mind for all the years to come.

Later, high mountains of the West played a part, but a broad expanse of water was the most lasting impression made upon my child's mind. The accounts of the people who followed the rivers were my introduction to history. Strangely, although I have written many books, I have yet to write the rich and romantic story of the rivers that so deeply influenced my childish imagination.

The house where I was born was in Alton, in the Commonwealth of Illinois. It stood on Prospect Street, high above the Mississippi on the bluff that bordered the river on the east.

Hundreds of small craft made their way north and south; canoes and skiffs and barges and steamboats chugged up and down river, to and from New Orleans. My only knowledge of that fabulous city was that each year the scourge of yellow fever visited New Orleans. Many people who lived there fled up river to save their lives. They came north by steamboat, disembarked at Alton, and spread out over the nearby country, towns, and villages. They were called refugees.

We liked it very much when the New Orleans folk came north. They were charming and spoke with love and enthusiasm of their famed city. From their talk I grew familiar with the French Quarter: Jackson Square, with its wonderful great houses bedecked with ironwork grilles on the balconies; the beautiful Cathedral, the Place d'Armes, and the French Market.

I learned about fine restaurants that had no equal in the world, save in faraway Paris. I learned about the Mardi Gras, with its gay parades by day and its balls by night. I heard most, however, about the St. Charles Hotel because the owner came each year to escape the yellow fever. We heard of the hotel's French furniture, red velvet curtains, and gilt-framed mirrors that extended from the high ceilings to the floor, reflecting fine ladies and gallant men. In my mind's eye I could see ladies in silks and satin, with ruffles and bustles and skirts that rippled as they danced on parquet floors.

It was to be many years before I visited New Orleans. By that time, the open sewers that had bordered the streets were gone, and the open canals that brought the virulent fever were closed over. But always, to this day, when I think of New Orleans I think of my childhood and the refugees who gave me images of narrow streets with white houses and overhanging balconies with iron grilles; and fences that only partially hid gardens of exotic beauty, with magnolias, camellias, and hedges of Cape jasmine.

A child's fancy created a dream city, close to fairyland, of cobble-paved streets and crowds in the early morning having coffee at the French Market after a night at a ball, gay with laughter and bright gowns.

The steamers that came up and down the river past Alton were, to me, floating palaces created for gay people. I gave no heed to cargoes, although sometimes when we went aboard to see a family friend, Captain Lysle, I remember seeing Negro stevedores unloading bales of cotton. They, too, were gay folk; they sang and laughed and danced jigs. They wore broad hats and often had a flower stuck over an ear. Their shirts were bright calico; their trousers were cut off below the knees. Some were barefooted, others wore homemade sandals of straw tied around their ankles.

29

They seemed carefree, those Negroes, apparently untouched by economic strain that obliterates the laughter and songs that I remember.

Alton was a real river town. There were many such along the Ohio and the Mississippi where freight, from north to south, was mainly river-borne. We had railroads, too, which puffed and whistled and sent up black smoke below us along the bluff; but it was the golden river that I remember best.

Just below our street was the flour mill belonging to our Uncle David. The boats came down river bringing the harvest of wheat in barges from Minnesota and Iowa and northern Illinois and Missouri. Those were names I knew well.

Our Uncle David and Aunt Anna lived next door to us. Mother would allow me to run over, by myself, to visit. I liked that. They were a family of five boys: two married, two younger ones of sixteen and seventeen, and Cousin Hodie, the middle son. He was a fabulous person who had just returned from school in Heidelberg, Germany. He wore elegant clothes which had been bought in London; he had bowler hats and a silk topper and an opera hat that crushed in and flew open at the touch of a spring.

I longed to play with that hat, but Mother said I was never to touch it. Sometimes, when Cousin Hodie was at the mill, the younger lads dressed up in his clothes and paraded about the house. They never dared to go out on the street, although I am sure they were tempted.

Mother had twinkling hazel eyes and long black hair. When she sat down to brush it, her hair touched the floor. I loved to watch her when, at night, she plaited it in two long braids. In the daytime it was rolled high on top of her head. Sometimes, when I was good, she would let me brush her hair; that is the way I learned to count to twenty-five, counting each stroke aloud.

I was well acquainted with my mother through constant contact. From her I received kisses and love when I was good and the back of a hairbrush when I was bad. I must confess that the hairbrush was in almost daily use.

My father was a stranger who came now and then and always went away early in the morning to catch a train. He was railroading—sometimes in Chicago, sometimes in St. Louis, and sometimes he had a three-day stopover in Alton. It was then that he took me downtown and bought candy, little black chocolate "mice" which I loved.

Sometimes we drove down to see my Grandmother Clark. (My father's name was Maurice Clark.) Grandmother lived in a great red brick house with a mansard roof. Her house was her livelihood, for she "let" rooms. She was a terrifying person with black eyes and a Roman nose, and when we called on her, I sat very quietly in a little maple chair with a cane bottom that had belonged to her and to her mother, also. (I have that chair today, in my bedroom.) She was a severe woman. "One has to be when one is a lone widow," she told us. "There are always folk who want to get the best of a widow." That may have been the truth, but I am certain no one ever got the best of her.

She was left a widow early. Her husband, David, had died of consumption and left her with four little children: Hannah; the twins, Napoleon Bonaparte and Joseph; and Maurice. She had brought them up in the fear of the Lord in heaven, and the ever present fear of Elizabeth Moray Clark on earth. She was a strong Republican and a great admirer of President Lincoln. Whenever a tramp came to the door begging food, she at once inquired about his politics. If he admitted to being a Democrat, she gave him a scathing lecture on his duty to his country. After she got that off her conscience, she had the cook give the now speechless man a piled-up plate of food.

One of the twins died young, and Napoleon Bonaparte became her greatest helper. During the Civil War, trains carrying Northern troops went through Alton. Grandmother Clark conceived the notion of sending Bonaparte down to the railway station to sell little pies to the soldiers. Cherry and apple and custard pies baked by her excellent Negro cook, Drusie, were sold for a nickel. Sometimes our father Maurice, the youngest boy, was allowed to accompany "Boney." He would beat on a little tin pan and cry out, "Pies for sale, cherry, apple, and custard pies and tarts, for a nickel, five cents apiece."

I often heard him say in later years that the proudest moments of his life were those when he went to the railroad station with Boney to sell pies. He remembered vividly the excitement of the trains clanging in the station; soldiers in blue uniforms with heads out of windows, guards marching up and down with muskets in their hands, the engines puffing steam, bells ringing, and the noisy crowds that came down to see the soldiers off to war.

To my father I think war always meant the railway station at Alton; the crowds, the noise, soldiers grasping the pies he held up to them, and the pride he felt when the great basket was empty and the nickels were jingling in Boney's leather pouch. They never left the station until the bell clanged, the conductor cried "All aboard," and the guards urged the stragglers back into the coaches. To cries of "On to Vicksburg!" the train pulled out on its southward journey.

A short time later Boney was in the Army of the North, a drummer boy. His mother raged and wept. She interviewed recruiting officers, claiming that her son was needed for her support, but the officers paid no mind. Drummer boys were needed and so Boney went away, leaving his little brother to peddle the pies alone. Maurice wanted to follow Boney, who in his eyes was a hero.

So my father got someone to put his name on a list. When his name was called, the recruiting officer had to stand up and look over his desk to Maurice Clark. "Little man, what are you doing here?" he said.

"I want to be a drummer boy in the army."

"How old are you?"

"Six, sir."

The recruiter laughed. "Go home to your mother, son. The army ain't that bad off . . . yet," he added as an afterthought.

The small hero ran home in tears. I have heard him say that he was too young for one war and too old for the next. He belonged to those years of peace between the Civil War and World War I, years when life still had values of simplicity and pleasant, leisurely living.

The father of my childhood was a vigorous man, and stern. He was sometimes gay, too, and made jokes with my mother. As long as he lived, he thought Mother was the most beautiful and finest woman in the world. He was proud of her ability as an actress and as a writer. She was in great demand at amateur theatricals. She also wrote little skits, doggerel poems, and children's stories. She had an innate sense of the artistic and creative, but perhaps her greatest asset, aside from her gaiety, was her ability at what we now call conciliation. She could create good feeling between rivals and smooth out differences of opinion. Her sense of humor was superbly quiet and subtle and was always put to use at the right time and place.

But this is an adult appraisal of my mother, not the feeling of my youth. I soon learned, with all the subtlety of childhood, that if I begged enough, I could get my way with Mother. But I never could with my father, the strange man who appeared now and then to disrupt the even tenor of our living.

Not long after my brother, Murray, was born, Father came home one day and announced that we were moving to Bloomington. I have not many memories of that city, which has since become famous as the home of the Adlai Stevenson family.

I do remember a little Italian greyhound named Gideon who trotted about the neighborhood and brought home presents—packages left by delivery boys at the back doors of our neighbors. By the time we received them, they usually contained only bits of meat or perhaps a loaf of bread, half eaten away. Gideon kept my mother and the cook busy looking for owners and making apologies.

One morning he dragged home a whole spring chicken, some-one's Sunday dinner. That was the end of Gideon. I grieved for my little companion and took out my anger on the cats. One I

33

almost killed by squeezing it in the waffle iron. The other I put in the drawer of the sewing machine. It leaped out when my Aunt Louise opened the drawer and sent her screaming down the stairs.

Bloomington meant little to me, yet I remember several other things concerning my life there. One was the "Normal" horse, as I called them. The Normal School was somewhere out beyond us and so was a big farm where beautiful big Normandy horses were raised. These two items were confused in my mind: I thought the horses went to Normal School and must be Normal horses. I remember very well sitting on the post at our front gate to watch the graceful animals go by. They held their heads high and arched their beautiful necks and manes.

My seat on the gatepost provided other pleasures. One day I asked each passerby for a contribution and had collected quite a little fund in my pinafore pocket before Mother discovered the source of my wealth and put an end to my solicitations.

I seemed often to be in difficulty of one kind or another— punching my little brother in the nose, or pulling his fuzzy hair, or trying to poke his eyes. One time, with nothing to amuse me for the moment and with nobody watching, I put my head into a tile umbrella rack in the front hall. That act was almost my undoing, for my head wouldn't come out. I screamed and screamed and brought Mother and Aunt Louise running. It must have been an amazing sight. There I was with my head stuck in the rack, down to my eyes, my little behind with ruffled petticoats and panties sticking up in the air.

They laughed, I'm sure, but the laughter soon turned to anxiety when they couldn't release me. They worked and worked and I screamed and screamed, all the time getting deeper into the tile. Finally, someone thought of the fire department.

Eventually firemen came, laid the rack and me on the floor, and worked to release me. By this time I was down to my poor little nose. At last, someone brought a hammer and broke the rack, very carefully, a bit at a time. When I was pulled out with no damage, save a few scratches, I was put sobbing to bed, where I went promptly to sleep. It is said that I was quite good for two days afterward. To this day, I have a strong aversion to tile umbrella holders.

During the Bloomington era, things were developing in the family of which I have no remembrance. My father was about to go to Canada, a long journey. If the family talked about this momentous decision, I have no recollection. In those days people did not discuss family affairs with children. They put fingers to lips and spelled out words and shook reproving heads whenever a child edged up close and serious affairs were under discussion.

This was a momentous decision for my father. He was going out to the far West of Canada with Sir William Van Horne to help build a railroad, the Canadian Pacific. Already the line was near a town called Winnipeg. My father would be gone months and months, maybe years. But it was a very important thing to build a railroad, and it took men of courage and foresight. My father would be superintendent of a division for Sir William Van Horne.

It was decided that we would all go back to Alton—Mother, little brother Murray, Aunt Louise, and I—while Father climbed into a train and went away to the far West, to his new work. I think that was the only time I ever saw my mother cry, and it made such an impression on me that I howled in sympathy, not knowing why. After all, Father was always coming and going; and Mother would have more time for me and little brother, to whom I still gave a sly pinch now and then to show he was not really welcome.

"He's such a good child, not a bit like this little h-e-l-l-i-o-n." (Spelling out the word.) This was Aunt Louise. Mother said, "She's not really bad, only too full of energy and imagination. She never does a bad thing a second time."

Aunt Louise said dryly, "If you use the hairbrush on her little behind."

35

Mother said, "What can you expect of a child who never crawled, just got up and walked?"

I knew they were talking about me, but I didn't mind. We were going back to Alton. I could run after Aunt Anna and sit quietly beside Uncle David in the library, and hear him talk about the Mexican War and his adventures going to California during the Gold Rush, and when he was a dashing captain of cavalry in the war with the South.

Aunt Anna and Uncle David were not my real aunt and uncle, Mother had explained to me. They were her aunt and uncle. That made them my great-aunt and -uncle. I didn't care what the relationship was, I loved them.

Each morning, Uncle David left for the mill right after breakfast was over. The mill was a wonderful place by the river where flour was ground. There was great confusion with wheels turning and rumbling, machinery squealing and groaning. Everything was covered with a fine coating of flour which rolled between great cylinders over something called silk bolting cloth which cost a lot of money. After a time, little round holes would appear in the cloth. These the head miller would mend with red sealing wax. When there were too many red spots, the bolting silk would be replaced.

Once they gave the great roll of red-spotted silk to me, and Aunt Louise made a little dress out of a clear bit of cloth. I loved that dress. It was trimmed with tiny ruffles, edged with narrow pale blue ribbon. No one else had a dress like that, and I was so proud that I strutted. As a rule, I didn't care what I wore. I was a strong, vigorous child, running, climbing over fences, in and out of briar patches, tearing socks and skirts, forever losing little coats and hair ribbons.

I had no use for dolls. I preferred playing tag or "mumbletypeg" with the neighborhood boys or stirring up bees' nests and killing the poor bees with paddles. Sometimes I caught bumblebees and tied black linen thread around their fat little bodies.

Then I carried them into the house in the pockets of my pinafore and turned them loose on the nearly invisible thread to hear the screams of the ladies of the family or the Negro cook. In other words, I was a tomboy.

There was another side to me, the side that loved to sit with the elders of the family and listen to stories of olden days. Particularly did I love to listen to Uncle David's tales of battles when he rode as captain in the Illinois cavalry. In my imagination I could see him riding a big black horse, slashing at gray uniforms with his great saber that hung now so peacefully over the fireplace.

Once I heard him say to Aunt Anna, "She has the most enormous black eyes I ever saw in a child. I wonder what will happen to her when she grows up?"

"If she don't mend her ways and quit telling those little stories, she'll come to a bad end."

"Not with her imagination!"

At times Aunt Anna and Uncle David would invite a girl relative to live with them, to cheer up the household of great long-legged boys. Cousin Belle was one. She came from up country to go to school for the winter. The lads of the household and their friends took a new interest in the house on Prospect Street, for Cousin Belle was a real beauty.

She resembled my mother greatly, but she lacked Mother's wit. Belle took herself and her looks very seriously. I liked nothing so much as to go to her room when she was dressing and help her pull her corset strings taut. She was as slim as a reed, but it was then the fashion to be even slimmer; a yard of silk ribbon would make two belts for her, she boasted.

She had dark eyes and dark hair which she wore in a knot at the nape of her neck. Sometimes she would pin a bright flower in her hair where the dark roll touched her white neck. She had a number of little fans which she used with telling effect on her numerous swains. I often think now that women lost a certain grace and elegance when they ceased to use fans. Belle told me

37

that fans had a language. I thought she meant that fans talked aloud. I was forever sneaking up on the vine-covered gallery to listen for "fan talk."

One other thing I remember about Cousin Belle: she taught me how to *faint*. Fainting was an important accomplishment of young ladies. She explained that if you looked at an object on the wall for a long time, you could make yourself fall over in a faint. "But never do it," she said, "unless you have a young man's shoulder to fall on. Sometimes when I am playing the piano and a young man is seated beside me, I sway gently in his direction." She laughed, a lovely, light, tinkling laugh. "But don't you try that, child. You are much too young."

But I did try it. I stared for a long time at a picture of Beatrice d'Este that hung on the wall. I tumbled over and hit my head on the brass fender and got a cut. That ended my desire to faint away like a young lady.

Two attachments came out of my early life in Alton that stayed with me the rest of my life: my love for running water and far horizons, and my great interest in battles, as told so vividly by Uncle David.

Father was still away in Canada when my mother decided to give up the house on Prospect Street, next door to Aunt and Uncle, and move to Edwardsville, twelve miles away, to be with her own people, the Chapmans. I was sad to leave, yet there was an excitement in moving.

I didn't want to leave Aunt Anna, who was always doing something kind for people; helping children at the orphanage or working in her church society. She was a forthright woman, tall and angular. In the afternoon she wore a black silk dress that swept the floor and a long gold chain around her neck. Sometimes she went away to Springfield, capital city of Illinois, and stayed while Uncle David sat in the Senate and made laws.

We heard him say that there are a lot of foolish people in the world, but the Good Lord made a few wise ones and they made the laws. Then he would give a great, hearty laugh and say, "For the foolish to break." And Aunt Anna would always say, "Now, David, you know you are not that wise."

One of the last things I remember of Alton was a cruise up the river with one of my cousins, Fletcher Sparks, to see the "Piasa Bird." It was a clear, beautiful day. Fletcher's boat carried fifteen or sixteen people; I sat up with Cousin Flet, who was steering the boat. Sometimes he let me lay my hands on the wheel for a moment. We passed the *Grey Eagle*, a beautiful side-wheeler, all white and gold. It was taking a party up river to Peoria. Captain Lysle, whom we knew well, saluted us with his big, deep ship's whistle, and we answered with a little squeak. The river was alive with boats going up to the twin cities of St. Paul and Minneapolis and southward to Baton Rouge and New Orleans.

I saw my first map that day, a chart, and Cousin Flet pointed out the great Mississippi River, running from the far north to the far south. He pointed out cities on the map: St. Louis, just across from Alton; Cairo, Memphis, Vicksburg, Natchez, New Orleans. To this day cities are to me dots on a map, as they were that day when I first realized the great length of the Mississippi River, draining a vast country as it swept downward to the Gulf of Mexico.

To me, the chart was almost as exciting as looking at the "Piasa Bird" which was painted on the high rocks that rose out of the river. The outline of the great dragon bird was clear on the high palisade. Someone told us the story of this creature that preyed on the Indians, carrying away young maidens to its lair in the rocks and devouring them. I thrilled then to this dreadful story and have never forgotten the impact it made on my childish imagination.

4

A famous professor once advanced the theory that the most highly civilized people are the most adaptable. Following that line of thinking, the child stands pre-eminent. Transferring me from Alton, which was my familiar home, to Edwardsville, which was the home of my mother's family, was accomplished with little or no trouble. A carriage drive of twelve miles for my mother, my little brother, and me—half a day's journey—and we were in the old Chapman Place in Edwardsville, a part of the large, lively, talkative family. There were Grandfather Joseph and Grandmother Rachel (she was a New Yorker from Onondaga County), two uncles, Edward and Joseph, and a confusing number of aunts. It took me some time to untangle them and put the right name to the right person.

Aunt Louise, the tall slim one, I already knew because she had stayed with us in Bloomington. She was artistic; she painted in watercolors and decorated mineral water pottery jugs (from French Lick Springs, in Indiana). The jugs were household ornaments and made excellent Christmas presents for friends who had no such ability.

Aunt Louise had other talents. She could cut out a dress and make it with no help except a picture from *Harper's Bazaar*. She designed clothes for the family and, with the aid of a seamstress who did plain sewing, turned out elegant dresses and hats according to the latest New York or Paris mode. If she had lived today, she might have been a famous designer, except for one drawback, a timidity regarding her own ability. People considered her reserved and snobbish because she held her head high and had a straight back, the result of walking about with a book on her head with one hand across her stomach, the other free swinging. This art of walking, and it was an art, she tried to teach me. But I was at the age to run, and I never acquired her stately carriage.

Louise Chapman was a beautiful woman, elegant, dignified, but remote. In spite of her timidity, she had courage. There is a family story that she and a friend of hers had waved the Confederate flag from a window when Yankee troops marched through the town. Also, she had a stubborn streak and in an argument held on to make her point "till the cows came home."

Aunt Etta was different. She loved people and constantly visited neighbors for morning gossip. She was wonderful with children and couldn't bake enough for us, little cakes and pies or other goodies to delight us. She was a superb horsewoman and rode or drove horses in county fairs. She and her older sister, the beautiful Mary Chapman, "took after" their father, who raised fine trotting horses. Mary died young, but she was kept alive in memory by members of the family who always talked of her as though she had gone away for a little visit and would presently return to the circle.

Then there were Aunt Nellie and Aunt Ada, younger than Mother, and two older sisters, Maria and Jane.

My grandmother's maiden name was Rachel Inglis; her grandfather, Andrew Inglis, had fought in the Revolutionary War as a captain in the Palmer, Massachusetts, troops and as an aide to General Washington in the winter of Valley Forge.

Grandmother Chapman was a typical New Englander who had baked beans and brown bread for Sunday morning breakfast. I remember little else about her, except that once she punished me for some misdeed by snapping her thimble against my forehead. I am sure she was a wise, good woman, plump and efficient, but the snapping thimble is my real recollection of her. How she survived and held domination over her large family (there had been twelve children, ten of whom lived to be adults) I can never tell, but she managed.

The "parlor" was always perfect. The square piano, with its golden design across the front, was never used except on Sunday nights when all the family came "out home" for supper and an evening of gay songs. I remember also great bowls of apples and popcorn, of hickory nuts and walnuts. Cider was the drink for our elders; tall pitchers of milk were set out for the children. We sang Stephen Foster songs: "Nellie Gray," "Old Black Joe," "Old Virginia," and a lovely ballad about an Indian maid and her lover who forever paddled a birchbark canoe in the lake of the Great Dismal Swamp.

My grandfather, Joseph Chapman, was a North Carolinian, born in Tyrrell County not thirty miles from where I now live at Bandon. He was a tall man, six feet four, and thin. All the Chapman men and women were tall, thin folk whom we now refer to as the pioneer type. They were easygoing folk, too, who had time for all the things they wanted to do. They sat long at table because eating was a ceremony. After the food had been removed, they would continue to sit talking, discussing and arguing everything—politics, books, religion. The family had plenty to argue about: my grandfather was a Unitarian; my grandmother and most of the children, Episcopalian. Also, my grandfather was a politician and there was much discussion of politics.

There is a family story about how my grandfather lost his judgeship. The night before election, the town was plastered with posters and broadsides distributed from door to door saying that Joseph Chapman did not need the judgeship—he had been to St. Louis and had bought a bed that cost $750. The posters were well-timed. It was too late to refute the tale and he lost the election. (He won another, later.) The truth was that he had ordered a special bed long enough to accommodate his full length. The bed cost $75.00. It is still at the old Chapman Place where the family has lived for five generations.

I have only one or two personal remembrances of Grandfather Chapman. I do recall being lifted up by him to pet a beautiful black horse with a blue ribbon and rosette on his head strap. Like most Southern men of the period, he loved horses. He had two prize horses, Black Douglass, a great trotting horse that won innumerable blue ribbons wherever he was shown, and a lovely little bay mare called Kitty Clyde. For many years the descendants of these prize trotters were to be found in southern Illinois.

Another recollection I have of my grandfather is of a tall, thin man with gray hair and beard sitting in a big chair, not long before his death. What I remember most vividly was a long blue-veined hand resting on the arm of a chair that was finished with two carved hound's heads. I still have the dressing gown that he wore; it is of flowered black mohair, lined with dark calico.

Other things I know about Grandfather must have been told me by my mother. He was very quiet, courtly in manner. He always got on his feet when a woman entered the room; he opened doors for his wife for fear her hands would be broadened by turning the doorknob. He was devoted to his plump little Yankee wife but he liked to tease her. She never quite understood, for she did not have the sense of humor inherent in the Chapman family.

My mother told me that her father never punished her but once in his life. That was when she, a small child, came running to tell the news she heard in school: "Old Lincoln is dead. Someone shot him. Goody, goody, goody."

He spanked her soundly. "Never say a thing like that again. That is a wicked thing."

"But I thought you didn't like old Lincoln," she cried, bewildered.

"A man can dislike another man's politics and disagree with his opinions but never wish his death." Mother never forgot the punishment or her father's words.

Grandfather was a Southern sympathizer. There were many in Edwardsville; men and women who had come from Virginia, North Carolina, Kentucky, and Tennessee. It behooved them to keep quiet, for Illinois had voted against slavery; but the state of Missouri, across the Mississippi River, a few miles away, was affiliated with the South.

The townsfolk were mostly Southern; tenant farmers, who were German, Swiss, and Czech, were on the Northern side. This was a tragic situation often repeated in border states. Even members of families sometimes held different opinions on the slave question and fought on different sides.

My grandfather did not have to make a decision on this latter question. He had fought in the Blackhawk War and an Indian arrow had pierced his foot near the heel, leaving him with a limp, unfit for soldiering.

He regretted the tragic death of President Lincoln in the same way he regretted the death of Elisha Lovejoy, the great abolitionist. But his belief in the rights of Southerners remained strong and firm, as strong as Grandmother's in the Northern viewpoint.

There was the same family division among Grandfather's brothers; two were in the Army of the North, two in the Confederate Army. Fortunately, they never met during the war. They all came out alive and all with the rank of major. All this I learned long years afterward, when I was grown.

I have rambled away from my story and written oddments

about the Chapmans without setting down my childish reaction to the old Chapman Place, which was my home for a number of years.

Alton had been a hilly town, built in layers like a cake. Edwardsville was in rolling country, comparatively flat to the east and north where it bordered on Illinois prairie land.

My grandfather's home was only four blocks from Courthouse Square, yet it was in the country. The rambling, whitewashed brick house was surrounded by twelve acres of land enclosed in a very high mock orange hedge. The grounds included an orchard, garden, barn lot, stables, two large pastures for horses and cows, and two ponds.

After the restricted area of the Alton house, this was a domain to be explored from early morning until suppertime. A stream (branch we called it) ran through the grounds. It rambled at an angle from the corner on the Hillsboro Road at the front of the grounds and joined a larger stream at the foot of a small hill, separating Chapman land from that of the next neighbor. Two rustic bridges crossed the branch along the path that led to Aunt Jane Hall's house.

A low place, below the rustic bridges, was covered with violets. In the spring, people from miles around, as far away as St. Louis, came to look at the violets. Sometimes, they were not content to peep through the Osage orange hedge but opened the wicket gate and came into the little valley and picked the long-stemmed purple violets to carry off to the city. No one bothered these interlopers. We were taught to look down on city folk, a mannerless group of people who knew no better. The aunts were (without realizing it) following their ancestors, Devon folk who had considered themselves superior to Londoners.

Chapman Place had been built by Mr. Prickett on his return from the Mexican War and it had the look of a Spanish house, surrounded, as it was, by gardens, with the orchard encroaching on the kitchen garden and the wellhead. In truth, the house had been set in a nursery, so that plants and bulbs and trees of all kinds grew under primeval oaks and walnuts and hickories. To the ornamental shrubs, my Carolina grandfather had added trees, bushes, and vines that grew in profusion in his native state.

In the autumn, the splendor of the sourwood, a gum tree of the Carolina pocosins, drew almost as many visitors as the violets of springtime. Hedges of yellow honeysuckle, fragrant and beautiful, divided the gardens; a bright orange trumpet vine grew on the wall of the kitchen and reached the second story. In season, long golden trumpet flowers made a mass of brilliant color against the whitewashed walls.

Years later, when I came to North Carolina, I found that sourwood and sweet gum trees are considered common. Also, farmers grubbed out the trumpet vines from their fields, for they were considered a pest, as was the beautiful yellow honeysuckle. But in faraway Illinois, they were rare and admirable plants.

Even though young, I was not too young to compare Chapman Place with the Alton home of our kin. First, the ceilings were not so high, nor the rooms as large. The furniture was different. In Alton, it had been walnut, carved and ornately Victorian. In Edwardsville, it was old, with the simplicity of Colonial days.

The Chapman hall was narrow, and there was no stairway with a walnut banister that curved and went far up to the third floor. This was a great loss, for I had loved to go to the top, mount the banister cross-legged and ride like the wind down three flights of stairs, to land with a thump at the bottom. This ride had brought me to the front door and the colored glass windows and the Mississippi River.

In Edwardsville there was no river. It was a full twelve miles away. But there were creeks. Cahokia, one of them, rambled through a meadow below Chapman Place. Cahokia is the old name of the town of Edwardsville, when it was Spanish and French and English. Three towns in the Illinois country, Kaskaskia, Cahokia, and Prairie du Rocher, go back many years to the great explorers like La Salle, who made his way down the Mississippi in 1682. These facts came to me, a little at a time, while I was listening to my elders. What a talking family the Chapmans were!

Aunt Etta was the one who knew the family from its origin in Devon down to all branches of the present line. She kept up a correspondence with Cousin This and Cousin That, but I was too young to listen. Now, I wish I had paid more heed.

We laughed when she told us that Sir Walter Raleigh was our kin through his mother, Katherine Campernown. We thought it a wonderful joke. But many years later, when I went to Devon to get material for *Roanoke Hundred*, I found it was true. I found also that there had been a Richard Chapman's shipyard in Appledore since the days of Queen Elizabeth. My great-great-grandfather had had a shipyard in Tyrrell County, North Carolina, before the American Revolution.

But I am rushing ahead through the years. It is difficult not to review scenes of childhood from the viewpoint of an oldster.

Back to the stairway at Chapman Place. It was a "hidden stairway," such as I have described at Bandon. It went up from a little alcove at the end of the long dining room, shut off by a door with an old iron latch.

There were two downstairs bedrooms and a large one over the kitchen for the uncles. The second floor, or attic, had bedrooms also.

When Mother and Baby Brother and I came to live at Chapman Place, several of her sisters were married. Aunt Maria, the eldest, had married George Leverett and lived with their two children, across town, on Piety Hill. Uncle George was an engineer, although most of the other Leveretts were teachers. They were descendants of Sir John Leverett, of the Massachusetts Colony, and his son, the first president of Harvard College. They taught in various colleges, one in the University of Michigan, and Uncle Washington was president of Shurtleff College, in Upper Alton.

Mother's sister, Jane, was married to Harrison Hall, of an old North Carolina family. They had a house on a section of the

47

twelve acres that made up Chapman Place. Uncle Harry was a politico, mayor of the town for years. To my young eyes, he seemed very grand because he wore a frock coat, high boots under his striped trousers, and a high silk hat, the prerogative of a mayor, I supposed.

Aunt Nellie had married a Pennsylvania German named George Fritz. They lived out West in Kansas, and later in the high mountains of Colorado. Aunt Ada, the youngest sister, was away visiting her, I think.

I am wondering now how much of family life I really took part in and remember and how much I know from my mother's stories. Several memories stand out.

Money was never mentioned before children. I am sure there was not much, for Grandfather, with so many to feed out of the meager salary that judges of the period received, couldn't have had much. Mother used to say that he had to buy a pair of shoes a week. At any rate, he had a shoemaker's kit set up on a bench in the brick-floored summer kitchen, where he pegged up the children's shoe soles when they began to flap.

We were taught by the aunts that we were second to none in regard to family background. In Virginia, from 1714 on, the Chapmans had always been gentlemen and ladies. In the past years these two words have gone out of favor, but in my youth they were still in vogue, and one accepted the designation as one's birthright. A lady or a gentleman was equal to any occasion, from meeting a queen to getting a direction from a Negro laundress. Modesty was important, for only second-rate people were purse-proud and assumed airs. I'm not sure but that these now out-moded ideas were basically sound concepts.

We were simple in our tastes. As Brother Murray grew older, we played together, hours on end, with only bits of broken pottery and china. We set up housekeeping among the gnarled roots of oak trees covered with soft green moss, or hunted bees' nests with flat paddles, or played baseball with the boys in the neighborhood. There were no girls.

I loved summertime and summertime storms. Southern Illinois is cyclone country, and whenever a heavy black cloud hung low on the horizon, old ladies of the neighborhood foregathered in the basement of Chapman Place to wait out the storm.

The basement was wonderful, whitewashed brick walls, a brick floor, and a brick platform about two feet wide and equally high running about the whole cellar. This was a fine place to sit and listen to old wives' tales of earlier storms and events.

It was good, also, to use as a base to reach up and get things to eat off the swinging shelves. The potato bin and the apple bin were in one corner, and the jellies and jams of the season were on shelves along the wall. On the brick platform were tall crocks of peach and apple butter and preserves.

If one could slip upstairs and look at the storm cloud from the back porch where the cellar steps were located, one could skip into the pantry and fill one's pockets with crackers to be used to dip into the preserve jars. No one saw this but Aunt Etta and she, always a friend of children, looked the other way.

It was here in the Chapman cellar that I had my first lesson in the history of the county. Names, without facts, stuck in my mind because of their strange, rhythmic beauty. Names like La Salle, De Soto, Marquette, Crèvecoeur, I discovered, were originally the names of exploring Frenchmen and not of the towns with which I was familiar. I found that Silver Creek, where we went hickory nutting each autumn, was called by that name because French voyageurs had found quantities of silver there which they sent home to France.

I heard even more history discussed on Sunday nights when all the married sisters and their families came "home" for supper.

As I have said earlier, the Chapmans were an argumentative family and strong in their opinions. They had the right to state them, and argue for them, but they must never lose their tempers. "When you lose your temper, you lose your argument" was the axiom of Grandfather Joseph. You were taught to be able to argue both sides—your own and the other person's as well. I think this fundamental idea is one of the most valuable I ever learned in my youth: to look at a question dispassionately and to weigh my opponent's opinion. This is a lawyer's point of view, but I think it is essential also to a novelist.

After a time, my father came home from Canada and the Canadian Pacific. He talked about things I could not understand, such as the development of the great West. A magnificent country was being opened up by the railroad they were building. Sir William Van Horne was bringing the people of Canada untold wealth.

The men of the family gathered around the dining-room table where maps were spread out to show the route of the Canadian Pacific, from the East to the Pacific Ocean, over fruitful prairies and high mountains.

My father had been superintendent of a division from Moose Jaw to Winnipeg, which would extend to Banff. But he was through with railroading now. He had signed a contract to sell railroad insurance for the Fidelity and Casualty Company of Chicago. My fears that we would move away from Chapman Place and go to the great city, Chicago, were groundless. Father had a territory from St. Louis to New Orleans and over into Texas, and we would continue to live at home. He would come home every two or three weeks and stay over Sunday.

I liked that, for when he came he always had a gift for me and Murray in his Gladstone. Sometimes he sent us kegs of oysters from the Gulf and many times flowers, gardenias, and once magnolias. The latter smelled of lemons, but when they came, they were not white. They had turned a lovely pale brown. I thought they were beautiful, in their bed of waxy green leaves, but the grownups said, "What a pity! They are so lovely when white." I longed to go to that country where the flowers were so beautiful and where I could see our old friends, the refugees who came up the Mississippi from New Orleans to escape yellow fever.

The attic was my refuge. I could hide there when I had been bad and punishment was impending. I could spend hours looking in trunks and boxes, where the clothes and hats of past years were kept. Then there were hundreds of old fashion books, such as *Harper's Bazaar*. I could carry up Aunt Louise's water colors and paint the ladies of fashion in dazzling hues. A favorite combination was pale green and burnt umber. (I still think it is an interesting combination.)

By crawling out the attic window, I could get on a wide porch which ran beside the windows of Uncles Edward and Joe. They were away in the daytime and I could play there for hours alone. Later, when I was older, it was still a refuge where I could hide and escape chores and read *Leslie's Magazine* and others which were piled high in the cupboards.

From the upstairs porch, I could almost reach my favorite apple tree where I had another retreat in the curve of a great limb where there was a small hole. Here I kept a reserve of salt so that I could eat green apples without howling with tummy ache.

Every day was carefree. I rode old Belle, the carriage horse, bareback, under the guidance of Aunt Etta. She would tell me stories of Aunt Mary, the beautiful Mary Chapman, long dead, who had sat a horse superbly and took many blue ribbons at county fairs. I, too, longed to ride superbly, without clinging to old Belle's mane. I tried this and sat up straight, kicking Belle's fat sides with my heels, holding my arms in the air.

This act was my undoing. Old Belle, annoyed by my thumping heels, trotted off toward the stable. I was delighted, for now I was a rider. Alas, I had forgotten a clothesline, and presently I was dangling from the rope while Belle trotted on, not caring that she had left me behind, hanging in the air, clutching the clothesline.

Aunt Etta helped me down. "That will teach you to watch where you're going, Miss. Never let your attention wander when you are on a horse's back." I little knew how often that advice would be used in years to come, when a horse was my only companion as well as my only transportation in the back country where I lived.

Presently I went to Miss Delphine's school, a sort of kindergarten, where I played through the days with girls, the daughters of my mother's friends. The school was in a long brick building of one story, halfway between Chapman Place and the main street of the town. Every morning, I walked the three blocks down the tree-lined street to the school, feeling very grownup and very important. Here I met the girls I was to have as friends until I married and moved away. We cut out silhouettes from paper, or made boxes from cardboard, or drew fruit on a blackboard. The competition was stiff in a class of twenty children.

I liked Miss Delphine's school. It was fun, there were girls of my age to play with, and so I passed lightly and eagerly from childhood to school age.

The next year came real school. I walked the long blocks to school in the morning, home for a hot lunch, back after lunch, and home at four; from nine o'clock to four, every school day, rain or shine. Mother often told me later that I never *walked* to school. I skipped, I hopped, I danced or ran, but never walked.

Then when I was eight and Murray six, a great change came. Father came home to stay and we moved into a house of our own. There were no more aunts, no uncles, just the Clark family.

A short time after this, in June, my sister Jean was born.

5

If a good fairy offered me one wish, it would be that all boys and girls could spend their early lives in a village or small town. The advantages are manifest: an open life in which the entire village takes part, healthful surroundings, the beauty of the countryside, and a truly democratic spirit.

I think of my days in Alton and Edwardsville with nostalgia. I have lived in many states in the Union, have visted many countries in Europe and Africa, and have observed many ways of living. But for a child, village life still seems to me the most wholesome and happy; a firm, solid foundation of fundamental manners and decent living is laid.

In the United States, country folk are sometimes looked down upon by urbanites. This is not generally true in England or in other European countries. The English people who make up the so-called upper classes live in the country. If they have wealth, they keep a town house in London, or a flat, where they go during certain seasons: for social life, for Parliament, the opera, ballet, or the drama. But their real life is in the country.

In America some pseudo-sophisticates think that rural areas are inhabited by half-educated folk. This is far from the truth. I doubt that city people read more books or hear more music or see more drama than country dwellers. Also, country folk make up for the loss of live theater by the little theater and home drama, by occasional concerts, and by what is now called "country singing."

My mother was an excellent natural actress. She belonged to a group that acted Restoration dramas. I remember when I was a child that she took, with great success, the part of Lady Teazle in *She Stoops to Conquer*.

She was one of a library board of twelve dedicated women who raised money to support the local library (housed above the fire station) by giving plays and operettas, such as Gilbert and Sullivan's *Yolanda* and *The Mikado*.

Our town had a population of no more than seven thousand people, one-fourth of whom were Negroes. The business section centered about Courthouse Square. Built prior to the Civil War, the courthouse was beautiful in its classic simplicity; it has been ruined by later additions to its simple, clean lines. The tree-lined streets were arched tunnels of green in spring and summer.

There was a lower town at the far end of Main Street, with houses that dated back to the town's beginnings. The old court-house was in this section. It was there that young Abe Lincoln pled his cases before Judge Joseph Gillespie.

In an old record book I have found the following item:

Madison County Court. March term, 1855; whereas, contrary to the wishes of a large majority of the people of this county, as the undersigned believes, the majesty of this court at this term, has passed an order to build a court house in the town of Edwardsville, and whereas there is no recourse left to the undersigned but to protest against this order, therefore the undersigned asks that his protest be placed upon the records of this Court.

(Signed) Joseph Chapman

Grandfather was then Clerk of the Court, and that order to build the courthouse in Edwardsville necessitated his removal from Upper Alton to Edwardsville. It was then, or a short time later, that he bought the house and twelve acres in the Hillsboro Road section at the southern end of town.

Here there were many old houses set in large wooded areas and surrounded by white paling fences. They were trim and lovely and "homey," with gardens in which a riot of bushes and plants flowered from spring to autumn.

In early times Southern folk lived in town; Germans from St. Louis were their tenant farmers. Now the farms are owned by descendants of the thrifty Germans, and the Southerners, who lived so pleasantly, so leisurely, have gone. Families have died or moved away, leaving only a handful of old residents and their descendants.

The street on which we lived bisected Hillsboro Road, angling off just beyond the school. I had friends who lived nearby, Nora and Clara Burroughs, and their elder sister, Miss Maude. I thought Miss Maude was the most beautiful creature I had ever seen, but she was too grownup to pay any attention to me. Their father, a judge, had come from the Eastern Shore of Maryland which, of course, became a far-off place of enchantment.

Shortly after I met the family, Miss Maude married a lawyer. It was he who gave me the nickname that I carried for a long time, "Bright Eyes." By this time, I wore my hair, which was straight, almost black, in bangs and the back hair in a bob. Now that cut is called a "page boy," but at that time it was a means of doing away with curlers made of rags, the wearing of which was a torture that beset straight-haired youngsters. I envied girls with blond hair and curls.

About that time, I began to write. I must have been ten or eleven when I turned the fairy tale of Snow White into a play. I worked long and hard over the script. When it was finished, I began casting it. Of course, I was the princess. I remember calling a meeting to read my play. With unaccustomed modesty, I kept quiet after the reading of the play, expecting my friends to be unanimous in saying: "Of course, Minna must play Snow White." Instead, all eight girls cried with one accord: "Irma! She has such beautiful long blond curls. *She* must be the princess."

I rallied. "I'll be the prince," I said. But no one heard me. "Leone will be the prince. She has such long, straight legs and is so tall she will be lovely in tights." Character by character the play was cast, until no one was left but the huntsman who comes in from the forest and kills someone with a wooden sword. Right there, I lost any desire to be an actress. No one even considered me, the author of the play.

Many years later, I had the same feeling of frustration. In Hollywood, writing a scenario, I found that the writer is the least important person in a studio. Anyone from director to actor to stagehand can say what shall be done with the script. The writer is ignored.

From the time of my first literary effort, "Snow White," until today, I have thought that a woman with good blond hair and wide blue eyes can defeat the best efforts of almost any brunette.

I kept on writing stories to the everlasting delight of my mother and my aunts. They all read my stories for the laughs they got from them.

My "novels" all had English settings and were replete with dukes and duchesses in great castles. I remember one heroine who wore a tea gown of white canton flannel. When she fainted, as she often did, she was carried off to hospital in an "amber lunch." Amber lunch became common usage in the family.

About this time my mother began writing children's stories for magazines. Sometimes I was the heroine, and this I did not like at all. Why should anyone else set down things that I said or did! Mother, I thought, had better stick to her verses which she turned out with little effort, witty little verses about people and events she knew. Unfortunately these verses were never kept, and her quick, spicy wit, her turn of a phrase, were all too subtle to repeat or remember.

My little sister did not bother me as Murray did. I didn't try to poke out her eyes, or pinch her to make her cry. I had another technique by then; I ignored her. But if I had to rock her cradle or wheel her pram I did so with short jerks or bounces. Her cries and tears soon released me from an obnoxious task.

Once my father said to me: "There are two kinds of courage; one is that of a person who is afraid but does what needs to be done, in spite of fear. The other is one who hasn't sense enough to be afraid. That is you, my child." I suppose he was right, for I was in and out of trouble most of the time. "Not really bad," the aunts said, "but high spirited, very high spirited."

One exploit that caused a minor sensation in the town was the matter of the pond at the county farm. An old friend of my mother's had married and moved to Denver. Every summer she came back to Edwardsville and brought her daughter Genevieve, who was near my age. Genevieve was very pretty and boasted of her city life. I was envious of such a superior person and took pleasure in leading her into trouble.

Five or six of us girls walked out toward the county farm, the main building of which stood on a slope in a grove of trees, with a little lake at the foot of the hill. We stopped to rest under the trees. Some gathered flowers, others sat on the edge of the lake to watch white swans gliding lazily over the placid water.

Genevieve said to me, "I dare you to go swimming."

I said, "I dare you."

"I said it first."

Never one to ignore a dare, I removed my shoes and stockings and walked into the water. It was not deep, but I stumbled over a root and was submerged. I came up in a moment, my face and hair wet and my new blue percale dress dripping. For a moment I was terrified, for I could not swim.

With accustomed braggadocio, I cried out, "The water is won-

57

derful, come on in." To Genevieve I cried, "I dare you! I dare you! Come in."

Genevieve glanced at my drenched clothes. She slipped off her pretty, embroidery-trimmed dress and laid it carefully on dry grass. In Ferris waist and ruffled panties, she walked in; she, too, sat down in the water. We called to the others to join us. One by one, stripped to waists and drawers, they stepped into the water.

Our splashing and shouting frightened the swans and ducks. They stretched out long necks and, hissing, protested our presence in the quiet lake. At this moment, a group of boys who had been fishing at the far end of the lake arrived on the bank. With whoops of joy, they hung our clothes on bushes. Every time we tried to come out, they drove us back in the water with sticks and little stones, shouting catcalls.

We made so much noise that the superintendent of the home came down the hill to see what was going on. He drove the boys away and ordered us out of the water. The girls, frightened and weeping, put their dresses on over their wet underclothes. Wet from my dress to my skin, I stalked along behind.

All the girls blamed me for their predicament. The next day their mothers wrote notes to my mother about her bad girl who had led their daughters into trouble, and I was in disgrace.

After a few days, Genevieve came to visit me, and I was restored to favor. It was Genevieve who promoted the correspondence that years later led to my marriage with John Fletcher, of Genevieve's home town.

Grammar school to high school was a simple transition because both were in the same building. But studies were not simple for me. I was never a good student. Mathematics and spelling defeated me, but history, English, chemistry, and geography were easy. There were fourteen in my graduation class and I was ranked number ten or eleven. In history or English whenever anyone came to me and said he did not know the lesson for that day, this was a signal for me to ask questions, well-knowing that Mr. Minor, our teacher and school principal, would go off on a tangent. The whole period would be spent in questions and answers, with good marks for all.

I have little recollection of the teachers in high school except for Miss Katie. Miss Katie wore wonderful dresses that she had made at Vandervort's, in St. Louis. Her dresses swept the floor and were lined with rustling taffeta that made a swishing sound when she walked. She also had a method of hitching them up at the side with a hook and eye, like a riding habit. This contrivance kept the skirt from gathering dust from planked floors.

About this time, Father went with the Union Casualty and Surety Company of St. Louis as general manager. His territory comprised Alabama, Mississippi, Arkansas, Louisiana, Tennessee, Kentucky, Missouri, and eastern Texas. He commuted to St. Louis every day along with other Edwardsville men who worked there. It was only twelve miles, but it was an hour and a half's journey to his office. The main line of the Wabash Railway, from Chicago to St. Louis, was some miles from our town and one took a little train called "the Dinky" to the junction. The regular commuters played bridge, going and coming, and sometimes had a rubber finished before the train arrived and landed them in the city, via the Eads Bridge.

Once when there was a cyclone, a train overturned on the bridge. Father was on the train that followed and was delayed half the night. Mother was nearly wild when she had no word from him, for all the telephone lines were out. It was the day following before he got home with a terrible tale of destruction in the city.

We went to St. Louis a few days later to see the wounded and damaged city. I remember little of it, except that nails were driven so far into telephone poles that they showed on the other side. I have never understood the force of wind.

At the time of the cyclone our family and the neighbors sought refuge in the Chapman cellar. We watched the storm clouds and the sky which had turned an awesome green. Great forest oaks crashed down about the house, which fortunately was not hit. I

59

believe that was the great cyclone of the century, but I have little memory of it, except for the peculiar green of the sky.

In recalling events of my high school years, I am reminded again of Miss Katie. Aside from prescribed courses, she taught us good manners and how to conduct ourselves in a ladylike manner under all circumstances.

Of course, Mother and the aunts had told us the same things, but we remembered better when Miss Katie instructed us. She demonstrated the proper way to set a table, how to sit on a chair properly, how to rise, bow, and shake hands. These things I remember to this day, as well as her admonitions to speak when spoken to, to rise when an older person entered the room, and to be kind to the aged and to "inferiors."

We loved to go down to the station to meet the "Dinky" at a quarter of six to greet Father and the other commuters. The street was crowded with surreys with fringe on top, dogcarts, buggies, and other horse-drawn vehicles. It was fun to watch the little engine drawing two passenger cars come around the curve, past the mill pond, and puff up to the station.

Many men lived within walking distance. You could see fathers with their young sons and daughters cross Courthouse Square and start for home. Many of the men whose families had not met them disappeared behind the swinging doors of a saloon for a quick mug of beer.

Cocktails were unknown; the drinks were beer, wine, and whisky. Gin was for Negroes. Wines were on the sideboard and few women drank anything but wine, served with dinner. There was a certain elegance and formality about dinner. It was the meal when Father was home and everyone had leisure to converse.

We children were encouraged to talk at dinner about events at school. Father would discuss larger events of the city and country as gleaned from the St. Louis *Globe-Democrat*. We were often questioned about places and people in the news. If we could not pronounce a word or did not know the city or country mentioned, we were sent at once for an atlas, dictionary, or encyclopedia. Often, the table was covered with books, to the annoyance of Mother, who wanted us to eat our dinner "while it was hot," and to the disgust of Lulu, Tessie, Martha, or whoever was maid of the moment.

I trace my lively interest in research to this early training by my father. He had a remarkable memory; for example, if you asked him how high any given mountain was, he would respond with an immediate answer. He was a wizard in geography too, and knew the location of obscure rivers and cities in faraway countries. My father lived before his time. He would have been wonderful on quiz shows or at working crossword puzzles.

He never ran for public office as Grandfather Chapman did, but the town political bosses used to be closeted with him, seeking advice. He liked to go to political conventions as a delegate or official of some sort, and we still have a boxful of badges of various conventions he attended. Father was a staunch Republican (the Chapmans were Democrats). He bribed me, at an early age, to be a Republican, by buying me little caps such as soldiers wore. Mother remained a staunch Democrat all her life. Nothing Father could ever say changed her loyalty to "the party of the South."

As soon as Father came to Edwardsville to live, he began talking about building a home. He bought a lot in Hillsboro Road, a part of Chapman Place. That suited Mother. Her sister, Jane Hall, lived nearby so that two of the sisters would be living on the old place only a step away from home.

Murray was a tall lad. He grew to be well over six feet, "tall, dark, and handsome." He played football and baseball, and later, in college, was a varsity jumper. He played the guitar very well and joined a group that played at school affairs and clubs.

After we moved into the new house, my little sister, Jean, formed a friendship with a girl who lived up the street in a lovely old red brick house. She and Amy were an annoyance to me, for they had the habit of sitting on the hall stairs and listening to the conversation whenever my boy friends came. They listened and giggled and kept on giggling, to my great embarrassment. No matter how I protested to Mother and begged her to do something, she always answered that Jean had the right to sit on the hall stairs just as I had a right to sit in the parlor. Mother, always strong for the rights of the individual, was a real conciliator.

Between a giggling sister and her chum sitting on the stairs, listening, and Father in the bedroom above, dropping his shoes promptly at ten o'clock, I had a hard time entertaining my boy friends (beaux as they were then called).

I was never a belle or an extraordinarily popular girl about whom the boys hovered. But I was the confidante of many girls and boys because I was a sympathetic listener. At dances, I never lacked for partners because the lads felt they must keep in my good graces. I don't think this could really be called blackmail, but it had the makings.

We had pleasant times going to football games. (I was the mascot of the school team and always had a big bunch of yellow chrysanthemums for every game). Tennis, track meets, and horseback helped to expend our youthful energy. Then there were school dramas and operas to give a tinge of culture. We went to St. Louis for the theater. The first play I ever saw was Palmer Cox's *Brownies*. The second was a Shakespearean play with Julia Marlowe and Edward Sothern as the leads.

One family in the town had a small orchestra. Sisters and brothers played for dances and gave concerts. We looked on the Schwartz family as something apart from ordinary folk.

Houses were furnished, as was Chapman Place, with Colonial furniture, china and silver, brought from Virginia, North Carolina, and Maryland. Other homes had Victorian walnut, some even oak. Mother's choice was Victorian, but as I grew older, I traded with my aunts for old family Colonial pieces. This was my introduction to antiques, the quest for which is still a vital part of my life.

My friends of this period were the children of old Southern families who made up a large part of the town's elect. But many German families were now moving from the farms to town. These thrifty Germans were descendants of the large group of refugees who came to St. Louis after the Kossuth Rebellion. There were old French families, also.

I well remember Carondelet, the French section, where one shopped in the French market and where Parisian French was spoken. South St. Louis was German, famous for its beer gardens, where one could see whole families eating picnic lunches, drinking mugs of beer, and listening to music by German bands.

The long-settled English had no definite characteristics, except those who were descendants of Western pioneers. Later, these three groups became fused into a mighty, commercial city famous for its factories and strong banking institutions.

We often went to the city with Mother on shopping expeditions. To go to big stores like Vandervort's and Barr's to buy spring or fall clothes was a major event. Sometimes we went to the fall expositions in a great barn of a hall, to see manufacturing exhibits and listen to famous bands such as Gilmore's, Prior's, or Sousa's. The last we liked best, for Sousa wrote marches like "High School Cadets" and "Stars and Stripes Forever."

I read books too old for a child, such as Dickens, who defeated me with his exactitude, and Sir Walter Scott. Their works in many volumes were in my grandfather's library, beautifully bound in calf. They were kept in a tall, majestic bookcase with glass doors and a key in the lock.

I was not allowed to take books from the shelf until one of the aunts discovered that I could read intelligently. Scott was my favorite, for even then I was headed toward romance. I still think Scott the greatest historical novelist of all time. No one, to my thinking, has ever approached him. Scott may not always be an accurate historian, but he never forgot that he was writing a story. Even now I reread him with a zest that I do not have for any other historical writer. His landscapes have life; spring, summer, winter, and autum have substance. The countryside of Scotland is before your eyes, but above all, the people are alive.

A neighbor began to take an interest in my reading habits. A retired lawyer who for some reason I did not know never left his house lived in his library among thousands of books. He introduced me to the seventeenth and eighteenth centuries, a thrilling period in literature. I have never really come out of those times except for a brief excursion into the period of the great Elizabeth. Through his library, I became acquainted with Swift, Addison, Johnson, Steele, Richardson, Sheridan, and Congreve. I reveled in the Restoration plays.

Some of my mother's friends were horrified at my extensive reading. Once I heard her reply, "She is too young to understand the things she ought not to understand, and her taste for good writing and good style will be formed." As I have said before, my mother had real wisdom.

To this day I have never held with what I call shock writing. Sex may have a definite reason for being in a story, but not words usually chalked on blank walls.

A Unitarian minister introduced me to the Greeks and thus broadened my reading considerably. When I finally discovered the Middle Ages, I was satisfied, long before I was eighteen, that I had explored all facets of reading!

Miss Sarah was librarian of the small library, above the firehouse, of which Mother was one of the twelve directors. Miss Sarah had a severe manner and quick eyes that we thought could penetrate the stacks. If we got behind the shelves and took down books of which she disapproved for the young, she would walk up behind us and, with a single word, take the book away. "Trash" was her one word, but she always put another book into our empty hands. Instead of a *Tempest and Sunshine*, we would find ourselves reading *The Scarlet Letter* or an Alcott story.

Some years later, Miss Sarah helped me out of a tight spot. I had been asked to a large literary dinner given by the Los Angeles

Public Library. Many famous people were present. I was seated next to Dr. Von Kleinsmid, President of the University of Southern California and Master of Ceremonies. Why I had this honor, I do not know. As the dinner progressed, my companion began to study the list of speakers.

I had thought my talk was to be about novel writing, my usual subject on such occasions. Suddenly, I had an uneasy feeling that something was not right. I leaned over and asked him when I was to speak.

"Directly after my introductory remarks."

Fear really overtook me then. "What am I speaking about?" I asked.

He consulted his program. "The relationship of the library to the public," he answered. "I'll talk about five minutes, then you come. You have twenty minutes."

I was really frightened. What was I to say? My mind went blank. Hundreds of faces were looking in our direction from the dining tables scattered over the large room. I closed my eyes. Suddenly I saw Miss Sarah bearing down on me behind the stacks.

When it came time for me to speak, I got to my feet and told the story of Miss Sarah, the librarian, and her relation to the children of the community—the hundreds and hundreds of young folk she had guided in the direction of good reading. That was, in itself, the relation of the library to the public, through the children.

I think I never had as much applause as I got that night. A day or two later, I had a note from the librarian of the Los Angeles Public Library. It was quite short. It said: "Thank you, and a wreath for Miss Sarah."

There is a small sequel to this story. Some years later, when I was visiting in Edwardsville, a tea was given for me at which Miss Sarah was a guest. She was old then with a wrinkled face and small figure, but she had retained her quick, birdlike movements.

I told the story of "A Wreath for Miss Sarah," thinking to amuse her and the group of friends. When I had finished, I glanced at her. Tears were running down her cheeks.

"I never knew. I never knew! I only wanted to make all of you young people read good books," she said. I put my arms around her frail body; I was near tears myself.

Miss Sarah died shortly after. I have always been glad that I told the story in her hearing. I am sure she then realized how much good she had done for the young people of her town and how they appreciated her guidance and devotion.

Some day I will write a story about the unselfish devotion of librarians and call it "A Wreath for Miss Sarah."

6

After we moved into our new house and Father began commuting to the city, life was a little more complicated. Father left on an early train so that we had a seven-thirty breakfast. When he came downstairs everyone else had to be at the table, fully dressed from the skin out, ready for the day. Breakfast was breakfast; the best meal of the day we were told.

"You have been ten hours without food. You must stoke the furnace," Father would say.

Fruit, porridge (which meant oatmeal cooked slowly on the back of the stove for three or four hours), bacon, eggs, and toast; milk for the children were the usual fare. Sometimes there was sausage or chops or a small steak. Broiled chicken came on Sunday and we had hot bread at every meal every day. A substantial T-bone steak in those glorious, forever past days cost fifteen cents. A farm-fresh fryer was twenty or twenty-five cents.

I didn't like bread crusts and found a little platform on the under side of the dining table where I could hide them. When my ruse was discovered, Father sent me from the table without breakfast. I enjoyed being sent to bed without a meal: I always had a book hidden away and I was certain that Mother, or the cook, would sneak up later with my food.

We had a series of colored cooks. Lulu, for one, brought her own fryers which she had for her breakfast while we ate bacon. Another was Mary who had visions and saw ghosts. She would leave the kitchen and go home whenever the stove lids "riz up." This, to her, meant that one of the dead wanted to have a rendezvous with her in her home. Away she would go, leaving a meal half cooked on the stove.

Then there was Martha who came in as an "extra," to cook or do laundry or to clean. Once Mother sent me to ask Martha to come to help. I did so and added, "if you can get away." (I had been trained from childhood to speak politely to Negro servants.)

"Yes'm, I can come. John's dead, no-count Taylor's in jail, and I's Scot free." (John was her husband and Taylor her son.)

About the time we moved into the new house, Aunt Chaney came up from Citronelle, Alabama. One of Mother's friends had written asking her to find work for Aunt Chaney. "She is a faithful soul. She's old enough to have been a slave before the war, but she is strong and willing. So, Flora, do what you can for her. She's bringing her son and daughter and granddaughter, and all want work."

Aunt Chaney became our cook; her granddaughter, Lillian, prepared vegetables and waited on her grandmother. Aunt Chaney was an indifferent cook, but what she really loved, and did superbly, was the laundry. I can see her now, standing be-side the ironing board as straight as an arrow, running a hot sadiron over ruffled petticoats (five or six we wore at a time, all starched stiff), a mammoth wicker basket piled high with snow white underclothes, smooth and beautiful. Ruffles were crimped on a fluting iron, myriads of tucks without a wrinkle. Aunt Chaney was proud of her work; she never complained about the number of petticoats and little panties she was obliged to wash

68

and iron. "A lady always changes her underclothes at least twice a day; three times if she's going to a party."

In the summer she liked to take off her shoes and heavy stockings and stand barefooted on the cool cement floor of the laundry. She often sang strange songs in some unknown tongue, the words being made by putting her tongue in the roof of her mouth. Years later, when I was in Africa, I heard those strange clicks in Zululand; they are an integral part of the Zulu language.

Aunt Chaney liked to talk about her people. She said she was the daughter of Zulu kings. I am sure she was, although at the time I thought her claim a matter for laughter. She had the black, shiny color and strong features of the Zulu. In Africa I later saw little children walking about with stones on their heads to teach them to balance burdens. I'm sure Aunt Chaney had carried stones on her head because she had such a proud carriage. We used to like to watch her put the great basket filled with fresh, clean-smelling clothes on her head, walk out of the laundry and up the steps to the kitchen, her arms swinging free. Aunt Chaney was a born aristocrat, with great respect for the amenities. She taught us proper manners and deportment. "Little ladies don' do that" was often on her lips.

Aunt Chaney would sometimes take me to camp meeting. These services were held in a grove outside of town. I loved the singing; full, rich, uninhibited Negro voices have no peer in group singing.

It is generally believed in this country that Negro songs derived from their slavery, but this is not true. The native African in his own country has songs: group songs for every occasion, river songs, hunting songs, planting songs, and war songs.

Camp meeting gave the Negroes an opportunity to sing at the tops of their voices. Some of their spirituals are known around the world; others, those more like native African songs, have been all but lost in modern jazz.

Years later, when I was about to be married, I told Jack that he must call on Aunt Chaney and get her permission. By that time she had retired and was living in her neat little house on the hill. My husband often says that seeing her was much harder than asking Father's permission to marry me.

Aunt Chaney approved, eventually we were married, and she came to the wedding. She sat up in front with our families, wearing a new black dress, with a bright-colored silk kerchief around her head. She was proud to be with "her family" and to see me settled in life.

But I am ahead of my story. In my age group, there were only boys in our neighborhood. I helped dig a deep shaft in Aunt Jane's yard, the start of a tunnel under the street into the yard of the Thurneau boys. But we never got as far as tunneling. The boys became angry with me for something and refused to pull me to the surface. I stayed in the shaft for a long time before some passerby heard my screams, let down the bucket, and hauled me to the surface.

The lads were punished, the shaft was filled up, and the project of tunneling under the street was abandoned. The boys were in disgrace with their parents, but I was in disgrace with the boys. I was given what the Chinese call "the living death." No one spoke to me; my companions passed me as if I did not exist. I was excluded from all games.

I was now forced to turn to girls, even though they were not nearby, and that necessity led to the death of the tomboy. From then on, my companions were daughters of my mother's friends, who formed the "gentry" of the town, daughters of bankers, judges, lawyers, doctors, newspaper editors, and other professional men. These people had no particular idea of being exclusive; they were a complete society within themselves.

About this time industry came to Edwardsville. N. O. Nelson moved his coöperative company, which manufactured plumbing and machinery, from St. Louis. On a piece of land just outside of the southern edge of town, called LeClaire after the great

French exponent of the coöperative plan, factories were built. Each worker built and owned his own home.

This was a new idea in living; a planned town with central clubs and community buildings, bowling alleys and tennis courts. Railroads were extended to the factory, stores started up, the population increased. The planned town became a show place to which people from all over the world journeyed. It was indeed quite different from the rambling old town that had grown from seventeenth-century Cahokia to be renamed after the governor, Ninian Edwards.

Nels Nelson soon built his own home, and his wife and daughter, Charlotte, came from St. Louis to live in LeClaire. Another daughter, Julie married to Louis Lawnin, came also, with two children. The advent of the Nelsons added greatly to local society. Charlotte and I became friends, and I often went out to LeClaire to spend the night.

When I was graduated from Edwardsville High School, I wrote a theme entitled "One Life Well Spent," a story of Helen Hunt Jackson's literary career. My own school career may not have been well spent because I had no honors. My only claim to fame was that I finished at the same school my mother had been graduated from some years before, and that fact was mentioned at graduation. It does seem to me now that I should have been able to secure one honor in a class of fourteen, but I didn't. I don't know what became of the honor students. That poses a question: what does become of honor students? I suppose if it had been the fashion to designate the one most likely *not* to succeed I would have had that honor. But I was rewarded, not many years ago, by having the high school yearbook dedicated to me!

Lack of recognition did not weigh too heavily on me because my years in school were gay, full of fun and jollity. What I lacked on the academic side, I made up in laughter, high spirits, and lightheartedness.

The question of college came up. As usual, the entire family

71

entered wholeheartedly into the discussion. Monticello had the most votes. I held out for Northwestern University, where one of my friends was a student. I did not want to go to a girls' school. I thought boys made more interesting companions; Northwestern was coëducational.

I was voted down by my father and went to Washington University in St. Louis, to the art school. I had a slender talent for drawing which Aunt Louise thought should be developed. I entered the School of Fine Arts the autumn after high school graduation. I immediately decided that I would be a sculptor and entered Robert Bringhurst's classes. He was a sculptor of note and an excellent teacher.

Anders Zorn, great Swedish painter and etcher, came to St. Louis to paint a portrait. His was a truly great talent, perhaps I should say genius. He painted magnificently, with sweep and boldness. Often in his portraits he laid on paint with a palette knife. One had to stand far back from his portraits, which at close up seemed to be smudges of brilliant color. Away, they became masterpieces of strong, bold portraiture. Today he is better known for his etchings, but he was a portrait painter of excellence.

Every day or so he would inspect the work of our class. For some reason he took an interest in me and my attempts. He would stand behind me, looking over my shoulder, criticizing my work; talking about various things that had to do with art. I liked the things he said; he seemed to have a bolder, broader concept than any of our other teachers.

One day he asked, "Miss Clark, what will you do? Will you go on working until you know something about drawing and form? Will you work to become an artist, give up other things?"

His question was more penetrating than anything I had ever asked myself. I gave some ambiguous answer, for I hadn't made up my mind.

He shook his head. "Too bad. One must know what one is going to do. Bad as some of your drawing is, there is always something interesting in it. The creative is there, the creative impulse."

He shook his head again and walked away. He still came to stand back of me and criticize, but I think his real interest was gone.

I did not realize then what a great artist he was or know his world-wide reputation. Years later, I saw some of his work in Prince Eugene's collection in his Stockholm castle. Then I knew the true greatness of Anders Zorn.

I went into St. Louis every morning on the train with my father. We arrived almost an hour before time to go to school, so I waited in the beautiful St. Louis station. I sat on a bench upstairs and looked over the rail at the beehive of activity on the main floor below. I was never weary of watching travelers and hearing the sonorous voice of the train announcer calling arrivals and departures.

I often noticed a young man at the cigar counter downstairs. Morning after morning he would be there, looking about, watching crowds, talking to the man behind the counter. Following my habit of making up stories about people, I decided he was a station detective.

He used to glance upward. Eventually he lifted his hat and came up to speak to me. He was tall, broad-shouldered, and very blond. He sat down and began to talk; this, I suppose, would be what we now call a "pickup." He was curious as to why I sat on the bench, morning after morning, at such an early hour.

I soon found that he was a reporter on the St. Louis *Post-Despatch*. The station was his beat; he came day after day to get stories of celebrities.

I had never known a reporter on a big city paper. I have forgotten what his last name was, but I soon called him Bobby, at his request. He was old to me, at least twenty, and through his eyes I saw the great movement of the city and the country passing before us. I decided I must be a reporter on a great paper and write fascinating stories about travelers and celebrities.

Of course, I made no mention of meeting Bobby. My family would have been horrified, and my father would have immediately dragged me away from art school. But that brief contact with

73

a person who wrote stories was my first real contact with the writing game.

I read the evening papers at night, searching for Bobby's stories and felt in close touch with a world which heretofore had been a closed book to me.

But I soon forgot Bobby, for another person entered my life at about this time—John George Fletcher, whom I married some time later.

My Denver friend, Genevieve, while visiting in Edwardsville, had a photograph of a lad who interested me so much that I stole the photograph. After Genevieve returned to Denver, John Fletcher needed a photograph quickly and 'phoned Genevieve, a near neighbor, asking to borrow hers. A search failed to produce it, and she told him that the last time she recalled seeing it was when she showed it to me. He was persistent, asked for my address, and wrote asking to borrow the photo. He never got it, but this was the beginning of a long correspondence. At that time, he was unhappily in love with a girl much older than he was, so that most of his letters were about her and the sadness of life in general.

Many a heart is caught on the rebound, and Jack (his mother and sisters always called him John) had enough curiosity to call me on the telephone when he was passing through St. Louis. (I do not think my reporter friend Bobby saw him at the station, or wrote anything about him.)

Not long after this, Jack went to California to carry on a mining career started in Colorado. On a trip to New York he stopped off to see me. We decided to get married on his return in two weeks.

The haste posed no questions in my mind, but Mother was horrified. The aunts were outraged. "Girls should wait at least a year before taking such a drastic step." But I was determined.

On a beautiful spring day in April, with Cousin Mabel Milmor as maid of honor and my brother, Murray, as best man, we were married in St. Andrew's Church.

The things I remember best: altar vases with sweet smelling

white narcissus arranged by Aunt Etta; Chaney in her new dress and turban; a friend's little dog following us up the aisle.

My sister, Jean, and her chum, Amy, hid in the back of the hack that took us to the junction and annoyed me mightily. (Jean immediately went to the stationer's and ordered new calling cards —Miss Clark, instead of Miss Jean—which indicated that she would now receive at Mother's receptions.)

We left amid rice and tears and laughter. A fast train bore us away to our new life. I little thought that I was moving out of one phase of life into another. But I was to have a thrilling experience, living in a mining camp on the top of a high mountain in California.

My remembrance of Jack's home in Denver, where we stopped for a brief visit on our way to Shasta County, is a kaleidoscopic panorama of snow-capped, mile-high mountains, invigorating climate, and parties and people—hundreds of people, for Jack had lived in Denver since early childhood and had many, many friends.

Girls, and girls, and more girls, came to call on the bride, expressing their "good" wishes: "I never thought Jack would settle down to one girl." "I'd be afraid I couldn't hold him. All the girls love Jack." "How did *you* catch him? I tried for years." "I was sure he would marry Dorothy, even though she *is* years older." "Have you met Valeria, and Ethel, and Rose?" And so it went.

I had one answer for all of them, which I gave with a smile (a little feeble, perhaps): "I'm a good letter writer."

Jack's oldest and best friends from his early mining camp days in Cripple Creek were the Fergusons and an Englishman named Edgar Messiter, or "Steppie," as he was known. Typically English, Steppie made a formal call one evening, talked for a few minutes, then delivered a dinner invitation from the Fergusons, for the following evening.

I learned later, after we had all become good friends, that Steppie had been sent to look me over. If he approved, he was to extend the invitation; if he didn't, he was to ride away.

Steppie was an out-of-doors Englishman, tall and lean and quiet. As I remember him, he seemed to be always on horseback, followed by a half-dozen fox terriers. He reminded me of an English hunting print, and I did learn later that one of his kin, his father or an uncle, had been M.F.H. of The Quorn, the oldest hunt in England.

The big event of our stay in Denver was a visit to the Fletchers' former home on Grant Avenue, a block from the State Capitol. This house was built when Jack's father, Donald Fletcher, counted his wealth in seven figures. The beautiful mansion, constructed of red sandstone from Manitou Springs in the 1880's, was one of the family's early sacrifices to the panic of 1893 that flattened many of Denver's merchants, bankers, and speculators in land.

My father-in-law was Scottish-Canadian. His father was a member of the clan Mac-an-leisdears of Glen Orchy, Scotland. When the clan moved from the glen, the members scattered. Some went to Argyll and founded the Fletcher family of Dunans Castle; others left Scotland entirely, among them Jack's grandfather who established the Canadian branch. Some settled on nearby islands and others went as far off as South Africa. Legend has it that Rob Roy was a member of the Fletcher clan.

Jack's father, Donald Fletcher, had been a Presbyterian minister in Evanston, Illinois, until his health failed and, in 1882, he moved to Denver with his wife, Julia Hay of Ottawa, and their small children, Florence, Ann, and John.

Mr. Fletcher had been a brilliant student at Knox College, Toronto, and Union Seminary, New York. He had mastered seven languages, including Hebrew and Sanskrit, and his thinking was broad and advanced. One would not expect a minister to enter the unknown business world and make a profitable career for himself, but Mr. Fletcher's venture into land development was fabulously successful.

77

The Fletcher house, when we visited it, was owned and used as a club by the Knights of Columbus. The former stables were now an auditorium, with a seating capacity of four hundred or more. In the house itself the third floor, previously the ballroom and servants' quarters, had been converted into a dozen bedrooms. The second floor remained substantially the same—the five family bedrooms with their baths, and a large sitting room opening onto a loggia. On the ground floor were six public rooms, including a large conservatory and a combination billiard room and art gallery. The latter was a one-story, completely fireproof wing.

Donald Fletcher had owned many fine pictures, including several of the French school, a superb Corot being the most valuable. He also had a large collection of Oriental rugs. After the crash, Mrs. Fletcher and Ann lived on the proceeds from the sale of the rugs and pictures. Florence was married, but Ann's years in Paris, where she studied art, were financed by her father's paintings.

Going through the old home was interesting for me, but Jack was depressed by some of the changes. In the large L-shaped reception hall, the beautiful grain in the Flemish oak paneling, which had originally been emphasized by a finish of nine coats of hand-rubbed shellac, was now buried under shiny brown varnish. And both the mahogany woodwork in the drawing room and the cherry in the library had lost their richness under coats of white paint.

But the magnificent view of the Rocky Mountains from Jack's bedroom windows was unaltered. As I looked out over the unbroken vista from Longs Peak to Pikes Peak and beyond, I thought with something of awe of the vision of the man who had been able to see in the flat land surrounding the small city his dream of the future.

Mr. Fletcher had borrowed money to buy unused land, which he subdivided and sold for homesites. Later, while serving (without salary) as president of the Chamber of Commerce, he was able to get the city ordinances amended. These amendments expanded the city boundary lines, prohibited the construction of frame buildings, and required that within five years all wooden buildings be removed beyond the city limits. It is owing to his foresight that Denver is today a city of brick and stone.

His construction of two office buildings in the downtown section marked the beginning of the boom that was to make Denver great. Even the later crash that wrecked business and industry and closed twenty-one of twenty-three banks could not stop the progress of the city.

Denver, like Los Angeles, was built on climate. In Denver, however, business took over and too quickly changed a country town into a metropolitan city. Mr. Fletcher early realized the danger of over-expansion. When the first signs of panic appeared, he was in London, consulting with Baring Brothers, the great London and Paris banking house. His objective was to float a bond issue to pay for the construction of a railroad from Denver, via Salt Lake City, to Sacramento. Years later, this was accomplished by David H. Moffat, the banker who had been instrumental in the building of the Union Pacific branch which runs from Denver to Cheyenne.

Mr. Fletcher was a brilliant man who made and lost two fortunes. When he died in California, medical experts who had known him asked to examine his remarkable brain.

The Fletchers were, and are, scholarly men of wide interests. *Who's Who in America* lists some thirty-nine Fletchers, many of whom have achieved success in the colleges or other professional fields and as business executives.

Ian, *The Fletcher*, of Dunans Castle, Argyllshire, is no exception. Nor is Sir Angus Fletcher, now retired from the British Foreign Service, in which he served for years. During World War II, he was Chief of the British Library of Information in New York. Afterward, he held various consular offices and participated in the work of numerous commissions. He also has a Seat in Westminster Abbey.

And, over the years, I have found that my husband is as true a Scot as though he had been born on the Fletcher lands in Glen Orchy.

79

The Denver visit was brief. I was glad to see the Fletcher home, but most of all, I was glad to see that my husband had no regrets for the loss of the home or the riches. He was interested in his own future, and ours. His future lay in mining. We were eager to start toward it. A few days in San Francisco and we would be on our way.

It was early morning when the Overland Limited set us down at the Oakland pier, from which we would board the San Francisco ferry. I fell in love with this fabulous city built on seven hills the moment I saw it. The sun sparkled against the Ferry Building and danced across office windows. Telegraph Hill, with houses which seemed to cling precariously to its sides, stood out vividly in the morning light.

I knew the early history of the Hill. On its summit, the Forty-Niners had built a station from which to speak to the ships that sailed between Panama and the Golden Gate. The Spanish discovered the Golden Gate in 1769 and since then thousands and thousands of ships have passed safely through the narrow entrance —ships from the Orient, from India, Australia, and Alaska. Two hundred years earlier, on his voyage around the world, Sir Francis Drake is reported to have passed the entrance to San Francisco Bay in a fog. He landed a little farther north, in a small, inconsequential bay which was later named for him.

We saw other hills, that eventful spring morning—Nob Hill and the Twin Peaks (called by the Spaniards, "a woman's breasts"), Rincon Hill, Russian Hill, and the lower hills to the east.

Northward, across the Bay, Mount Tamalpais reached majestically toward the sky. It seemed higher than the mountains of the Continental Divide, for it rose out of the sea to dominate the coastal hills.

The ferry was crowded with commuters from the East Bay cities, but we found seats in the bow and watched the city unfold before us. Jack knew San Francisco and pointed out buildings of interest.

Market Street cut the city in half, from the Ferry Building to Twin Peaks. It is a great broad thoroughfare, wonderful for colorful parades during festivals. San Francisco is a city of festivals. Fiestas, they are called, for the real soul of San Francisco is Spanish. The spirit of the early Conquistadores hovers over her, guarding her as a father guards a loved daughter.

The lure of San Francisco begins when you step on the mainland. Even the "made" land at the Ferry Building entices you as a natural part of her beauty. During the morning she has a cool, sparkling, energetic air. In late afternoon, when the fog rolls in through the Gate, she seems to be vested with mystery. One seeks the origin of her charm but never quite fathoms it.

In later years we lived in San Francisco, but I never felt that I had reached its inner heart; it always evaded me. I came to believe that only the Spanish, sons and daughters of the true settlers, really knew San Francisco.

After three wonderful days we left that loved, fabulous city and journeyed north toward Shasta County and the Mammoth Mine on Bahamatosh Mountain.

We left the Portland sleeper at Redding at six in the morning. We were the only passengers to get off the train. I stood for a moment watching the train pull out of the ugly, forlorn station and looked around at the little town. A few half-awake men leaning against the wall looked at us with sleepy eyes. They wore broadbrimmed felt hats, high laced boots, blue flannel shirts, and corduroy trousers, the trade-mark of mining men.

A bus marked "Golden Eagle" waited beside the platform. Jack went to look after our luggage. Our small bags had been put off several car lengths away; our trunks were even farther up the platform where they had been dropped off the baggage car.

It was early in May, but already, at six o'clock, the sun was hot on the red baked earth. Across the street there was a long, low building, a combination livery stable and stage depot. Jack told me that twenty-six stage lines ran out from Redding to nearby towns and to mining camps in the high hills. A big sign listed the schedule: Old Shasta, Weaverville, Trinity Center, Lassen, Bully Hill, etc.

A stage with six horses drove out of the blackness of the wide open door to the stable, stopped at the entrance to pick up a few passengers, and was on its way. In a moment, another stage followed. A third came dashing out to stop by a foreign-looking man in mining clothes who was standing on the platform beside a mound of luggage. The driver pulled up with a flourish and stopped abruptly just short of the platform. I was reminded of Charley Fish and the stage at Apex, Colorado, and of the tricks of the driver who had as his motto: "Always enter and leave a town with a flourish." It was like the old coaching inns of England, without the drama of the coaching horn.

Jack soon joined me, followed by a porter with our bags. "That was Baron Lagrange," he told me. "He's on his way to Trinity County to visit the Lagrange Mine, the biggest hydraulic mine in the world."

I didn't know what a hydraulic mine was, but I asked no questions. I had earlier discovered that if one kept quiet or didn't make too many inquiries one soon learned things without appearing ignorant.

The bus bounced along the dusty, unpaved streets for a few blocks to the Golden Eagle Hotel. The sleepy night clerk at the desk rang a bell for the porter, but no one answered. After repeated ringing, he said, "I guess he hasn't come in yet. He'll be here by the time you get your breakfast."

The dining room was completely empty. Its bare walls made it seem even larger and more deserted than it was. But Jack, knowing the ways of the hotel, pushed open the swinging doors that led into the kitchen and called out to the cook. I heard the answer, "Why, Mr. Fletcher, you here? I thought you were cavorting on Broadway, New York."

Jack came back to the table, followed by a tall, buxom, bleached-blonde waitress. "This is my wife, Tessie."

"Pleased to meetcha, Miz Fletcher. What'll you have?"

Jack answered for both of us. "Fruit, chocolate, and toast for Mrs. Fletcher. Coffee, eggs, and toast for me."

Tessie returned with canned peaches, burnt toast, and coffee. "Cook say, 'No chocolate.' Cup of tea?"

"Milk will do," I hastened to reply.

"The milk will be canned," Jack told me, "but you might as well get used to it. That's all you will get from now on."

"Oh, I don't mind. You know they make wonderful canned milk at Highland, a town close to Edwardsville. 'Pet Milk,' they call it. It's really good."

Jack's breakfast came. The plate held three fried eggs, a pile of greasy fried potatoes, and a slice of ham. This was followed by a stack of hot cakes. After I saw his food, I couldn't eat. It took me some time to accustom my stomach to mining camp cooking, but I did it and before we left the camp I could eat a regular miner's breakfast, complete with a large "stack of wheats."

In the afternoon, we visited a store that served all the mining camps within a radius of a hundred miles. The walls and floor of the huge warehouse were crowded with things that I had never seen before—miners' supplies, such as dump cars, drills, T-rails, Visalia saddles and bridles and harness of many other kinds, and coils of fuse for setting off the boxes and boxes of dynamite. Dynamite frightened me, but I was told that the sticks were not dangerous until cap and fuse were attached. It took me a long time to get used to the explosive, and I never did feel at ease when the miners put the round sticks of dynamite into the tops of their boots to thaw them out.

Jack ordered groceries and mine supplies for a month, case after case, to be sent up next morning. They would go on the train with us to Kennet. The little mining village was not far up the canyon where the Sacramento River cuts its way through the high, rocky walls.

We were on our way, the last stage of our journey.

The mining world is a thing apart. It offers to man a chance to ful-
fill his dream of work and wealth under the inspiration of far
places. It is a life so far removed from that of the city dweller that
there is no common meeting ground. Only those who work alone,
away from crowds, can share the miner's experiences, such as the
explorer and the cattleman, the timberman, or the army man
stationed in the hinterland of the Far West of the old gold rush
days—Arizona, New Mexico, Colorado, Utah, Montana, Idaho,
Washington, Oregon, and California.

This is a breed of forward-looking men whose lives are not set
in patterns of the old. Each man is a law unto himself. He develops confidence, judgment. He learns the laws of nature, for with
nature is his greatest fight. He has wide vision to match his wide
plains. The man who stands at the door of his mountain cabin and
looks across a valley a hundred miles to snow-capped hills has little time for petty things that plague the town dweller. Miles from
a railroad, in the high hills, he relies on himself and his own in-

genuity. The plumber, the carpenter, the mechanic are not at the end of a telephone.

He usually has no doctor, but he must "make do," under all circumstances. A medicine book, sometimes one that is for the care of horses or mules, is often his only guide. If a mine accident is severe, then the patient must be carried on a crude litter to a railroad or company hospital, sometimes forty or fifty miles away.

But hill men develop self-sufficiency. There are no specialists. Every man or woman must learn to provide for himself. The rule of survival of the fittest is an essential part of life in the mining world. The fight against nature is hard and grim, but surely it is a nobler fight than that of man against man in the city. These men learn the hard way that a man's word is his word and always to be trusted. In my many years in mining camps, I can remember only one scalawag. He sold bogus mining shares, but then many more bogus shares have been sold on stock exchanges of the world.

It was into this world that I was moving, a young girl, wide-eyed and eager to enter into the romantic life of a mining camp.

My husband grew quieter and quieter as the little train chugged up the valley toward the mountains and the canyon of the Sacramento River. Gradually I, too, became silent, for he was obviously concerned about something; perhaps he was thinking of the long weeks ahead and the difficult problems that would arise at the mine.

When after a time he said, "I hope they have cleaned our cabin," I laughed in relief to find that his anxiety had been for me and over such a minor detail.

We were coming to the outskirts of Keswick, a small village which had been built up around the Rothschild's great copper mine and smelter, Mountain Copper. They employed about a thousand men and operated the largest smelter in California, the yearly output running into staggering figures. Except for the miners, the entire staff came from London, from the general manager down to the office clerks.

From our open car window we watched as two men got off the train. They stood beside their many-labeled traveling bags, waiting for a company surrey to take them to the office up the hill. Their clothes were similar to those of the other mining men I had seen, except that they were better tailored. The Bond Street touch was evident, even if one didn't hear the clipped British accent.

As they passed our window, one of them said, "He's in Johannesburg now. There is some sort of a deal on with the American engineer Henry Butters. They say Cecil Rhodes is behind the whole thing." They passed on and I heard no more, but I had a feeling of strangeness, of unreality. Here we were in the mountains of California and people were talking casually about mines in South Africa and that fabulous figure, Cecil Rhodes, the empire builder.

What I did not know at that time was that famous engineers from all over the world would visit us at our mountain mining camps—men to whom China and India, Russia, Korea, South Africa, London, and Paris were as familiar as San Francisco or St. Louis or New York.

The train pulled out and continued its climb up the canyon beside the Sacramento River. The mountainside was a mass of greenery with gay splashes of blue lupine and yellow spring flowers. Above the dense undergrowth, gnarled bushes of red-trunked manzanita were almost covered with clusters of small white flowers. Pine, fir, hemlock, and cedar towered to great heights above the hardwood, as we made our way up the mountain to Bahamatosh on the bare summit.

The Sacramento was wider here, and more quiet; earlier, as it had cut into the canyon it had been narrow, deep, and rushing. Over boulders, it had roared in whirls and eddies.

Kennet was the name of our mining town, and here we left the train. I looked around at the small village clinging to a high bank; it was my first close-up of a copper camp. The prospect was not pleasant. The narrow, unpaved street paralleled the railroad. On one side, rising abruptly into the hill, was a small hotel, a general store, the post office, and two saloons. On the lower side was a long, low, unpainted building with many doors, all of them now opened to the street and each occupied by a woman in one of various stages of undress.

Jack told me that the rooms in the building were called "cribs" and the occupants were "ladies of the night," who dispensed their favors to the miners when they came down from the hills on payday. Some of the women lived there, others came up from Redding and Red Bluff just to take care of the brisk payday trade. Some were young and pretty, some were old and raddled hags; but as the saying has it, "All cats are black in the dark."

Next to the cribs was a row of saloons and dance halls. We arrived early in the morning so there were no sounds of gaiety or music, and since it was not payday, even the saloons were deserted.

Only a few itinerant miners, with their load of blankets, sat on the wooden sidewalk, waiting to get a ride to outlying mines or to catch a mine foreman or superintendent to ask for a job. If they weren't lucky enough to get a ride to their mine, they would eventually shoulder their blanket rolls and set out to walk the five miles, a thousand foot climb, to the Shasta King, Trinity, Balakalala, or Mammoth.

Jack was superintendent of the Mammoth. It belonged to a development company with headquarters in Boston.

We went up the hill to the hotel, a frame building with a gallery. We walked through the barroom to the office, where Mr. G., an old man with kindly, twinkling eyes, greeted us with enthusiasm. He clasped my hand with both of his and announced that I had "got a fine man, one of the best, the very best." He called to an old, decrepit porter, who smelled strongly of liquor. "Take Mr. and Mrs. Fletcher to the best room in the house," and, turning to me, "A kind of bridal chamber," he said.

About this time there was a heavy thumping on the floor above. The landlord hastened away, explaining, "It's Mrs. G. She'll be wanting something. I must run."

The best room in the house was a sorry place, boarded in pine. There was a double bed that sagged in the middle, two plain kitchen chairs, a bureau, and a washstand with a china bowl and pitcher. A slop bowl stood at one side.

Jack said, "The facilities are out back," and that was my introduction to the necessary houses on the hillside. I was later to meet up with all sorts and conditions of these little houses, some loosely extended over a rushing stream, some snugly built of planks. For the most part, however, they followed an accepted pattern in design—a seat, four poles around which burlap sacks had been sewn together and stretched, with the top open to the sky and the elements. I've been rained on many times, even hailed on in a heavy thunderstorm. Eagles have flown over me, and once a grouse in flight fell in upon me. I could write a tale on necessary houses!

"The best room in the house" had two windows overlooking the main street, in particular "Slim Warren's Square Deal Saloon." The most exciting thing in the room was a large painting which took up most of the wall space on one side. Brilliant in color, it pictured a straggling village at the foot of a mountain. The sky was red, the village was red, and so was the mountain. I at once titled it, "Vesuvius In Eruption." That name stuck. For years, whenever we met people who had been in Kennet, the first question we asked was always, "Did you have the Vesuvius room?"

Mrs. G., the landlady, came to welcome us. She was short and stout, with very black hair and snapping black eyes. She informed us that she had painted the picture. "My dear, I told Mr. G. to put you in this room with my very first painting."

After this, she looked me over, and said, "I can see that you are a city girl who knows nothing about mining camps. You won't last long." After this pronouncement, she departed, her walking stick tapping on the uncarpeted hall boards.

I glanced at Jack. There was a look of such dismay on his face that I burst out laughing. He pulled up a chair and sat down beside me. He took my hand. I could see that he was troubled by the woman's words.

"Maybe I have made a mistake, not telling you more about life in a mining camp."

"But I have been in a mining camp, in Colorado. Remember?"

"I remember, but that is not the same thing. Apex is a mining town with houses, real homes."

I brightened. "Oh, we're going to live in a tent. I've always longed to camp out in a tent in the mountains."

He brushed that aside. "We've got cabins, but they are shakes and logs. It isn't that. I don't know whether you will like it, so far away from everything. It's very primitive."

"But you live there," I said.

"A man's different. He doesn't mind a rugged life. Maybe you had better stay here, or at Redding. I could come down once or twice a week."

I was indignant. "I can be just as rugged as a man. Aren't there any women living in mining camps?"

"Of course, but they are the established camps, where they have good houses, not an undeveloped mine like ours."

"Isn't there a woman in your camp?"

"Only a cook."

"Well, she stays there, why can't I? If you think I am going down to Redding and stay at the Golden Eagle or sit here looking at Vesuvius erupting, you are really mistaken. Anyway, how could we pay for a hotel on ninety a month?"

I was so emphatic that Jack's face lost its look of deep gloom. When he smiled I said, "I have a confession to make. I don't know much about cooking, but I can make wonderful salads." Then I added, "You know our cook didn't like us to mess around in her kitchen."

He laughed. "You won't have to cook. We will eat at the mess."

"With the miners?"

"I'm afraid so. There are only ten of them. I don't think we should eat later. It would make more work for the cook."

"When do we leave for the mine?"

"In the morning. I've got a pack train to take up the mining supplies and the stuff we bought in San Francisco and some groceries. I've an extra mule to carry our bags."

"But my trunks aren't here! How can we go without my trunks?"

"The livery stable man has orders to bring them up. I've given him the checks."

"But our wedding presents? There are two barrels and a big wooden box!"

"They will all come along in a few days."

I had to be satisfied with that. I wouldn't have started off so blithely for the mine the next morning had I known that the big box, the two barrels, and the trunks would be dumped down beside a roaring mountain stream and remain there (sheltered only by a tarpaulin) for three weeks before the freshet subsided and the packer could cross the stream. In the meantime, my silver and my china and my Paris dresses sat in the mud at the edge of Kennet Creek.

But this I did not know that lovely May morning when we mounted our horses and rode off to the mine on the first leg of my great adventure in mining life. This was the beginning of "Pay, Pack, and Follow," which I was to learn was an integral part of the life of a woman in the mining world.

It took us more than two hours to reach the mine, up a narrow, winding trail which led through acres of wildflowers and flowering bushes into a forest of tall pines and firs. As we rode that narrow trail, zigzagging through bushes and trees, I was dazzled by wild beauty. At times we meandered through a leafy tunnel, green and mysterious; at others we were in the open, twisting around and over great outcrops of rock, with glimpses of the valley below. As we climbed toward the ridge, we paused by a little stream to let our horses drink and rest.

We walked out to a rocky point and looked over the valley. On the other side, snow-capped Mount Lassen, the live volcano, rose high above. A streamer of smoke trailed across its white summit.

Jack took me by the shoulders and turned me toward the northeast. I caught my breath in ecstasy. There, before my eyes, was the great white cone of the giant, Mount Shasta, cutting upward through the clear blue sky. It stood regal and alone, not a peak lifting its head above its fellows in a range but a mighty mountain rising straight from the floor of the valley. We could see its wide platform of false summit lying below the proud cone of the real summit which lifts its snow-crested head over fourteen thousand feet above the plains.

I have seen mountains in many parts of the world—the panorama of the Alps from the balcony of the Dolder Grand in Zurich, Switzerland; the terrifying, blood-red Drakensbergs in South Africa; the summit of the Canadian Rockies; the Cuillins in Scotland, rugged and craggy; Mount Kenya rising out of the plains; and Kilimanjaro, the wonderful, the mysterious, heaving its great bulk toward the sun—but never have I felt the excitement that I experienced when I first saw Shasta standing out against a cerulean sky, alone above the world.

I have no idea how long I stood clutching Jack's arm, filling my eyes and my soul with the mountain's unearthly beauty. Jack, too, was silent. He was happy that I felt the spell of the mountains that were so much a part of his life.

Born on a lowland river, I only now began to comprehend the lure of the hills. I think it was at that moment that the mountains took hold of me, and I have been in their thrall ever since.

We mounted our horses and rode on in silence. When we stopped to rest the horses again, Jack pointed down the narrow trail. My eye followed the winding path. From far below, I heard the faint tinkle of the lead pack animal's bell and saw the packer and his mules moving slowly up the steep path.

Presently we were in an open space, and Jack pointed to a hollow, filled with round stones. "This is where the rattlesnakes live. I've seen a dozen lying in the sun."

I kicked my horse's ribs and hurried by. Not only did I loathe snakes, I feared them.

We crossed the ridge and followed the trail downhill. Soon glorious Mount Shasta was lost to view. We entered the wooded slope of the canyon and approached Mammoth Creek. We were close to Bahamatosh Mountain now, almost at the foot of it. We could look upward and see where the timber line ended. This giant outcrop had broken out of the mountain side many thousands of years ago. It might have been a great eruption that poured rocks and boulders out of the depths. Some geologists claim that the country from the coast to the Sierras was once the bottom of the ocean from which the high peaks rose as islands.

The mine was on the side of Bahamatosh Mountain, beyond a ridge and now out of sight, but below us we could see the camp where we were to live—a little cluster of six or seven cabins, clinging to the hillside, with a narrow platform of bare earth in front of each, just wide enough for benches and rustic chairs. A small stream ran directly through the camp and emptied into Mammoth Creek hundreds of feet below. A gust of wind blew up the canyon, carrying the pungent fragrance of pines and the scent of wild flowers.

"The wind blows up the canyon in daytime, and down at night," Jack told me, as we rode in single file down the narrow, rocky trail.

"Which is our cabin?" I asked, as we drew near.

"The middle one, between the men's bunkhouse and the cook-and mess-cabin." It looked very small from the distance, but I noticed there was a wider earth platform before it—large enough perhaps for one to have a small spot for flowers.

"How many rooms?" I asked.

"One. But it's a big one."

A woman came out of the cookhouse and stood looking up at us, her hand shading her eyes. Suddenly she started walking swiftly up the hill toward our cabin.

A few minutes later Jack called to her, "Well, here we are, Mrs. Thomas. This is my wife. Is our cabin ready?"

The woman, a thin, pioneer type with red hair, said, "We didn't know you was acomin', Mr. Fletcher."

"I sent a letter from Denver and a telegram from San Francisco."

"No one's been to Kennet. We haven't had mail for two weeks. I'll hurry and take my chickens out. One of the night shift men will help me clean up."

I heard Jack swear under his breath. I glanced through the door. A cock strutted about and several cackling hens were pecking at some grain that had been scattered on the floor. Jack did not look at me. He was off his horse and striding into the house.

"Get those damn fowls out of here, quick."

"Yes, sir. I will, sir."

If Jack had looked at me, he would have seen that I was choking with laughter. What a home-coming for the bride!

We were clearing out the last evidence of chicken occupancy. The walls had been brushed down and the floor scrubbed with lye and many buckets of creek water, when we heard the tinkling bell of the pack train. It had crossed the ridge and started down the hill.

First came the old gray bell mare (pack mules are traditionally led by a gray mare with a tinkling bell). Next came a black mule with a double bed box mattress lashed across the pack saddle.

The two men of the night shift who had been scrubbing out leaned on their brooms to watch the descent. It was a ridiculous sight, the poor little mule completely obscured by the bed, which was scraping against bushes and brambles as it tilted from side to side.

The men laughed hilariously. One of them said, "It's a good thing the packer didn't use Old Nig to carry that bed. He surely would have rolled on his back and got the whole thing off down the mountain."

By the time the pack train reached our cabin, the floor was

clean and still slightly wet, but not too wet to set up the bed on four wooden cracker boxes. Although I knew little of "hand work," as Aunt Chaney used to call it, for it had always been done for me, I worked hard that day, and by dinnertime we had the washbowl and ewer unpacked, a Scottish plaid over the bed, and a small wood stove set up, for the nights were cold at that altitude. Folding steamer chairs and two wooden kitchen chairs finished us off.

Later, we covered the walls and ceiling with green denim and the floor with Japanese matting. One of the Fletchers' Oriental rugs, a genuine museum piece, added a touch of elegance to the simple mountain cabin. Paintings and prints added color. We had a room that was talked about from Redding to the Bully Hill Mine and at every other mining camp in the region.

But that first day we had fun. Jack grumbled a bit about the cook and her chickens, but I laughed it off. Cleaning the floor with a hoe had been wearisome, but how was one to scrape off chicken droppings except with a shovel or hoe?

I was too tired to go to the mess hall for dinner that night but had a cup of tea in the cabin, boiling the water in our chafing dish.

Night descends early in the mountains, especially in a canyon. For a long time after it was quite dark on our hillside we could see bright sunshine on the summit of Bahamatosh. At dusk, we walked up to the ridge. The snowy crest of Mt. Shasta was blood red in the light of the setting sun. A little walk up to the ridge to watch the sun go down soon became a daily habit with us.

The mountains at night become a different world. The noises of the day are many and varied, but the night has its own special sounds. Owls hoot mournfully in the trees, nightjars fly about, bats whirl through the air, and the small, plaintive call of quail and grouse break the stillness. Somewhere in the distance, a fox barks. The cry of the mountain lion, like the cry of a suffering child, penetrates to one's very depths.

I shall digress a moment to speak of these animals of terror,

95

the mountain lions, for whenever I think of the night sounds in the mountains, the cries of these despicable creatures come to mind first.

Once Jack was trapped in a mountain cabin in a heavy blizzard with a mountain lion prowling around and around the cabin, waiting. And he had no gun. Fortunately, his companions on the trail were able to kill the beast, but I can never think of his frightful experience without a shudder.

One hears many tales of their craftiness, following men on horseback, jumping from limb to limb, waiting to pounce on the traveler when he comes to a tree-covered turn in the trail. They hamstring the horse and tear the rider to ribbons. Most wild creatures face their enemies and fight, but mountain lions track and trail, waiting for a chance to jump the victim in the dark. They attack deer and smaller game in the same way. They can easily kill a doe, but sometimes a buck will trample and gore a mountain lion with his razor-sharp hooves and pointed horns.

Some years later, in Africa, I saw lion hunting, but I never saw a lion sneak up on a human. It faced danger and attacked its enemy, snarling and fighting. Only small members of the cat family hide in trees and spring without warning. To me, the name "mountain lion" is a misnomer, and in some sections of the country they are called, more appropriately, cougar, puma, or panther.

But during our first summer at Mammoth Mine, a Redding woman shot five mountain lions in one tree—a large male, a female, and three cubs (or kittens). The whole countryside rejoiced; first, because it was magnificent shooting and, second, because of the destruction of five lions, for which she was paid a bounty.

I dreaded the first meal at the mess with the miners, but it had to come. At six the following morning, I was awakened by an unaccustomed sound, the cook striking a triangle made from an old drill steel to tell us that "grub" was ready. Jack was up and dressed in his mine clothes: corduroys, flannel shirt, and high-laced boots.

I jumped out of bed, hurriedly twisted my long hair in a knot at the nape of my neck and put on a gingham dress.

Before the bunkhouse the miners sat on their haunches (a typical attitude of miners and woodsmen) awaiting the signal. As soon as the triangle sounded, they tramped down the trail, single file. It reminded me of the early bugle call for mess which I had often heard on visits to friends at Jefferson Barracks near St. Louis.

The men were seated at the long table taking their first swallow of coffee when we came into the mess hall. Jack introduced me. The men turned and stared, unsmiling. It seemed to me that their faces expressed suspicion. Only one man arose, a giant of a man with a mass of unruly red hair and a beard. "Pleased to meetcher, Miss," he said, and sat down.

I was downcast. They don't like me, I thought, they resent a woman in the camp. We walked to the two vacant places at the end of the table. There were no chairs, only rough, homemade benches that ran the length of the long table.

I stood for a moment not knowing how to get my feet and legs over. Jack said, "Slide in." I sat down, back to the table, and awkwardly inched my legs over. I learned after a time to flip my legs and sit down with one quick movement.

The men were eating oatmeal porridge. The cook slid a soup plate of it in front of me. "There's your cream," she said, nodding toward a can of condensed milk.

I never ate porridge at home, but I was afraid to refuse. I had had instructions from Jack to fit myself into the miners' ways and not make myself conspicuous. "Miners are suspicious," he told me. "They are always looking for people to be critical, so don't act superior."

I had never acted, nor even felt, superior in my life. But I had sense enough to know that, here, I must make no errors. It was bad enough to have a woman in a development camp; to have a critical woman would cause trouble for Jack.

I did not speak. I ate what was set before me, a regular miner's breakfast. I even swallowed the bitter black coffee. I had never drunk coffee or tea before I came to the camp. I was used to milk, but I knew there was only the condensed milk that was used on the "mush."

The men were soon through, and taking their greasy old caps off the pegs on the wall, went out, picked up their lunch pails from a bench beside the door, and tramped off up the ridge trail that led to the mine.

When a moment later Jack said, "Finished?" I nodded, for I did not know what to say to break the silence that had lasted throughout the meal. At our cabin he picked up his cap and kissed me in an absent-minded way. "I haven't been in the mine for a month. Burt tells me they are approaching the ore body in Number Three tunnel. We may get a strike there."

He was off and away. With a sinking heart I watched him overtake the last of the miners and stride swiftly along. I was alone in a great new world of mountains and trees, where people did not even speak to one another. I was no longer my husband's first thought; I had taken second place to a lode of copper.

I don't yet know how, young and inexperienced as I was, I managed to have enough native wit to understand that I was facing one of the fundamental problems of married life. A wife must be able to share her husband with his work and, often, the work is given precedence. As I think back, I can attribute it only to my early training by a mother who had the wisdom of the ages. "Always use common sense," she would say. "Try to think of the other person and be courteous."

Although I had found it difficult to follow her advice—given as I was to quick and impulsive actions—I must have been guided by it more than I realized. For now as I walked along the narrow trail through the woods, I realized that I must adjust to a new world, a world in which another person's values were of equal importance with mine.

Before I came back to the cabin, I had made up my mind that I would learn all I could about my husband's work so that I could share the excitement he found in it, and that I would enter into the life of the mining camps with enthusiasm. It would take time, but I had all the time in the world.

I never deviated from that decision. Many years later, in 1938, when my husband retired and I told him I was going to be a writer, he in turn agreed with enthusiasm to live my life. And so it has been over the years.

On that bright May morning, however, sitting on a log under the great pine trees watching two chipmunks gather nuts against the winter, such a future was far from my mind. When Jack came home at noon, my first words were, "Did we reach the ore body in Number Three tunnel?"

The days passed swiftly. I roamed the woods and the hills carrying my little .22 rifle, to be startled occasionally by the swift upward flight of a ruffled grouse or the downward swoop of a bald eagle. Once, for three days, pigeons flew overhead, breaking off tree limbs, darkening the sun. In the valley below, they had already left the grain fields desolated. I had no idea that I was witnessing an historic event of nature and that the carrier pigeon would soon be extinct. The miners scooped up the birds by dozens and we had pigeon pie to vary our limited diet.

The cooing of pigeons and the flutter of wings remained in my ears long after the flight had passed. I never saw the phenomenon again, but whenever I hear the cry of the mourning dove in the evening, it is not as a prediction of rain but rather as a reminder of the early days of my marriage when I made my decision to share my husband's work and his enthusiasm for mining.

July Fourth was a holiday. Usually, work in a mining camp meant every day of the week, Sundays included, but the Glorious Fourth and Christmas were true holidays. The common practice of underground miners was to work until they got a "stake," then quit and go to the nearest town for a big drunk. The wiser ones deposited a certain amount of money with a saloon or hotelkeeper, who would hold it for them until they sobered up.

In Kennet, Slim Warren was the honest saloonkeeper. After he had locked a man's money in his safe, no amount of pleading, cursing, or threats would induce him to give it up until the owner was cold sober.

Sometimes the holding would be enough for the miner to move on to another camp. More often he would go back to the mine he had left and repeat the performance. Miners in those days, like early agriculture workers and printers, were a migratory lot. In the copper mines their range was between Montana and Arizona, with seasonal stops in northern California, Idaho, and Nevada. Most of their talk was of the mines in which they had worked, what they thought of the operation, the foremen, and the superintendents. Uneducated for the most part, they were shrewd observers, with a sort of wisdom that comes to men who live close to nature.

Jack had a deft hand with all kinds of tools, and we spent that first Fourth of July at the Mammoth building a wide veranda around two sides of our cabin. With a special tool from the mines called a "frow," he cut a "shake," a kind of rough shingle, from a sugar pine trunk. He had previously made the framework and the roof. Now all he had to do was nail the shakes to the roof frame. I tried to help and after some experimenting, I was able to hack out shakes of a sort. By nightfall, the roof was covered and we sat down to admire the result of our hard labor.

The porch extended across the front of the cabin and around the side that overlooked the steep slope down the mountain. It was like a house in the Swiss Alps, with a superb view of great trees and Mammoth Creek below and the crest of Bahamatosh above. We were well pleased with our Fourth of July. I doubt if we ever put in a more profitable day.

The steamer chairs were restful after a day's work. Jack would change from his mining clothes and we would both lounge in comfort, our hearts and eyes filled with the peace and quiet of the trees above and below us.

Shortly after, Mr. G., the Redding representative of Mammoth

Mines, visited the camp. He was loud in his praise of what we had done with the old "chicken house." By this time, our trunks and boxes had arrived, after sitting out in the weather on the creek bank for three weeks while the packer waited for the freshet to recede enough for him to cross and bring them to the mine. Our silver and china had been unpacked (as well as my Paris dresses), and now I even had a tea table, where I could serve Jack a cup of hot tea as soon as he came home. Mr. G. approved of this custom also, and he and Jack sat out on the veranda overlooking the mountainside, drinking tea and talking mining.

While I was in the house writing letters for Mr. G. to take to the post office when he left in the morning, I heard snatches of conversation—Mr. F., the president, was trying to raise money in Boston, Mr. K. was in New York on a similar mission. The Boston officials were trying to make a deal with the great financier, Thomas W. Lawson, to whom they had sold their previous development, the Shasta King Mine, after Jack had developed pay ore. If Lawson bought the Mammoth, there would be plenty of money for development. It was up to Jack again to strike the ore body.

I heard Jack say, in his quiet voice, "We have struck ore in Number Three tunnel, but we don't know the extent. Another month will tell the story. And we are running a raise in Number Five that offers encouragement. We started this raise when the east drift went beyond the stream of water we had been following. A few feet more and we may tap the bottom of a substantial lens of ore."

"Good! Good! I'll telegraph Mr. F. tomorrow. He may be able to make the sale at once."

Before Mr. G. went to the bunkhouse, he announced that the mine would have visitors next week: Mr. and Mrs. Holmes, stockholders from Boston. A tent would be put up just behind our house to accommodate them.

I offered to let them have our cabin, but Mr. G. laughed. "The Holmeses are set on camping out in the mountains and living in a tent. City folk love to camp out. They have all their own equipment. All we have to furnish is a tent."

Jack said, "I'll have it set up tomorrow. We must do everything to please the stockholders."

Please the stockholders! How often I was to hear those words during our mining life. This first time, though, I confess I was nervous. Suppose these stockholders were not pleased? Would they withdraw their support? Would the mine be closed down?

I need not have worried about the Holmeses. They were charming. Mr. Holmes was a grandson of the poet and a nephew of the Justice. They settled themselves in their tent with the ease of experienced travelers. They had been everywhere and they taught me many of the amenities of successful camp life. For instance, bathing at the mine had always been a problem for me. Either I took a sponge bath or went down to the creek for a swim. The Holmeses carried a bathtub! Made of rubberized canvas, it folded into a little case no more than eight inches wide. When it was unfolded it sat flat on the floor. The sides were eight inches high with whalebone supports, and it was large enough to sit in. One could fill it with hot water and have a real bath. When the Holmeses left, they gave me the tub, and we carried it with us for years. The Holmeses were the first of a series of visitors. Mining experts came from all over the world, and our little cabin with its overhanging veranda became famous in a small way.

The miners, however, continued to be remote and suspicious of me until the day I shot a grouse through the eye with my .22 rifle. Although it was purely accidental, the miners invested me with the reputation of a marksman that traveled all over the mining camps of northern California. "A woman at the Mammoth Mine shot a grouse through the eye with a .22 caliber rifle," they boasted; and they were delighted to live in a camp where there was a woman with such skill.

From then on, all barriers were down. I was spoken to. I received small presents—a bunch of wild flowers, a bird with a broken wing, a stray cat. They even laughed with me when I thought the skunk I saw in the storeroom was a black and white kitty! Having them laugh with, and not at, me was real progress and I was filled with pleasure. So was my husband.

I still walked through the hills and read the books that came by pack train from Paul Elder's in San Francisco—twelve novels a month. I finished them all the first week and reread them the rest of the month. I had not read many novels of the American scene. I liked biography and eighteenth-century novels and Restoration plays. I thought many of the contemporary novels dull and over-written, but they had been selected for me and I had nothing else to read. I often thought I could write better ones myself. But it was some time before I wrote my first mining camp story. It was refused by the *Ladies Home Journal,* but very cordially, with a long letter that ended: "The Editor would like to see more of your work."

The summer passed pleasantly, with many visitors, a large majority of whom were mining engineers who came to "expert" the mine. At first I enjoyed seeing new faces, but so many came that it grew to be a bore.

"A 'mining expert' is a man from another district," Jack said one night after a particularly stupid engineer had gone down the trail. But still the experts came. The multimillionaire, Mr. Thomas Lawson, had not yet bought the mine.

10

As I said earlier, I have an active fear of snakes, rattlers in particular. I paid no mind to Jack's theory that a rattlesnake was a gentleman, for he always warned you when he was about to strike. Whenever I went by that rocky section of the trail where Jack said there were so many rattlers, I shied away like a frightened pony. My experience with a rattler one August morning, though, had two important results. It forever freed me of the fear of snakes, and as an unexpected by-product I was taken to the heart of the miners forever.

Our cabin, which was between the bunkhouse and the mess hall, had been built on a large platform cut out of the steep hillside. The slope itself, which was about 30°, was covered with low bushes, manzanita, scrub oak, and small rocks. On the uphill side, however, the cutbank was about ten feet high.

The morning of the event, Jack had already left for the mine and I was tidying up our cabin when I heard one of the miners shout, "Mrs. Fletcher! Mrs. Fletcher!"

I ran to the door. The miner was standing before the bunkhouse door, waving his arms excitedly. "Rattlesnake! Rattlesnake, coming your way down the bank. Stay in the house."

Automatically I grabbed a long-handled shovel standing by the door. (Jack kept it there for just such an emergency.) It was a mine shovel, curved and very sharp. I had only a moment to decide whether to retreat or to go forward to battle, boldly. I did the latter. Armed with the shovel, I went to meet the enemy just as it came over the cutbank and dropped on the ground, almost at my feet.

I am usually a calm person, but at that moment my temper took over. What business had that vile reptile to invade my privacy? I whacked at it furiously, hitting it squarely across the back with the sharp shovel. I suppose the snake was harmless then, with a broken back, but my rage was so intense that I kept hacking away, scarcely knowing that I was doing so until one of the miners caught my arm.

"Mrs. Fletcher, stop! You've killed it. There isn't a piece as long as an inch left!"

I came to then, but I was shaking with excitement. Several of the miners had gathered around me. I think they thought I was going to faint, but I only looked at the snake, its back broken in a dozen places, and said, "Oh, I didn't know it was so easy to kill a snake."

Everybody laughed. I had not only broken a snake's back, but I had broken down the last shred of prejudice the hard rock miners had against a woman in camp. The men cut off the rattles, seven of them, and nailed them to the door of the cabin.

One of them said, "Your husband will be proud of you. You are a real mountain woman, not afraid of anything. Why, I don't believe you'd bat an eye if you met a 'bar'. What *would* you do if you met a 'bar'?"

"I'd throw my hat at him," I said, to the delight of the men. (It was years after this that I saw a man throw his wide-brimmed felt hat at a lion that he had met unexpectedly in a narrow path. The lion ran.)

The story had to be retold at supper when the day shift came in. I received so much praise that I began to think of myself as something of a hero. But, hero or not, I had lost all fear of snakes.

The long hot summer slipped into autumn and cooler weather. The raucous cry of the bluejay cut through the forest, and the call of mountain quail was everywhere. I had not left the camp or even gone down the trail to Kennet since we arrived six months ago, but we were not lonely, nor had we lost touch with the outer world.

Among our many visitors was Mr. F. who, in addition to being president, was also financial adviser of the Boston syndicate. I didn't like Mr. F. from the first moment we met. He had narrow, tight lips and hard, black eyes. Jack thought he knew little of mining and had incurred the old man's dislike because he did not say, "Yes, sir," to all his pronouncements. On one occasion they had a long argument about drifting along a change of formation where there was a definite selvage and considerable flow of water from the roof. Jack had run this drift on his own initiative and had passed the point where the water was falling. He had then started work on an upraise, confident that he would encounter the bottom of an important lens of ore. (This was a characteristic of the presence of ore bodies in the district, which were not fissure veins but lenticular masses.)

Mr. F. had always been critical of Jack, and had been quoted by his associates as thinking him "much too young." (Jack was twenty-two.) On this occasion Mr. F. had said, "You follow my orders, Fletcher. I do not like superintendents at my mines who do not do as I tell them."

Jack had a natural faculty for interpreting the meaning of changes in rock formations, as well as good experience in both Colorado and California mines. He had discovered the first pay ore in the Shasta King Mine (later sold to Thomas Lawson) and it proved to be big.

Now, he thought the old man was off on the wrong foot and said so. He never played up to him, for he was honest and candid and could not say "Yes" when he thought "No." He listened to the old man's orders, but followed his own judgment.

One November day, I was astonished to see Jack coming toward the cabin in midafternoon. His first words were, "We're going down the hill in the morning. We'd better get to our packing." Then he told me that the old man had arrived unexpectedly at the mine and found that Jack had disregarded his orders in two respects.

"He blew his top!" Jack said. "Blew his top! I let him rave and then told him, 'Save your steam. You can't fire me, I've quit!' "

I was frightened. I looked at Jack's white face and set jaw and knew there was trouble. I had sense enough not to ask questions but started packing. Jack was ripping the green denim off walls and ceiling. The ripping of the cloth seemed to calm him. After a time he said, "I'll walk down to Kennet tonight and send up a horse and pack train for you in the morning." Then he kissed me and went out the door.

I wondered what we would do. I hoped we would not stay in Kennet. I didn't think I could stand to live with "Vesuvius in Eruption." There was a new hotel building in Redding. Perhaps we would go there. I finished packing by midnight and went to bed and slept soundly. I did not know it but I was entering the second round of "Pay, Pack, and Follow."

Because of this blow-up with the old man, Jack was not the one to bring in the great volume of ore in the Mammoth Mine which made it one of the great copper mines of the West, but, as we came to know later, it was by following through with Jack's plan that the lens was discovered.

Later, after the Mammoth was sold to United States Smelting, Refining and Mining Company, Jack met the superintendent of the Mammoth and asked him how far he had gone in the upraise in Number Five before he struck ore.

"Seven feet, and the biggest lens we have yet."

"How about my crosscut Number Two in the upper level? How

far did you have to go to strike the hanging wall? I was in low-grade ore there when the old man blew up and accused me of ruining the mine."

"We've never reached the hanging wall, and we're in 1,600 feet, in good ore all the way."

"Do you call that a crosscut?"

"I call it a mine, Fletcher. It was called crosscut on your old map. From those two ore bodies, we get the greater part of the three thousand tons that come out of the double-track electric railway and go to the smelter every day. So it is really your mine, for you were the one who had faith in it when everyone else had given up."

But this we did not know when I went down the trail for the last time.

I was a downcast girl that day. I had yet to learn the comings and goings of the mining world. The miners worked without contracts, completely independent men. If things did not suit them, they "hit the trail."

I had been writing long letters home each week, telling the family of my adventures. Mother answered, always giving me quiet advice. Of course she hadn't any idea of the way we lived. I never told her about the chicken house or killing the rattler. I skimmed the surface and described the beauties of Mt. Shasta or the erupting of Mt. Lassen.

I told her about meeting an old prospector and his burro on the trail and finding out that he was from Madison County, Illinois, and knew old Judge Chapman. We had invited him to lunch and sent him on his way with a bundle of Edwardsville *Intelligencers* which she had sent me.

Although I thought often of my family and our friends, I was never homesick. There were too many new things in my life for me to regret the old. My philosophy of "always welcome change" has helped me over many a hurdle.

The new hotel in Redding was indeed a change, for we had a bathroom of our own. The owners had to send out for a ledger so we could register, for we were their first guests.

I occupied myself reading and walking while Jack hired a horse and visited various mines in search of a job. He had to find work soon because even though we had saved our money at the Mammoth, it would not last long. Jack had received ninety dollars a month and his board and our cabin. I had paid twelve dollars board a month and ten dollars to Elder's in San Francisco for my books. We had had no other expenses, except our insurance and the ammunition for my little .22.

At the hotel, however, money went faster and I began to worry. "What if you don't get a job?" I asked fearfully.

Jack was surprised at my question. "Of course I'll get a job. I've had jobs, good ones, ever since I was seventeen. I've already turned down two. We can go to a gold mine in the Mother Lode right now, but I don't want to. I like Shasta County. Don't worry, my dear."

Don't worry! Christmas came and went and still he was not settled. Shortly thereafter, though, in early January, Jack returned one morning smiling broadly.

"Pack up," he said, "we're leaving for Old Shasta. I've accepted a job at the Mt. Shasta Gold Mine."

At four o'clock we were on the stage, riding along the road that led to the famous ghost town of California, Old Shasta.

11

Old Shasta was indeed a ghost town, living on her historic past—a winding street, empty houses, and only a few stubborn souls who would not give up. There had been a time when Shasta had been the center of a great gold mining district, but that was far back, almost in the days of the gold rush, but not quite.

One of the stories told around Shasta was about Joaquin Miller, the poet. As the tale went, he had panned gold in the creek, gotten drunk, and had been put in the log jail. Later, he had been rescued by an Indian woman. Whether she had been his legal wife, his common-law wife, or only a well-wisher varied with the teller. But they all agreed that she did manage a jail break. Perhaps the sheriff or his men closed their eyes, for Miller was well-liked in the town and the mines nearby, and getting drunk was a common fault of miners.

From a busy, exuberant town of reputedly eight thousand, Shasta had now become an almost empty shell with few more than a hundred people. Houses, formerly important, had been abandoned and were falling into ruin. Stores were boarded up, many with iron shutters. A general store which carried groceries and mining supplies, a bake shop back of the one saloon, and a drug store were all that was left of a once thriving gold camp.

Just outside of town the stage driver whipped up his six horses, entered the main street at a gallop, and pulled up beside the depot in a cloud of dust.

It was my first journey in a real Concord stage, with the express messenger seated on top, a double-barreled shotgun in his hands. For we were now in a country of stage robbers. We were on the road to Trinity County where there were still great mines which shipped out gold bullion by Wells Fargo Express. And that meant road agents and stage holdups.

There is a certain excitement about coming in on the stage. The town folk, old-timers, even the women, gather at the depot to collect express and mail, packages ordered from the Redding stores, or just to watch and listen to bits of gossip picked up along the way by the stage driver and the express messenger. Altogether it is the event of the day.

People seemed to know who we were. Mr. Z., from the mine, greeted Jack. "Good evening, Mr. Fletcher. Your house is all ready. Shall I walk you over?"

Various characters seated on the "whittling bench" looked us over. A couple offered to carry our bags and boxes. Another man drove up with a spring wagon and two mules. He loaded our trunks and heavy bags and started down the road. We followed on foot, Jack deep in conversation with Mr. Z.

I was at once delighted with the little old town. Although the abandoned houses had a pathetic look, those that were occupied were well cared for. There were neat lawns behind old paling fences, well-trimmed hedges, and many old trees.

We walked up a side street, under a tunnel of live oaks, to a house set in a wilderness. A hedge of laurestine enclosed the grounds, where in the neglected flower beds and garden plots some hardy plants still struggled for existence.

It was a low, spreading house, with a gallery across the front and side, onto which high French doors opened. A great oak tree grew on one side, its branches spreading over the roof. The house had a pleasant, friendly look. It was our first real home, and while the men were unloading our gear I ran about exploring it. There were six rooms, a springhouse, a woodshed, and out-buildings, all in good repair. I liked everything I saw.

The furniture belonged to the late Victorian era, slightly ornate, but not too bad. Considering that we rented both house and furniture for eight dollars a month, I thought we were quite lucky. That was before I learned that it was supposed to be haunted!

I unpacked feverishly, putting clothes in the ample closets, getting the kitchen in order. I wanted to have our first dinner in style, in the long dining room with the French doors opening onto the gallery.

A cleaning woman had left things in order. The springhouse, set deep into the hillside on one of the three terraces at the back, was stocked with milk, butter, and eggs. There were kindling and firewood in the woodbox.

The contrast between this home-coming and the chicken house at the Mammoth Mine was so great that I sat down at the kitchen table and began to cry.

Jack found me bawling, wiping my eyes with a kitchen towel. His face expressed his dismay. "What's wrong, dear? What's wrong?"

"Nothing, nothing. I'm just so happy. It's all so wonderful."

"Well, buck up, Missie. Suppose we scramble some eggs. I have to go over to the mine. I'm taking over the night shift."

The shock of this news dried my tears. I was facing a major problem. I had never stayed alone a night in my life. I suppose my terror showed plainly in my face, for Jack said hesitantly, "Perhaps I could get the cleaning woman to come over."

"No, no," I said hastily. "I'll manage. I've just got to have a little time to get used to the idea."

I was too busy worrying about a night alone in a strange house to enjoy the eggs that Jack scrambled, but I had too much pride to say so.

"Where is this mine?" I asked, hoping that it was nearby.

"Oh, four miles or so. The trail goes up the mountain right behind the house."

"How will you get there?"

"Walk, of course."

"Four miles over and four miles back?"

"My dear child, we're not in the city or a town, but a mining camp. Pack up a sandwich or two and I'll be off."

After Jack had gone I locked every door and window, a useless precaution, for if anyone had wanted to get into the house all he would have had to do was punch in one of the French doors with his fist. But the locking-up routine comforted me. I looked around for lamps. The lamps were there but no kerosene. I rummaged about and found a few candle snubs, enough to last the night if I went to bed early. And that is what I did, as soon as it was dark. I had put chairs in front of the doors and I had my .22 at my bedside. That was the longest night I ever spent. The wind moaned and groaned, the trees bent and twisted. Lighted by the moon, their shadows appeared and disappeared across the windows. A dozen times I crept out of bed to listen fearfully to strange noises.

Jack came in about seven in the morning. I got out of bed to make him coffee. Half asleep, he ate his breakfast, yawned, and said, "I'm for bed. Be sure and wake me by four this afternoon. I've got to be at the mine by five." With that he climbed into the unmade bed.

The day passed somehow. I went into town after lunch (which I ate alone at the kitchen table) and found the bakery at the back of the saloon. There didn't seem to be any other entrance so I paused hesitantly at the saloon door. A couple of men stood at the bar, drinking beer. The bartender helped me out. "The bakery is down there, at the end of the room," he said.

113

I found the baker taking fresh, fragrant loaves of bread out of the oven. "I'm through baking every morning by twelve, Miss Fletcher," he said. "On Wednesdays and Saturdays I have pies too."

I thanked him and put the loaf under my arm.

He smiled. "Better hold it in your hand. You'll have it all squoze up. Hot bread wants tender handling."

The baker and I became firm friends, as time went on. I met other town folk, too, and found many of the women charming. Most of the men worked in the nearby mines. A number of women came to call. We sat on the gallery so we would not disturb Jack's slumbers.

I learned a great deal about the old days in Shasta. Many a man had made his original fortune in the old gold camp. Some had gone on to become great names in San Francisco. Others had ranged as far as New York, there to turn their Shasta gold into golden stocks.

Judge Dangerfield, the famous jurist, had built the house where we lived. Some of the Wells Fargo men and pony express riders who had ridden trails to Trinity County had made their homes here. One could shut one's eyes and see the Forty-Niners roaming the streets, coming in from the nearby diggings with their pokes full of gold dust and nuggets. After a rain, it was said, one could pick up small golden nuggets in the streets. But it was not the gold nuggets that had made men rich, it was the hard rock with gold-bearing veins. Even in our time a respectable amount of gold was still being taken from the veins of quartz.

Jack would sometimes awaken about lunchtime, saying that he had had his sleep out, and we would walk about the hills that rose behind our house. One day he slept only an hour or two, then went off to Redding to look for a horse. Up to now, he had walked the four-mile trail to and from the mine. He came back about five o'clock, riding a short-coupled horse called Bay Billy. Bay Billy had belonged to the Modoc Indians and had evidently been abused, for he shied away from everything that was strange to him. He waltzed down the road like a circus horse, Jack talking to him, patting his silken neck, gentling him.

My husband had a way with horses. I have never known anyone who could tame a wild, frightened horse as quickly as he could. He didn't "break" them, he gentled them. They would do his bidding, follow him like a dog, nuzzle into his pockets for sugar, and come when he called. He trained them so that I could ride them, but no one else. When a stranger insisted on riding one of Jack's "gentle" horses, he was likely to go over the horse's head. We could never understand this special talent of Jack's, but I suppose a horse, like a dog, instinctively knows a friend.

It was the day that Jack brought home Bay Billy that I first heard we were living in a haunted house with an authentic ghost. I was standing on our gallery watching Jack ride up the trail toward the mine just as the sun went down. The tall trees had shut him off from view and I had turned to go into the house to wash the supper dishes when I had visitors.

A woman from the village had brought her husband to call on me. We sat on the gallery and as evening approached I could see that the woman was growing nervous. Several times she interrupted the conversation to say that they must go. The husband, absorbed in his stories of early days in Old Shasta, paid her no mind.

Presently the woman stood up. "Everett, we must go. I don't want to be here after dark."

I turned, puzzled by her words and her nervous manner. "I'll light the lights," I offered.

She turned to her husband. "Didn't I tell you Everett, that she was the bravest woman I'd ever heard of?"

I was now completely at sea.

"Shut up. I told you to keep your mouth shut," the man said.

The woman grew angry. "No need to talk to me like that!"

"Don't you see she doesn't know?"

Now I was curious. "Please tell me what you are talking about."

The woman, angry with her husband, snapped out, "He told me

not to say anything, but I'm sure you know anyway that this house is haunted."

I felt my knees tremble. I leaned against the rail of the gallery. I said, "No, I've never heard anything about its being haunted. Besides, I don't believe in such nonsense."

The woman turned to her husband. "There! Didn't I tell you she is the bravest woman I've ever seen?"

I appealed to the husband. "Please tell me what your wife is talking about. If there is a legend about this house I ought to know it."

"Sit down, Mrs. Fletcher. I'm sorry, very sorry, that the story has to come from us. But too much has been said. I may as well tell you the whole wretched story."

I listened to the whole wretched story, trying not to show my alarm. No matter what I said, I was as superstitious as one could be. I had had superstition instilled into me by my Negro nurses since I was a child. But I was determined not to show it. The woman had said I was brave. Well, I'd be brave.

It seemed that back in the days of '49, the man who had lived in the house was a heavy drinker. He went on sprees every month or so and, as the saying went, "shot up the town." He had a Chinese cook who looked after him. This was, of course, in the old days when Chinese wore their hair in a long queue tucked under an embroidered cap.

The man came home drunk one night and chased the cook around the house, threatening to cut off his queue. Now the Chinese believed that when he went to his heaven he must be complete, with his hair intact. Cutting off his queue meant cutting him out of his heaven. The drunken man caught up with him and with a butcher knife hacked off the queue. In the tussle, the Chinese was killed. The neighbors found them the following morning, the Chinaman dead, the master in a drunken slumber. When the man had finished, I managed to smile. "But who haunts whom?" I asked.

"Why, the queue-less Chinaman, of course. He runs around and

116

around, a butcher knife in hand, chasing his master and looking for his lost queue so that he can get into heaven."

They went away, leaving a terrified, frightened woman alone in a haunted house. One thing consoled me—I hadn't allowed my visitors to know that I was frightened. It wasn't eight o'clock, but it was dark. I locked all the doors and windows, climbed into bed, and covered my head with the sheet.

It was a long night. My vivid imagination was hard at work. I could see the wretched Chinese, butcher knife in hand, running round and round, in and out of rooms, seeking his queue, swearing vengeance. I must have dropped off toward morning for when Jack came in, he found me asleep. He put his hand on my shoulder and I woke up screaming, "I haven't got it! I haven't got it!"

"Haven't got what?" His voice brought me fully awake. I rubbed my eyes. "I guess I've had a nightmare." I sighed in relief and went back to sleep, no longer afraid.

I didn't tell Jack that the house was haunted. He would worry about me. One of us worrying was enough.

About this time, he brought me a young collie pup for "protection." The silliest little dog I ever saw, he was afraid of his shadow and at the slightest sound would rush to me and hide behind my skirts. He followed at my heels all day long, and when I went to bed I tied him to the bedpost where he cried and whined all night long. I had other protection though, my little .22 rifle and a baseball bat. I can't imagine why I thought a bat would be protection against a ghost, but there was something about its solid sturdiness that gave me a feeling of comfort.

Although the nights brought their peculiar terrors, the days and early evenings were filled with activities. I enjoyed the people in the village and nearby mines. Like other folk removed from cultural centers, we made our own entertainment. We gathered at different houses, for cards, games, charades, and such. We gave concerts in the old town hall, for a small entrance fee which we used to renovate it, and we even gave a play, for which I was costume director. This was not an easy task, for the play chosen

117

was the old melodrama *East Lynne*. We played it fully. Villains were black villains, and the good, as sweet and syrupy as sugar candy. People came from nearby camps and the play was a tremendous success, from the standpoint of both acting and finance. We made money, a lot of money, which went into stage properties after we had given a certain amount to local charities.

I had about settled down to living peacefully with my ghost when the Trinity stage was robbed of several thousand dollars, not far west of Old Shasta. The ghost faded into the background, overshadowed by this new danger of desperate stage robbers possibly hiding in the vicinity.

I heard of the robbery one morning when I went down to the depot to watch the stage drive in. I enjoyed the theatrical approach of the stage. To me, it spelled the romance of the West. When I saw the grim, determined express messenger in his place on the box, his double-barreled shotgun across his knees, I used often to think of an old Scotch ballad: "Ere she see the Earl of Morey Come sounding through the toun!"

The stage and its guardians came "sounding" through the old town of Shasta that morning. When I saw the crowd gathered about the coach, I knew something had happened.

"The stage has been robbed, ten thousand dollars taken . . . robbers escaped to the hills . . . well planned escape on horseback . . . It must have been the Catlin brothers . . . looks like their work. Tom Catlin's in Red Bluff jail . . . his three brothers are loose." Over these snatches of conversation a man called loudly for a posse.

The sheriff got up on the driver's seat of the stage. He was a real sheriff of the old West, two guns sagging from his belt, star on his vest, broad-brimmed felt hat, and a straggling mustache stained by tobacco juice. His powerful voice reached to the edge of the crowd. "People will attend to their own business, and the sheriff and his deputies will attend to theirs. I don't want no 'amatoor' posse underfoot. They might get shot in the backside, and their widows come complaining to me."

A shout of laughter rose from the crowd. "That's right, Sheriff, you tend to the robbers. You can do it."

"I sure can." The sheriff climbed down and the man who had called for a posse disappeared.

I was caught up in the excitement. We had a real stage robbery to deal with, not something to read about, such as the stories of the early Mother Lode, of Black Bart or the Bristol gang, the "Robin Hood" tales of Joaquín Murrieta.

I asked a neighbor if she thought the robbers were hiding nearby. She thought not, they would probably be far away by now, in Sacramento, or more likely, in San Francisco. Why would they stay here? she asked sensibly.

A man answered, "They might if they are local people. They could stay here until the hue and cry dies down and then take their loot to San Francisco."

The Wells Fargo man looked grim and worried. It had been his responsibility to guard the treasure, and he had failed. He would have to appear before his company in San Francisco. How could he explain that he had let robbers get away with the gold? How could he explain why he hadn't filled the robbers with buckshot? No wonder he looked worried.

The robbery had occurred some miles west of Shasta, where the road went through a small creek. The robbers had hidden in the bushes on the bank and attacked just as the stage pulled out of the water. They held guns to the messenger's back, took the strongbox off the stage, and rode away. The messenger quickly turned and shot, but he had no chance of hitting the fast disappearing horses.

When Jack came home, I was eager to tell him the news, but he had already heard it from men on the trail. He laughed at my excitement. A stage holdup to him was something that might happen any time. "The robbers are long gone, now," he said, "maybe north on the way to Portland, south to San Francisco, or east to Nevada. Don't worry your little head about it. You've enough to occupy your mind, with your Chinese cook."

He had heard about my ghost! I had been so careful to keep my night fears from him. "Why didn't you tell me you knew about our house being haunted?"

"I don't believe in 'hants,' " he said, matter-of-factly.

I burst into tears, angry that I had tried to be so noble when he already knew about the ghost. Jack was astonished at my tears. He had not yet learned that I cried only when I was angry, never when I was afraid or hurt.

That dissipated to some extent—I never really dismissed all my superstitions—my active terror of the ghost, but there was still the problem of the whereabouts of the holdup men.

In spite of Jack's insistence that the robbers were "long gone," I was worried. Every day when I went to the saloon to get my loaf of bread I gathered a new set of rumors from the barkeep. We had become friends. Neither he nor I took "strong drink," but we would often have a glass of milk together.

He thought the robbers were still about. "I'm sure it's the Catlin gang," he would say. "That's the way they always operated —a man by the road to flag the stage, and the gang hidden by the roadside, ready to hop when the stage stopped. This time they didn't have a man waiting to flag the stage. They knew the driver would rest his horses, directly he pulled out of the creek and got firm on the bank."

Sometimes I believed the barkeep. I thought Jack was trying to keep me from worrying, by saying that the robbers were "long gone."

Jack continued to work the night shift, riding away on Bay Billy at sundown. I always stood on the gallery to watch him ride up the trail behind the house. I never completely conquered my fear of the long lonely nights; there was always a tight ball in my stomach.

One late afternoon, after Jack had gone to the mine, the sheriff called. He asked me many questions. Where were we from? Where had we lived in California? What was my husband's business? Where was he now? I was annoyed. We had been in Shasta

The Clark family in Edwardsville, Illinois:
Murray, Inglis, and Jean with their parents

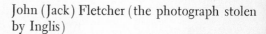

John (Jack) Fletcher (the photograph stolen
by Inglis)

The Chapman Place in Edwardsville, Illinois

Bully Hill Mining Camp, California

Inglis Fletcher in the mountains

In a camp along a western trail

Inglis and Jack Fletcher at Dangerfield House,
Old Shasta, California

Inglis in Nyasaland, British East Africa

One of Lt. Billy Mitchell's training planes at
North Island, California, before World War I,
in which the Fletchers made their first flight

Inglis Fletcher, from a charcoal drawing made at
the time of publication of *Men of Albemarle*

Aerial view of Bandon Plantation, near
Edenton, North Carolina

Front entrance to Bandon

Mr. and Mrs. Fletcher playing with their dog Nipper

Parson Daniel Earle's schoolhouse

Kitchen fireplace, Bandon

Inglis Fletcher today

long enough for him to know the answers to these questions. Half jokingly, I said, "You don't think we are the stage robbers, do you?"

This apparent frontal attack embarrassed the sheriff and he hastened to deny such a foolish idea. "We think the men are still about. This is routine. We are asking everyone the same things."

I didn't believe him, but I said no more. He was now obviously convinced of our innocence.

He asked, "Haven't you someone you could get to stay with you at night while your husband is at the mine?"

"No, I haven't anyone, and I don't need anyone. I've got a .22 and a baseball bat."

The sheriff looked astonished.

"And my dog," I added.

The sheriff glanced at Nero, crouched timidly behind my chair. He raised his eyebrows questioningly.

"Besides," I ended triumphantly, "I've got my ghost to protect me. Nobody will go into a haunted house at night! You're a comparative stranger here, Sheriff. Perhaps you don't understand, but people around here don't like ghosts."

The sheriff looked at me. "Do you, Miss?"

"I don't exactly like my ghost, but I've learned to live peacefully with him. He goes his way and I go mine."

The sheriff exploded with laughter. He patted my shoulder in a fatherly way. "I guess I needn't worry about you, Miss. You can take care of yourself, with your baseball bat and that fierce dog of yours."

I joined in his laughter. Nero, pleased with the sound of gaiety, wagged his tail and licked my hand, and the sheriff rode away.

That night the Chinese cook walked more than usual, or perhaps, since the wind had risen, the branches of the giant oak tree scraped the roof more frequently. But a new sound was added, a sort of furtive thumping which seemed to come from the spring-house.

Nero stood stiff-legged, the hair rising on his back. Perhaps, after all, the ghost story was true. I had heard that animals had acute perceptions, that dogs saw things invisible to humans. In spite of all my whistling to keep up my courage, I was really frightened.

In the morning, I found that dogs, or something, had gotten into the springhouse and made off with half a leg of lamb. The noise continued for several nights and each morning food was missing from the springhouse.

I had reached the point where I felt I must get someone to stay in the house overnight with me. I went down to the village to see the mail coach come in. The Wells Fargo messenger, my friend the sheriff, and two deputies went into the office.

Rumors were afloat. The officers were about to make a kill, someone said. But no one really knew what was going on.

I bought my loaf of bread. The baker knew nothing except that the barkeep had been sworn in as a deputy.

I dreaded to see Jack leave that night. I had an uneasy feeling that something was wrong, but I let him ride up the trail without speaking.

When he came home at daybreak, he brought the news. The robbers had been surrounded that night in an old mine tunnel in the hills behind our house, not a hundred yards from the trail that Jack traveled every night. He tried to laugh it off, but I could see that he was somewhat shaken. I was appalled at what might have happened. Any night they could have attacked him as he rode by.

He said, "I was always whistling or singing. I suppose they knew that I had no idea that they were holing up in the old tunnel, so they let me go about my business. Besides, if they had attacked me, it would have been a dead giveaway. The sheriff would have been down on them like a flash."

"I hate them!" I said. "They had no business stealing our leg of lamb." I had to tell the whole story then about the noises in the springhouse and dog's behavior.

He was quite annoyed. "You should have told the sheriff at once. He might have captured them a week earlier."

I held my ground. "How was I to know it wasn't the Chinese ghost making all that noise?"

Jack looked at me in disgust. "I never heard of a ghost eating a leg of lamb."

1 2

The Bully Hill Mine in the hills of northern Shasta County was one of the great copper mines of the West. When we first went there, it was owned by Captain J. R. Delamar, who operated other properties in the West and later won fame and fortune in the Nipissing region in Canada. Captain Delamar was one of those fabulous men who passed out twenty-dollar gold pieces to the Japanese boys who did his rooms at the guest house. The table boys and the cook at the mess house were also recipients of his princely generosity. Today, we have his counterpart in the oil-rich Texans, but at that time, he was a phenomenon. About the time we went to Bully Hill, that first occasion, he was arranging a sale of the mines and smelter to General Electric Company, so that a succession of famous mining experts was visiting there.

I can't remember why we left the Mt. Shasta Gold Mine. Possibly because it closed down. (Mines were often closed down suddenly, usually because stockholders' money ceased to arrive.) Or it might have been because of Jack's desire to work in one of the great copper mines in the district. He had become enamored with copper mining. It was the most challenging of all mining, to his mind.

Jack had spent several years with the development company, which opened up a mine to the point where big money was necessary to bring it to full capacity, build a smelter, etc. Then the property was sold to those with operating capital. But he had had no experience in the operation of a large mining and smelting property, and he had much to learn about methods of blocking out ore and timbering up "stopes" for reserve so that the ore bins at the smelter could be kept filled at all times.

We left Shasta a little sadly, and once more we were in Redding, looking for a job. But this time I knew something about Jack's work, and he discussed his plans with me. He needed experience underground, he said, so he would get a job as a timberman at Bully Hill Copper.

This plan presented problems. The large mines had something that resembled a caste system, with the manager, engineer and assistants, and office force at the top. Next came the underground foreman and shift bosses, and after that the miners and timbermen, although timbermen were in a higher pay bracket than ordinary miners. So were drill machine and hoist operators.

Jack knew the manager of Bully Hill, John Keating, but didn't want to ask him for a job "below." The miners, with whom he would work, looked with suspicion upon men who knew top officials and treated them as spies.

Then there was the newly organized I.W.W. growing strong in the West and trying secretly to get a foothold in the larger copper mines. Jack didn't want to be forced to join any such organization, for he planned to work underground only long enough to get the experience.

We had a long talk before he went to Bully Hill to apply. Two things we would have to face: a serious reduction in pay and our social position there. We could not expect recognition by the staff, and we didn't intend to be associated with the miners. They were for the most part a mixture of mid-Europeans, with some Welsh,

Cornish, and Italian. Good, sturdy, upstanding people though they were, they would afford little companionship to me. Again Jack wanted me to stay in Redding at the hotel. I didn't intend to do that, but I let him ride off to Bully Hill on Bay Billy without telling him so.

In two days he was back. He had a job underground. I did not have to make a fight to go to Bully Hill with him after all, for through the mine foreman he had found a little house, just the right size for us—bedroom, living room, and kitchen, with two porches.

Again, it was "Pay, Pack, and Follow." I was on the stage bound for Delamar, the little town below the smelter. Jack had gone ahead on horseback.

The only thing of interest on the long drive was my talk with the express messenger, Dan Haskell. He was a pleasant, mild-mannered man who wanted to retire and raise sheep in Nevada.

Later, the story of Dan Haskell and his tragic death defending the strongbox gave me the idea for my first literary effort that brought me real money. A moving picture company in Hollywood bought the script and made a picture for an actor of Westerns, named Neil Hart. For the story I received one hundred dollars, probably the most important money I ever received, for it was then I began to think seriously that I could earn money writing.

When the stage, following Squaw Creek, turned toward the town, I was horrified. It was bare country, no trees or bushes, every vestige of life killed off by the withering, poisonous fumes of the smelter. The only green thing for miles was poison oak bushes. Only when timber line was reached on the mountains beyond the town were the pines and oaks undamaged.

As the stage approached the camp, I was intensely interested in its physical aspects. It was the largest and liveliest camp I had ever seen. The town was made up of many small houses on a couple of straggling streets along the creek bank. But it was the giant, sprawling smelter that took up the foreground—dark structures of steel frames and iron roofs, open to wind and weather.

126

Great fires burned under the enormous roofs, fires that shot green and purple and red flames into the air. It looked like an inferno, which indeed it was. The small human figures moving here and there, gnomelike under the gigantic buildings, were an integral part of a Dantesque scene.

The mine buildings were halfway up the long slope rising to the mountains. Tunnels had been cut into the hill and there were tremendous waste dumps. Little ore cars ran out of the mine, dumping ore into huge bunkers from which a narrow-gauge railroad carried it down to the smelter. There was activity here, the activity of a producing mine.

On the opposite side of the hill there was a group of half a dozen small houses. Farther up, perhaps a quarter of a mile, six or eight larger houses nestled in a crescent. These were painted white and seemed more pretentious.

From Jack's description, I knew this was where the manager and his staff lived. The mountain behind them cut upward abruptly. It looked as though it would tumble down and smash the houses with great boulders. This section was above and out of the path of the prevailing winds and the smoke, so the trees were tall and green and inviting.

Roads crisscrossed the long open area between the smelter and the first group of houses. I was sure that one of the group was our future home.

As usual, the stage drove into town with a flourish. Haskell jumped off first and carried the strongbox into McCormick's store.

These mining camp stores were unique in that besides selling hardware and mining equipment, groceries and clothing, they were also stage depots and banks. They gave credit to miners, as well as catering to all their needs. They were workingmen's clubs, where the off-shifts would gather to discuss mining affairs or their personal problems. McCormick's was a branch of the large Redding store. The storekeeper and the stage driver served as buying agents for both the men and women of the town. The stage driver would bring in a spool of thread as readily as he would a case of dynamite.

I've always thought there was a real and vital story in the social implications of a small store in a mining community. It is the eighteenth-century coffee house, the home of the exchange of ideas, as well as the center of gossip. The ideas which originate there may be good or bad, but its influence is strong in a community which has neither church nor civic leadership.

Jack was waiting for me at the store, and we walked up the hill to our home. Again our house was unfurnished, save for a small iron cookstove and pots and pans for the kitchen. Our bedsprings had taken another mountain journey and were again set up on four wooden cracker boxes. Steamer chairs unfolded, a scratch meal out of tins (sardines are anathema to me to this day), a cup of tea, and we were ready for bed.

I slept so heavily that I did not hear Jack get up, make his breakfast, or leave for the mine. When I awoke and found him gone, I felt guilty and quickly set about unpacking and arranging our belongings. This time, we had walls of pine boards in the living room and bedroom, so our prints and paintings showed up well. The straw matting for the floor I left for Jack to lay when he came home.

In late afternoon I looked out the window and saw a man dismounting from a big black horse. I opened the door to a tall, black-haired, black-eyed man, with a pleasant smile. He introduced himself as John Keating, the general manager. He said the Wells Fargo messenger had told him that an attractive young woman had come up on the stage.

He laughed at my surprise. "News travels fast in a camp," he said, easing his long, lean body into a steamer chair.

"I just heard from my mine foreman that your husband is working in Number Three. Why didn't he come to see me? I think I can find something better for him than underground work."

"Oh, no, Mr. Keating. That is exactly what he wants. He says you have wonderful methods of timbering heavy ground in your mines. He wants to learn."

I insisted that he have a cup of tea. By then, I thought a cup of tea not only pleasant but a panacea for everyone.

Later, "J.B.," as he was called, told me that he had a hard time to keep from laughing. A good drink of Scotch would have suited him better.

He told me he was from Helena, Montana, had gone to college at Ann Arbor, and married a Michigan girl. "Sally is in San Francisco, but she will be home in a week. She will ride down to call as soon as she gets here."

He left then, and I watched him ride up the hill, sitting tall and easy in the saddle. He was a real Westerner and I thought him delightful.

That visit was the beginning of a friendship that has lasted through the years. It was through him, the men who surrounded him, and the experts who visited the mines, that I had the rare privilege of early contact with brilliant, creative minds.

During my writing years, many people (and two publishers) have thought I was a man. The name Inglis Fletcher helped, but perhaps I learned, through my associates in the mining world, to think as men think, to make quick decisions, then go ahead and try to carry them out.

I had no idea, that afternoon at Bully Hill, that our whole future would be influenced by this casual visit. John Keating and his wife, Sally, became our intimate friends. They were beside us in gay, carefree days. They were beside us in the sad days when our first son died before he was three weeks old. I think we have never had closer friends, nor ones I think of with deeper affection.

That same afternoon, after J.B. had ridden up to the staff houses, I had another visitor. He was a Cornish miner by the name of Amos Treloar. I had trouble understanding his broad Cornish accent, for my ear was not attuned to the rhythm of the dialect. He was a craggy-faced man, with a tough, lean body and incredibly blue eyes under overhanging brows. He brought me two small meat pasties, just out of the oven. He said he lived in the house above, the one with the bright blue door. "My pardner, Uncle Dick Eva, painted the door blue to keep out evil spirits. I don't know as it do, but it keeps him happy."

"Where is 'Uncle Dick'?" I asked.

"He's down at McCormick store," he said evasively.

I thanked him for the pasties, he touched his miner's cap with one finger, and walked briskly toward the mine.

When Jack came home, he was pleased when I told him that J.B. had called, and he laughed about Amos and "Uncle Dick."

"Two characters, known all about the mining world as tops in hard rock mining. They have a pact; only one of them can get drunk at a time, the other must stay at home to mind the chickens."

I enjoyed Uncle Dick and Amos. Gossip had it that Uncle Dick was "bought and sold" with the mine, like the old white mule. There was an old tale that Uncle Dick was called by the coroner as a witness to an accident in the mine. The coroner asked his name. "Uncle Dick," was the reply.

"Uncle Dick? Is that all of your name?"

"Uncle Dick Eva, sir. But I was born an uncle, so I've always been Uncle Dick."

The coroner said, "Mr. Eva, I understand you are a miner."

"No, sir. Ain't no miner, You."

"But I understand that you work in the mine. How long have you been working in mines?"

"Oh, come fifty-six, fifty-seven year, You, but ain't no miner."

Amos and Uncle Dick were our only near neighbors. It was a quarter of a mile to the staff houses up the hill, and a little more to the village below the smelter at the bottom of the hill, on Squaw Creek.

It was Amos who showed me how to build a refrigerator box, to keep milk and vegetables cool. We made a door for an old crate and covered it completely with burlap sacking. On top of the crate we placed a flat baking pan, about four inches deep, filled with water. Two long strips of felt were placed in the pan so that the ends fell over the sides. This permitted a constant dribble of water to run from the felt strips to the burlap sides, keeping them wet. Evaporation kept the inside of the box cool. This was a successful method of refrigeration, not quite as cold as a freezing unit, but it sufficed.

Speaking of the box reminds me of the cow that ate our Christmas dinner several months later.

As I had told Jack, I knew nothing about cooking when we were married, beyond making a salad, but I was learning, with the aid of the *Boston Cookbook* and some family recipes one of my aunts sent me.

I believed then, as I do now, that anyone with a grain of sense can cook if she follows the rules set down in a cookbook. I have no real facility for cooking. I don't like it, but I can do it if I have to.

At Bully Hill I had to cook, for there was no one to hire to cook for me. No smiling colored woman to take over as I had found in Old Shasta. The staff families up the hill had a mess with an excellent Japanese chef and three mess boys. In addition, each staff family had its own cook for the times when they didn't wish to eat at the mess.

But the people down the hill had no such luxuries. The women fended for themselves, cooking, for the most part, good substantial Cornish dishes.

Christmas was coming, so I got out my *Boston Cookbook* and began on plum pudding. I made six and steamed them in six of Jack's tobacco tins. They were beautiful and I put them in the bottom of the cooler.

We had fresh vegetables only on occasion, when the vegetable peddler came in from Redding. He arrived unexpectedly just before Christmas so I bought more lavishly than my budget would allow—bananas, oranges, lemons, celery, asparagus, beans, spinach. Happily, we were in California where vegetables were to be had the year round. These, too, I packed in the cooler.

By this time I was well-acquainted with the wives of staff personnel. Sally, J.B.'s wife, rode down frequently to see me. The

Hanleys, the Mays, and the Schoonovers were frequent visitors at our little home halfway down the hill. The bachelors, company engineers, and the company doctor also visited us. I had invited them all for Christmas Eve dinner.

Bully Hill had certain traditional ceremonies. One was bringing home the yule log and Christmas trees for every household. Ten or twelve of us rode off into the pine forest to get trees and to cut the wild California holly for decorations. There was much gaiety and laughter, and we sang Christmas carols as we rode homeward, the yule log dragging behind two horses.

The night before my dinner everything was in readiness: the turkey stuffed with oyster and chestnut dressing, celery cut, and hard sauce made (with plenty of brandy), all in the cooler on the back porch. I went to bed happy and content that all the real work was done.

In the middle of the night, I heard strange noises, grunts, and heavy movements at the back of the house, then a loud crash. I sat up in bed and shook Jack's shoulder. He made a protesting sound and buried his face deeper into the pillows.

"Wake up! Wake up!" I said. "There's a mountain lion on the back porch. I can hear him prowling around."

"You've got another nightmare. Go to sleep."

I couldn't get him to move, so I got up and lit a candle. I was deadly afraid of a mountain lion, but I had to know what had happened.

As I came into the kitchen, there was another loud crash. Suddenly I realized that the cooler had been turned over. I was no longer afraid. I was angry. I flung open the back door. By the light of a full moon and my feeble candle I saw a large dark animal finishing off my Christmas dinner with a bunch of celery. It was not a mountain lion, but a cow. That made me even angrier. I ran into the house for my .22, determined to shoot the beast.

By this time the noise had roused even Jack. He took the gun out of my shaking hands. "Calm down. You can't shoot the neighbor's cow. You'll go to jail."

"I don't care. It can't eat my Christmas dinner," I wailed.

Jack went out and shooed the cow away. It lumbered off, the bunch of expensive celery dangling from its mouth. I started after it with a broom. I hit it a few good solid whacks before Jack could bring me back to examine the remains of my Christmas dinner.

The turkey was intact, but all the vegetables were gone. Gone, also, were two of my precious puddings, and every bit of the hard sauce had been licked from the pan. A dozen fresh eggs, hard to come by, had been broken.

Jack said, "Go into the house. I'll clean up the mess."

But I stayed to view the devastation. It wasn't as bad as I had at first thought. We had the turkey, there were cranberries in the kitchen, so I still had the fundamentals of a Christmas dinner. I could salvage enough to round it out. We would have no fresh vegetables, tinned would have to do. There were enough puddings. I made fresh hard sauce.

The story of the invasion of the cow gave a hilarious start to the dinner, that and a gallon of Chianti we had bought from a vineyard down the valley. My friends, to this day, still talk about the cow that ate the Christmas dinner.

After a time, when I got over being angry and could laugh, I wrote the story and sent it to *The Ladies Home Journal*. I got my first letter from a real editor. Mr. Balmer sent it back, but his refusal was so pleasant that I was almost as happy as though he had sent me a check. He wanted, he said, to "see more of my work." I never sent him another story. I was too busy living to set anything down on paper. That came later, a long time later.

Bully Hill was now in the throes of being sold. By this time I understood the quick sales that take place within a development company. But selling a great mine, two lesser ones, and a smelter— a going concern—was a different thing. The place swarmed with experts: mining experts, smelting experts, and business experts.

I don't remember who they all were, but they were all top brass in their fields. The only one I remember well was Dennis Matthew Riordan, who came out of the deal as Mister Riordan, President of B.H.M.M. & S. Co. (Bully Hill Mining, Milling and Smelting Company.)

Mr. Riordan was a tall man with a mop of white hair. He was built on heroic lines, and with his classic features, blue eyes, and ruddy skin, he reminded me of Jove. He was big in all ways, in body and in his thinking. He had at one time been Indian Agent for the Navajo Tribe.

Wherever he went, he was followed by a retinue, from a tall, statuesque secretary to engineers and office men. His luggage was multitudinous, twenty-five to thirty pieces; there were bags, suitcases, Gladstones, briefcases, all numbered. His secretary had a check list, and she could tell in the twinkling of an eye just where every item was. His arrival in a private stagecoach, followed by a luggage wagon, created a great diversion in the camp.

Mr. Riordan took over the large guest house in the center of the crescent of staff houses. His retinue took another. The Japanese boys at the mess rushed about in excitement, catering to his every need. Perhaps they were remembering Captain Delamar and his twenty-dollar gold pieces. I do not know anything about Mr. Riordan's gratuities, but he was always sending off to the Navajo Reservation at Fort Defiance, Arizona (via Gallup, New Mexico), for bales of Indian blankets. There was always great excitement when the blankets arrived. After he had taken those he wished, he distributed the others lavishly, so every home had floor coverings of beautiful Navajos—none of your aniline-dyed modern "tourist bait" blankets, but authentic weavings dyed with vegetable and mineral dyes. These blankets were like Oriental rugs in that they became more valuable as they aged.

Everything about Mr. Riordan was in the grand manner. He liked people and people liked him, and the camp looked forward to the new regime. To both staff and miners, General Electric was Mr. Matthew Riordan, and therefore the best.

Mr. Riordan's coming provided us with additional opportunities for entertainment. There were more luncheons, dinner parties, tennis matches. Once we had a tennis tournament for men and women from nearby mines. A dozen people came to Bully Hill and stayed for a week. I suppose business was discussed among the men, but the women gave no thought to anything but pleasure. Everyone had horses, and we took long rides up the trails to picnic in forests undisturbed by smelter fumes. Our visitors came from the Mammoth (now building a smelter), from Trinity Copper, and Balakalala.

I have never known anything gayer, or more elaborately planned, with the exception of the "Sports Week" I spent in Nyasaland in 1928. (All of the English government officials and their wives met for a week of festivites in the capital city of Blantyre where they were entertained by the governor and his wife, Sir Charles and Lady Bowring.)

By late winter Jack was ready to leave Bully Hill. He had learned what he had come for. For some time, a consulting engineer friend, "Sonny" Elmer, had been urging him to come to Snow Creek Mine near Sumpter, Oregon, where there were problems of heavy ground on which he could use the experience he had acquired at Bully Hill, and he decided to accept the offer.

So, again, it was "Pay, Pack, and Follow."

Before taking off for Oregon, we decided that it was time for me to go home for a visit. I was of two minds whether to go to see Father and Mother and Jean and Murray or to accompany Jack to Snow Creek, but I had been away from St. Louis nearly two years. Even when Jack put me on a train for the East, I went with a sinking feeling in my heart, and when I got back to Edwardsville I realized, much as I wanted to see my family, my real home was with my husband.

In the two years I had been away, there had been many changes, of course, but home life was familiarly pleasant. Father was still commuting every day to St. Louis. He still wanted to see everyone at the seven-thirty breakfast table, completely dressed, no negligees. Mother still instructed me in my conduct, but the emphasis was now on how I should behave as a married woman.

Murray was a man, eighteen, dark and handsome, with a quiet, poised manner and beautiful brown eyes. He was studying engineering at Shurtleff College, in Upper Alton, the college where Uncle George Leverett's kin held sway. He had spent the summer with a group of engineers, building a railroad in Missouri. He held the school record for running high jump and broad jump. Like all the Chapman men he was tall and thin, over six-foot-two.

He and Jean were close, and although he was two years her senior they went about with the same group, attending the same cotillions and other dances. He played the guitar, and with two friends had a trio that often entertained at informal gatherings. He had a pleasant, untrained voice, and with his companions sang many of the old folk songs. Murray's early death from an infected hand a few years later when he was twenty-one, brought the first break in our family, our first real tragedy. Mother took it the hardest, and it was years before she could bear the mention of his name. She locked him deep in her heart and kept him there. The loss of her only son was a sorrow she could not talk about; I used to try, for I thought it would relieve her heartache, but she would only turn away.

In my two years' absence, my little sister Jean had grown up. She was now a young lady, well-established in the social life of our world. From an annoying little sister who sat on the hall stairs and listened to the conversation of my beaux, giggling loudly, she had developed into a very pretty young lady, with a reserved, assured manner. Like Mother, she had a fine sense of humor and laughter came readily. She, as the other young people in her group, spent much time at house parties, visiting friends in St. Louis, Alton, and other nearby towns.

At the moment, she was quite interested in a young engineer, who had been graduated from the University of Illinois and was now engaged in building a section of the Wabash Railroad, with headquarters in Edwardsville. His name was Lloyd Alder Chenoweth, and a few years later they were married, one of the truly perfect marriages.

After I had visited all my family and friends a curious thing happened to me. I found that I had changed. I still loved my family, but I was no longer vitally concerned with the affairs of my unmarried friends. I thought them young and uninteresting. I was eager to go back to my much more exciting and romantic life in the mining camps of the Far West. I was homesick for Jack.

The Snow Creek Mine was in the Blue Mountains of eastern Oregon. What impressed me most when I arrived was the gigantic size of the pines, firs, and cedars; the pack rats' nests in the mine tunnels; and the "Polygamy Central" Railroad, so called because of the large number of Mormons who lived in the valleys and Mormon stockholders who participated in its building.

The little narrow-gauge railroad rambled through the valley from Baker City on up into the mountains. It twisted and turned and almost crossed back over its own tracks to gain altitude. "Crooked as a snake's back," was the common description. In one place, the passengers got out and walked up a hill while the engine puffed and panted back and forth to make the grade. It was quite out of breath when it reached us at the top. The conductor and trainmen piled on wood from a reserve by the track, and we finished our journey. I say "finished," for that was as far as the rails went. We had a mile or more to travel by stage to reach the mine.

I was fortunate to arrive in clear weather for, later, Jack showed me slashes cut in giant trees, twenty feet from the ground, which marked the winter trail over the snowdrifts.

Jack had almost finished the work he had come to do, which was to solve a timbering problem that had been delaying production. His experience at Bully Hill had made him an expert, and he received a large bonus.

His friend, Sonny Elmer, who had brought Jack to Snow Creek, now asked him to go with him to "expert" a placer-mining property near Juneau, Alaska.

We talked it over on the Fourth of July, attending a miners' celebration in a heavy snowstorm. We sat on a bench watching a competition in hard-rock drilling, with snow falling so heavily that we could scarcely see the men drill their holes.

Mr. Elmer suggested that I stay in Seattle, or go to San Francisco, since this was to be a three months' trip. I set my foot down hard. I had no intention of being left behind while they went off on the steamer to that fabulous country. Both of the men put up good arguments, but I was adamant.

Sonny said, "I have no place in my budget for a woman, only for a cook."

"Then I'll sign on as cook." This was surely a joke on Mr. Elmer, for although I had cooked at Bully Hill, I was a little feeble at it. But that is how I went.

We traveled by way of Seattle and I was enthralled with that beautiful city. Even Mt. Rainier seemed glad that I came, for she sparkled in all her icy grandeur the whole time we were there. We intended to put our baggage on the steamer *City of Topeka* the night before we were to sail, but I wanted to see a show, so we went to *The Pink Lady* instead.

That night the *Topeka* sank at her dock, with all the freight and baggage (other people's!) in the hold. We sailed on the *City of Seattle* two days later.

The cruise up the Inland Passage is beautiful, enthralling, magnificent, and all the other praiseful adjectives you can find in *Roget*. Every American should take the journey, at least once. Only the Norwegian fjords can compare with the strange and thrilling beauty. The almost vertical mountains are all green and heavily timbered, green moss covers the granite, the rivers are waterfalls, tumbling straight down like Yosemite's Bridalveil Fall but in far greater dimensions.

Juneau, our destination, clings to the side of the mountain with a precarious foothold. It was then a quaint, quiet spot, part American, part Indian, part Eskimo.

We lingered but a day and went on westward in a small motorboat to Lemon Creek, a mining camp in the shadow of the Mendenhall Glacier—Jack's new assignment.

13

The camp on Lemon Creek was delightful. The country west of Juneau was almost subtropical, like the climate of Seattle.

The manager's house was a well-built cottage with four bedrooms, a large living room, and ample kitchen. Although I had signed on as cook, fortunately for me—and the miners, too!—there was a Japanese cook and a waiter for the crew of twelve men. The mess and bunkhouses were down the hill from us, on the bank of the stream in the narrow valley.

Everything was green, with the strange, eerie effect of a tropical jungle. Heavy vegetation grew in rank splendor, fern trees were ten feet high, and giant leaves, like elephant ears, met above narrow trails. It reminded me of Hudson's *Green Mansions*. Even the ground was green, covered with a thick carpet of moss called tundra. In some places, the tundra had grown over old mine shafts which made it dangerous to travel off the beaten trails.

There were other dangers, too, from wild animals. Great bears roamed the woods, a danger not to be laughed off. Shortly after we arrived in camp, one of the miners opened the door of the bunkhouse directly into the face of a bear. The giant animal, standing on his hind legs, towered above the man who gave a mighty yell and fell back into the room. The bear, equally as frightened at the sudden appearance of the man, grunted and rushed away into the darkness. This story was told me half a dozen times, the object being to keep me from wandering off the trails into the woods.

For my protection, I was given a cartridge belt and a holstered German Luger pistol, not that it could kill a Kadiak bear but so that I could signal the camp to come to my rescue. I never gave the signal for help, although once I heard a large animal crashing through the woods, and at another time I caught sight of a bear. I hollered and yelled and made a great commotion throwing a piece of wood at him. The bear paid me no mind, but ambled away into the gloom of the trees.

I fancied myself a primitive woman, trudging about looking for food. I killed "foolish hens," a type of grouse, with a stone, and chased rabbits. But my real contribution was fish. The little brooks and the creek teemed with trout. I had no fishing tackle, but I used a bent pin; a bit of chalk line tied it to a reed, and with a snip of fuzz from my red woolen beret, I was ready for fishing.

The brook trout usually rose to the bait as fast as I could throw the line into the water, but one afternoon, for some reason, they were not biting. I kept at it until the sun had left the canyon, although it still shone brightly on the hilltops. I did not want to get caught in the dark, but there were still not enough fish for supper so I fired two rapid shots into the stream with my Luger. Fish showered on the bank, stunned but still breathing. I gathered up a dozen or so and threw them into my basket, the rest I pushed back into the stream. I was on my way home when I met three miners tearing down the track. They all carried rifles.

"What's happened?" I called out. "Anything wrong?"

The oldest miner glared at me. "You gave the signal. Two shots! Why did you do that?"

I was overcome with embarrassment. "I forgot about the signal. I was shooting fish. They wouldn't bite."

"Don't do that again!" the old man said gruffly. "You liked to scared the life out of us. We thought a Kadiak bear was after you."

One of the younger fellows from California said, "There ought to be a law against dynamiting fish. Some day this country will have game laws and game wardens."

"But I didn't have any dynamite. Just my little Luger."

"My God! Just her 'Little Luger'!"

I didn't know why they all laughed, but I was glad they stopped scolding me. After all, they had come to my rescue.

I knew little about the mine examination, except that it showed there had been a great deal of gold taken out of the creek in the early days. A Pittsburgh group had an option on the property. They would take over the abandoned mine if Elmer recommended it.

What I did not know was that the problem was quicksand, dangerous to tunnel through. Already two men had died in the effort. It was some time later that I learned that Jack had been asked to come there because of that very problem of sinking through quicksand to test the gold values at bedrock. Because of his experience at Bully Hill he had been able to salvage the Snow Creek Mine in Oregon, and that was the reason Elmer had selected him to come to Lemon Creek to try to lick another problem where others had failed.

He got the shaft down sixty feet to bedrock without incident, by double timbering, double-driven lagging, and driving down the floor of the shaft with two-inch square, sharpened pegs, each a foot in length. This enabled them to control the inflow and to bail and hoist out the sand. But at bedrock they discovered that the gold was not in sufficient quantities to justify a favorable report.

Shortly before we left Alaska, Jack had an extraordinary experience. While the shaft work was moving smoothly, he walked up

Lemon Creek to its source under the great Mendenhall Glacier. While he was studying the bare rock formation at the foot of the Glacier, he noticed that chunks of ice were falling from the four-hundred-foot high vertical face of the glacier.

With a slight sense of warning that his position could be dangerous, he turned and climbed up the opposite hillside to a height almost equal to that of the face of the glacier and sat down to relax and to observe.

He had not been there long when the whole face of the great mass of ice tumbled with a roar on to the floor of the canyon. The air was filled with tiny particles of ice. After it had settled and all was quiet, he came down from the hillside and followed the creek through a large arch under the glacier. Underfoot the surface was smooth, polished granite. Overhead was a large dome across which stretched iridescent rainbows. He did not feel it wise to tarry long, but when he described his experience he said, "For once in my life, I knew that I stood on a spot of the earth's surface where no human foot had trod before."

When we were waiting in Juneau for return passage to Seattle, Jack presented a letter of introduction to the manager of the enormous Alaska-Treadwell Mine on Admiralty Island, and was permitted to spend a day in the underground with a foreman making his rounds.

Years later, that day was of especial value to him. It was at a hearing in a Federal Court where the defense was claiming a similarity to Alaska-Treadwell. When Jack described the workings of Treadwell, in minute detail from personal observation, the defendants lost their case.

We took ship back to Seattle. On the trip, many of the passengers became sick each time we crossed the open sea (especially down the Gulf of Georgia) and took to their bunks, Jack among them.

I am a good sailor, so I walked the decks enjoying the rough seas, and went to every meal. The only thing I didn't enjoy was Tonka and the dreadful odors that hung over the place. The tides met there, and the offal from a fish cannery polluted the air so that it was almost impossible to breathe.

While Jack and I had been shuttling around mining camps, my father had bought some hotels. He had a theory that since he had lived so much in them, he knew how to run one properly. His idea was to buy old hotels cheaply, put them on their feet, and sell them at a profit.

And this he did. He had hotels in Edwardsville, Oklahoma City, and Denver. He was ahead of his time in this idea, and was successful until he had a stroke in 1924 and had to retire.

But there was nothing wrong with the idea. Although today great hotel chains, such as the Hilton, are immensely successful around the world, they were almost unknown when my father made his attempt.

When we returned from Alaska, Jack went off on a series of brief "experting" jobs, first to a mine in Central City, then to Hayfield in the valley, from there to Mexico. While he was away, I joined my family in Denver where they had a charming apartment.

The owner's late husband had a collection of eighteenth-century literature, and I was in my element with the novels and the plays of the Restoration at my hand. I read day and night, pausing only long enough to eat or to look at the beautiful panorama of the snow-capped Rockies.

My sister, Jean, was married to Lloyd Chenoweth while I was in Denver, a quiet wedding with a few old friends. As I said earlier, it was, and is, as near a perfect marriage as I have ever known. At that time, Lloyd was working with a firm of engineers in Michigan.

I was happy over the marriage because we were all devoted to Lloyd. He is one of those men who have the happy faculty of thinking of other people. He still thinks of Jean's wants before she herself is aware of them. Men, women, and children adore him, and the years have been good.

The life of an engineer is as roving as that of a mining man, so Jean and Lloyd moved about almost as often as we did. From Colorado, they went to Ohio, then to Massachusetts, and finally

California, where they stayed with us in Riverside, until Lloyd joined the Southern Pacific Railway. When he left them, after a brief interval, he became associated with our old friend "J.B." in the Byron-Jackson Pump Works. And there he remained until he retired a few years ago.

Jean was always very active in civic and social works. During World War II, while they were living in Santa Ana, she and a friend headed up a volunteer service for the Red Cross. They were in direct contact with the Army Air Force, the Navy, and Marines, all of which had tremendous installations in Orange County. She was also president of the Assistant League, a well-known California organization founded in World War I by Mrs. Hancock Banning and some Los Angeles women. The organization is similar to the Junior League (only the women are not as young), and they have done an enormous amount of good work. The Orange County branch was organized by Mrs. James Irvine. Her husband owned the famous Irvine ranch, a vast operation of over one hundred thousand acres, with its origin in an old Spanish grant.

Now Lloyd and Jean have bought Belvedere, a beautiful Colonial estate on the Perquimans River, about twelve miles from Bandon. The present house was built in 1725 (but thoroughly modernized by the previous owner).

While I was still in Denver, Jack went on from Mexico to a mining camp in the Kawich Mountains of Nevada, some sixty miles east of the flourishing mining town of Tonopah.

That's where he was in midwinter, when I received a telegram from his brother-in-law, Paul Webster, a mining engineer in British Columbia, saying that Hugh Rose, one of the Guggenheim managers, wanted to know if Jack would be interested in taking over the management of the Golinsky Copper Mine near Kennet, California.

This offer was manna from heaven, for Jack was developing a gold mine where the snow was deep, the temperature around zero, and he and his crew living in tents. California would be heaven for him, and the Golinsky mine he knew well. Kennet was the little mining town where we first went after our marriage. I knew he would want the job. What to do?

I hadn't had a letter from him for weeks. There was no mail service to the camp; only if someone from Tonopah happened to be coming out to the camp and think of the mail did they have any letters.

I thought about the telegram overnight, and came to my conclusion: I would wire the Guggenheims over Jack's name that the offer would be acceptable if the salary were right.

So I telegraphed to Paul Webster and to Hugh Rose. Among other things, I said that he was familiar with the mine and the problems, that he had brought in the Mammoth to the point where it was sold to United States Mining and Smelting Company, and that previously he had developed the first pay ore in the Shasta King. All this over Jack's signature.

Then I set about trying to find Jack. I tried several ways without success. Word came from Tonopah that that section of Nevada was snowbound and probably could not be reached until spring.

Finally, I thought of Dr. Eugene Wheeler, who had operated on me for appendicitis and who had later left Denver to take charge of a big hospital in Goldfield, Nevada. I wired him about my difficulties. He sent a man in to Jack's camp with an order for Jack to come out and proceed at once to Kennet.

In the meantime, I carried on my telegraphic negotiations with the Guggenheims in New York. Everything was settled, including salary and time of arrival at Kennet. I still had no word from Jack, only a telegram from Dr. Wheeler telling me not to worry.

I worried all right, day and night. I had not even told Jack's brother-in-law that I had been dealing with the Guggenheims in Jack's name. I was afraid that if he knew, he would say something to someone in authority and the deal might be ruined.

The waiting seemed interminable; in reality, it was less than two weeks. I had a wire from Jack. He was in Tonopah. It read: "Leaving on midnight train for Kennet. Love and thanks." I think I have never been happier in my life. It was weeks before I learned the full story, when I joined Jack in Kennet. He told me of the trip out from the Kawich region. It sounded pretty grim to me, but he made light of it.

When Dr. Wheeler's message came, he searched for some form of conveyance but none was to be had, so he set out alone in zero temperature and trekked the sixty miles in about sixteen hours. After he got down the mountain, the dry snow was only ankle deep and the going was easy, except that he had to hold back his speed to keep from getting overheated. He carried a lunch pack and a thermos of coffee. The only habitation in the entire region was a stage station, about halfway. Here he rested briefly and got a refill of coffee.

We lived that summer in a two-room shack of corrugated iron. The temperature would drop from around one hundred during the day to eighty at night. I used to dip sheets in a tub of water, wring them out, hang them like a tent, and sit inside to try to keep cool.

We were in a narrow canyon, near a limekiln. A fine white dust permeated the air, coming from the lime rock as it went through the big crushers.

The only pleasant things were the operatic evenings. The workmen were Italians and every night they dressed in native costume— black velveteen trousers and white shirts; around the waist a gay colored sash, worn like a cummerbund; little, tight-knitted caps that hung to the shoulder, tasseled at the end—and sang Italian operas. They had beautiful, liquid voices, and we would sit out on the hillside while the day-shift sang through one opera after another. Many Italian operas were quite familar to me through the limekiln workers long before I heard them in San Francisco, at the auditorium and later at the Memorial Opera House.

Kennet had grown in the years we had been away. The great

Mammoth smelter was running three thousand tons of ore daily. A company hospital had been built in the valley. Our old friend, Dr. Chester Teass, was at the head of it. Trinity Copper had built a large company house up the hill.

At the Balakalala, miles up the hill to the south, the mine was going full blast and shipping ore on an aerial tram to their own smelter at Coram down the mountain. They had added new houses for their employees and a big house, the finest in the county, for their new manager, who had come out from New York. Roy Bishop was a Columbia graduate from Decatur, Illinois (the home of my brother-in-law).

The mines were all producing and the copper market was high. The district was booming. The town was alive with experts coming and going. Miners filled the saloons, and the "cribs" were thriving.

From my little iron house, I could watch stages going to the Mammoth—they had a real road now—and pack trains going to other mines.

Jack was busy reorganizing the development at the Golinsky and preparing to build a tram road for shipping the ore to Garfield, Utah, where the Guggenheims needed it as smelter flux.

The company sent up an office man, George Gibson, who had just come up from their mines in Peru, Cerro de Pasco, I believe. It was through him that Jack had an offer to go to Peru, to a mine at an altitude of 14,000 feet. The offer was fabulous and I wanted him to accept it. He turned it down. He had had enough high altitudes, not only mile-high Denver, but one or two of his Colorado experiences had taken him even higher, where it was difficult to keep miners because of the heart strain.

Anyway, the company wouldn't allow women to go. One of the things which had attracted me was the story that the native women found gold nuggets while wading in the creeks. I thought that while Jack was working I could go tromping the creek sands, picking up gold.

In the spring, there was some special excitement in Kennet. Roy

Bishop had married a New York girl whose father was one of the original Standard Oil officials. He was bringing her out to live at the Balakalala Mine.

One day Jack said, "I think we should ride up to Balakalala and call on the bride."

I demurred. I didn't want to go. I didn't want to meet a New York girl. I knew enough people. . . .

But we went. I rode a wild little sorrel Modoc Indian pony that Jack had bought and "gentled." Only he wasn't gentled very much. I could ride him, but in order to mount (he didn't like my divided skirt), he had to be blindfolded and cheek strapped for a flying mount. Once in the saddle, I had to get my feet in the stirrups in a hurry and check his wild whirling. Around and around he would go, trying to get rid of his rider.

Jack had taught me to grip with thighs, as well as knees, and get a firm seat in the saddle. I would let the little sorrel whirl until we were both dizzy, then pull up on the curb. By that time Buster was discouraged and would settle down and be a good horse for the rest of the ride.

Once he took it into his head to run up the mountain. He was out of control, but I managed to keep my seat. But I was angry, really angry. When he stopped running, I turned him downhill. He went down quite cheerfully, but when we got to the foot of the hill, I whirled him around and headed him uphill again at full gallop. Whenever he indicated that he was ready to stop, I whacked him with my quirt. I ran him all the way up the hill to the spot at which he had given up before, whacking him all the way. Then I let him stop. He was in full lather and puffing like a steam engine, but he never tried to run with me again.

Despite my reluctance to go, the visit to Balakalala was a great success. The bride was delightful. She liked the West and made a splendid Westerner. I came to the conclusion that Eastern women fitted into mining camp life more readily than Western women. Perhaps it was the novelty that intrigued them.

148

Soon after this, the district manager came up to examine the mine. He was pleased with what he saw and indicated that Jack had satisfactorily fulfilled his assignment. He explained, however, that the company was curtailing their explorations and closing down several mining properties, including the one he was developing personally. Since his contract had two years to run and since Jack had declined to sign an employment contract, it had been decided that he, Brayton, should take over at the Golinsky. He did ask Jack to stay on as foreman, but it suited us to move.

This worked out very well, for J.B. was about to build a railroad from the Sacramento River along Pitt River and on up Squaw Creek to the Bully Hill smelter. He wanted Jack to join him as construction superintendent, to work with the chief engineer, Frank Dearborn, who was an old friend.

So we were soon back at Bully Hill. This time in a less humble capacity, for J.B. built a house for us (from my design and plan) in the staff crescent on the hill.

The railroad had been a headache from the time it was started. There had been thirty fatalities, and the summer heat in the canyon plus a driving attitude, had made a difficult labor problem. Major Hood, Chief Engineer of the Southern Pacific Railroad, had looked over the prospect and estimated that it would take a thousand men two years to build the road.

We went in at the beginning of a winter of one hundred and five-inch recorded rainfall. High rubber boots and rubber saddle coats were the almost constant costume.

There were six hundred men on the job when Jack undertook the task, and the work had progressed to a point where the rock hillsides called for mining practices, rather than the teams and scrapers which had been used on the lower stretch. Jack had a plan for easing the labor situation. He assembled the twenty gang bosses—Greek, Italian, Slovenian, Montenegrin, etc.—and explained it to them. The laborers would be supplied with shelter. They would receive a fixed price per carload, with a higher figure for the uphill side of the cut and a higher figure also for night shift. A tally light system would record their production.

He added to this what he called the "bait"—a solemn promise that no matter how much money each man made per day at these rates, the same rates would be paid to the end of the job.

The result was that these immigrant laborers, the majority of whom understood no English, who had been sending home most of their two-dollar or two-and-a-half-dollar daily wage and felt that they were getting rich, suddenly found themselves earning five and six dollars, sometimes even seven or eight; and they were almost ready to fight to remain at their places after a twelve-hour shift.

With this new impetus, the crew was gradually reduced from six hundred to less than three hundred. Those mid-European immigrants did yeoman service for "Mister Fletch," and he was able to place many of them after the railroad and the rebuilt smelter were in operation. They called him "the Padrone" and were hurt when he refused to take money from them. They were accustomed to the "padrone system," under which they were required to send money to their respective consulates in San Francisco every payday.

The first locomotive reached the smelter on the first anniversary of construction.

I can't forget those dreary days when the men from the staff crescent went down the hill in the driving rain, and came back up the hill in the driving rain. Jack kept two saddle horses tired. He would change horses down the line, and often came home so weary that he threw himself on the bed and was asleep in a moment.

How well I remember an experience in returning from a visit. Where the McCloud River emptied into the Pitt, there had been an old wagon bridge, but this had been removed to build a steel railroad bridge. During its construction, there was a temporary suspension bridge over the McCloud, the floor of which was only two planks wide and the side cables almost beyond reach.

While I stood contemplating this uninviting situation, the civil engineer, Frank Dearborn, came down the grade. He led my horse

Buster across by the cheek strap. I followed tremblingly, to the accompaniment of a flow of advice.

"No danger. Don't look down. Keep your eyes on your horse."

The good firm earth of the eastern shore was a welcome haven to my faltering feet. I mounted and rode on to the mine.

It was about that time that the express messenger, Dan Haskell, was killed by bandits. As I said earlier, he was the hero of the story which I later wrote and sold to the movies and for which I received the first hundred dollars I ever earned with my pen.

For some time, there had been trouble when the payroll was brought in through the mountains from Redding. Dan was a Wells Fargo man, brave, courageous, and bold. He had more than once fought off stage robbers. He seemed to have a charmed life. But one day, armed men ambushed the stage. In the strongbox was thirty thousand dollars, wages for the men at the mines, smelter, and railroad. Dan, with his box, sat in the back where he could watch the road but be partially concealed. This day, when the robbers appeared, the driver slowed down and was about to stop the horses, but Dan held the shotgun at his back. "Drive like hell!" he shouted. "Whip up your horses!" The driver was more afraid of Dan than the robbers and used his whip frantically. The horses plunged ahead. There were four miles to go to reach McCormick's store in Delamar. He made record time, driving so fast that the robbers gave up and turned back.

Dan Haskell attempted to put the strongbox into the hands of the storekeeper, but the attempt was too much. He dropped it and fell across it, covering the gold with his body.

People rushed to help him. The doctor came running from his office across the street. He was too late. Dan Haskell was dead. He had been shot through the body. True to Wells Fargo tradition, he had brought in the strongbox. He had lived long enough to deliver his charge before he allowed himself to die.

The town was in an uproar. A posse rode out, armed and furiously angry, for Dan was everyone's friend.

They caught the robbers hiding in the rocks. The sheriff took them to jail in Redding. That was wise, for had he brought them to Delamar they would have been hanging from a tree in half an hour.

I suppose Dan Haskell's ride to Bully Hill with the payroll is still part of the legend of that country.

Our first son, Maurice Clark, was born in the Mammoth Hospital at Kennet. A lovely, fine boy, he lived only three weeks, before he died of an infection that modern medical science would have been able to control. It took me a long time to become reconciled to his tragic and unnecessary death. It was during this time that Sally and J.B. proved their deep friendship. I've never forgotten their kindness.

The stock market entered into our lives. Speculation in metals forced the market down, and at the same time the United States Forestry Service was threatening suit for damage to forests by smelter fumes. Mines were closing down all over the West. Copper reached its lowest price.

One day word came from New York that Bully Hill would be closed. This meant another move.

Jack decided that he had had enough of copper. He turned down an offer to manage a silver, lead, and zinc mining and smelting company in New Mexico only because key men were leaving Bully Hill almost daily and he felt that he should stay with J.B. to the end in appreciation of his many kindnesses.

When it was over, we went down to San Francisco, where Jack made a profitable sale of his Bahamatosh mineral property. At the same time he received an inheritance from his grandfather and an offer to join a large real estate company in Oakland.

I was again pregnant. I was determined not to have another child in a mining camp. I wanted to be where I would have care and comfort. We found a nice home in the Adams Point section of Oakland, and Jack was soon doing well selling real estate.

We furnished the house with furniture I bought at antique stores along the waterfront. It was all Victorian walnut. I bought it, not because I liked the period (my real love was eighteenth century, with which Chapman Place was furnished) but because it was cheap. Chairs that now bring a hundred dollars, I bought for a dollar and a half. A fine dining room table to seat sixteen cost ten dollars. My drawing room furniture came to about fifty dollars.

Much to my surprise the effect was delightful. My treasure was a Chinese Chippendale tilt table, which I still have. It is my choicest piece. There is one similar to it (but smaller) in the drawing room of the Palace at Williamsburg.

Antique buying was a delightful experience. In the mining camps we had had only the crudest furnishings, makeshift. Now we had a real house and the old walnut made it a dwelling of substance.

This venture into antiques started a trend that has lasted all my life. But in the twenty, and more, moves we have made, most of the early Victorian has been sold or given away. I have, however, added other pieces, and our home at Bandon is overflowing. I have almost come to the place where I long to sell everything and start over, just for the excitement of discovery.

Our mining days were over, although we did not know it at the time. We thought panic conditions would soon pass and we would go back to the hills. We never did. Jack rejected offers for examinaton work, but he did accept an appointment to the Board of Directors of the California State Bureau of Mines and Oil. It took only one afternoon a month and was routine, but during that term of service his mail arrived addressed "Honorable," which he found amusing.

Now much of the copper country of our early experience has been inundated by the waters of the great Shasta Dam.

In July, 1911, our second son was born in Oakland. Mother came out from Oklahoma City. The baby was slow in coming, and Mother told me to take long walks. I was too unsightly to go out by day (so I thought) but in the evening Jack and I walked down to the lake and back. One evening we were not far from our house when screaming sirens bore down on us. We were at once surrounded by police who began to question Jack.

He told them that we lived in the neighborhood, only a few doors up, but they were suspicious until they turned their flashlights on me. "Get her home quick!" the lieutenant said. "Two burglaries have just occurred in this district and there may be shooting. Get her home!"

We hurried to our house as fast as we could. Later that night, the nurse sent for the doctor, and the following day John Stuart was born. He weighed nine pounds and came feet first. Slightly delirious from the prolonged and difficult labor, I kept crying out to keep the police from shooting me.

The nurse said he was a beautiful baby, but I was bitterly disappointed because he had a mop of heavy black hair. I had thought all babies were bald. Now he is a great tall man, six-feet-three, and a commander in the United States Navy. But to me, he is always the small child I held against my breast, helpless, dependent upon me for food and life and love.

PART TWO

14

The mining period of my life covered a number of years, twenty or more moves, and many mines which I have not mentioned.

I thought when we reached Oakland that we would settle down into a conventional way of living. I had in mind a growing family, schools, and the attributes of a pleasant, easy life.

I was never more mistaken.

Jack had sold a fine property in Rockridge to Mr. Wells, a wealthy sugar planter, who had many interests. One of them was a chemical works on the Olympic Peninsula, a few miles south of Port Townsend, Washington. This was a new enterprise based on patents bought from a French company. Mr. Wells had taken a fancy to Jack, had looked up his record, and wanted him to go to Washington to take charge of the plant. They were having a variety of troubles, including excessive costs and delays in construction, and wanted a complete change of management.

Jack considered the offer seriously. The idea was challenging and the offer flattering, financially.

The trouble was I. The baby was only three months old, and I was in hospital for an operation. My mother had returned home and Jack's mother had come out to see her only grandson. She had been living in Paris, where her daughter Ann was studying art.

I assured Jack that I had recovered sufficiently to be able to join him at Hadlock in a few weeks, so off he went to the new venture.

I had thought I was through with "Pay, Pack and Follow," but here it was again; furniture to be stored and the house given up.

Hadlock was miles from a town, on the wildly beautiful Olympic Peninsula. Stretching out into the waters of Port Townsend Bay and Puget Sound on a background of high, snow-covered mountains and covered with twenty-foot rhododendron bushes ablaze in pink and purple bloom, the Peninsula was to me a new country of profound beauty.

We lived near the plant, at the bachelor's quarters. Our Chinese cook, Oh Sam, took an immediate liking to Baby Stuart. He would wheel the buggy out into the kitchen, and I would hear him talking to the child in unintelligible Chinese. Later, when Stuart began to mumble words, Oh Sam was delighted; he insisted that the baby was talking "China talk."

Our days were pleasant. There was a fifty-foot yacht to travel up the sound to Seattle or around the bay where the plant was located.

I had a rowboat, and I used to lay the baby in the bottom and row about the bay while the bachelors were "crabbing" for the fine big crabs that are native to that part of the country. Dungeness Crabs they are called, and they were a delicacy in the city markets. The men would fill washtubs with them and cook them under a jet of live steam in the engine room. Oh Sam would have a great bowl of mayonnaise ready, and we would all feast.

There were always troubles in the plant—mechanical and chemical problems—always new ones cropping up. Since one of the products was alcohol, there were always two Internal Revenue agents in attendance, and locks and seals on all pipes and outlets.

I never knew much of what was going on (I was too busy being a mother), but one of the experiments produced a kind of cattle and chicken feed from treated sawdust.

Large ships would come in and tie up at our dock, carrying molasses from Hawaii, oil from California, sulphur from Japan. Huge barges brought sawdust from the lumber mills, and at times there was much activity.

One of the pipelines, through which they pumped molasses, burst and sprayed the sticky stuff all over the dock. I could hear the cursing clear up to the house.

Breakdowns were frequent; much of the equipment was unsuitable for the loads required. The plant which produced sulfuric acid was constantly developing leaks, and the fumes were terrific when the wind blew our way. At times there were other nauseous gases.

Finally, after months of lowering costs and increasing output, still unprofitably, Jack sent his assistant to France to learn what was really wrong with our operation.

Jack told me of one unnecessary expenditure which made him suspicious. The foundations under the machines were of an excessively heavy design and weight, and the sand and gravel for them had been brought more than a hundred miles when there was ample supply right here on the property. He was uneasy about it and reported to his company in San Francisco that he could not find an answer to such extravagance, but he was told to carry on.

One of the men of the laboratory staff had been sent over from Alsace-Lorraine. One day he got a batch of foreign mail. I could see he was worried. He confided in me that he must soon go home; he was in the French Army and had been called back to service. He said he hesitated to tell Jack. I saw no reason why he should hesitate, and said so. Finally, he talked to Jack and urged that his reason for leaving be kept confidential. Jack respected his confidence, even told me nothing about it, but I believe he did clear it with someone in authority, who paid no mind.

What came out a few years later, during World War I, was that

Germany owned the so-called French patents, the chemical works were camouflage, the heavy foundations were for artillery emplacements. From this plant heavy guns could command the three forts that protected Puget Sound, and also cut off the water supply of Fort Flagler and Fort Worden; command the Strait of Juan de Fuca, and, thus, isolate Seattle, Tacoma, Victoria, and Vancouver. The farsighted plan was one of many the Germans had for world domination.

Naturally we knew nothing of the coming war at this time. All we were supposed to know was that a man from Alsace-Lorraine had to leave Hadlock "to go to his dying mother." If we had had the foresight, we might have recognized a key to World War I.

Shortly before Jack made up his mind to resign from the plant, his mother had a sudden stroke and passed away. It was a great shock and sorrow to all of us. She was a kind gentlewoman of great elegance. Since she had been born in Canada, she had asked that she be taken back to Ottawa, her girlhood home, and buried in the Hay family plot.

It was impossible for Jack to get away at the time, so there was a temporary burial in Port Townsend. We will never forget the kindness of the people there. Within an hour or two, a delegation of the Masonic Lodge arrived and took over all arrangements, including the advising of friends and acquaintances of the final rites.

Although reports from Jack's assistant investigating in France indicated that Hadlock was far advanced over the European plants, by now there were so many complications that Jack was determined to get away and had trained a man to take his place. He didn't want to be present at the "finish" (which came less than a year later).

Dr. Takamine, the famous Japanese chemist (consultant for Parke-Davis and reputedly the foremost authority on fermentology), asked Jack to go to Japan and try the process there. He argued that labor and materials were favorable to success in Japan.

But Jack declined. He was thoroughly fed up with "infant industry."

We spent a few days in Victoria and a day or two in Vancouver where one of Jack's schoolmates showed us about, then started east on the Canadian Pacific with his mother's remains. It was a long journey with a small baby, but Jack's sisters had wanted their mother's request to be fulfilled. As for me, I think differently. The old proverb suits me best: "Where the tree falls, let it lay."

When we returned to the West again, in 1914, we lived for a time in Pasadena. Jack had accepted an offer that came through J.B. to join the Standard Oil Company of California. He had hoped it would be in production, but he was assigned to the sales department in the Los Angeles district.

Again we were on the move, for Standard sends its men here, there, and everywhere. Our first stop was Riverside. That suited me, for Riverside was one of the most delightful towns in the nation. It was small when we lived there, for that was before the military moved in with its great air base.

We found a house in an orange grove, on famous Magnolia Drive, between Riverside and Arlington. We were delighted with the life. Jack drove around Riverside and San Bernardino counties but was home every night. I was invited into the various clubs that made Riverside in winter a tourist Mecca. The tennis club was a stone's throw back of our grove; the polo club only a short distance away. Then there was the Glenwood Mission Inn, with dinners and dances on Saturday nights. Bridge clubs supplied daytime entertainment.

I found a wonderful cook and nurse for Stuart. One day when I was walking down a street in Riverside, I saw a colored woman with a wicker basket of clothes on her head. She was smiling and humming a song. I stopped her and asked her what her name was.

"Carvilla, ma'am."

"Where are you going, Carvilla?"

"To deliver this wash to Mrs. Jones."

"I want you to deliver the washing and then come and work for me. I've got a small boy and I haven't a soul to cook for me or look after him, and I don't know what to do. Will you help me?"

She was truly astonished. I think the direct attack confused her so that she consented. She insisted upon only one thing: she would have to have time to see William. William was her husband who worked away from home all week.

"You can go home on Sunday," I told her, and the bargain was made. I have had good fortune all my life in finding capable, faithful cooks and nurses, and Carvilla was one of the best. She stayed with me until her husband's work took him far away; then she found a young girl whom she trained to take her place.

The social life in this resort town was delightful, but I enjoyed the polo games most of all. We had an excellent team, splendid riders and superior players. Some of them were Englishmen whose health suffered in the damp climate of England but flourished in the small orange and lemon groves around Riverside.

The Riverside Polo Club did not have the wealth of the Los Angeles and Pasadena clubs, but played Midwick, Santa Barbara, and Redlands. Nearly every week there was a game. We served tea in the rambling little clubhouse and met some of the greatest players in America.

After a time, we found a house in town, a big, old rambling house with a huge pepper tree growing up through the broad veranda. The crown of the pepper tree was so large that it shaded the whole house.

At this time, not only did the mines remain closed, but railroad building was being curtailed. Lloyd was engaged on the erection of a railroad between Boston and Montreal; he and Jean lived in Webster, Massachusetts. When his company laid off all construction employees, Lloyd was out. We prevailed on them to come to California. Shortly after, Mother and Father came out, also, and the whole family was together in Riverside.

But the Chenoweths soon went to Imperial Valley, where Lloyd had an offer from the Southern Pacific. The Valley was wonderful in winter, but the summers were so hot as to be almost beyond endurance. They stuck it out, however, until Lloyd joined J.B. in his pump manufacturing company.

We loved Riverside. After the restricted years I had spent in mining camps, it seemed to me the peak of fine living. But another move was in prospect, and with our projected move came word that Belgium had been invaded by the German Army.

My last memory of Riverside is of a big ball with tableaux which we gave at the Inn for Belgian Relief. This was preceded by a polo game at the club where we went about among the spectators selling little Belgian flags.

From the pleasant, mild climate of Riverside, Jack was sent to Spokane, Washington, in midwinter.

Stuart, who was now six, talked all the way up about snow. We were going to live in a country where snow lay on the ground from October until May! He could have a sled and build snowmen! We talked snow and its pleasures, until he could scarcely wait to get to the snow country.

We arrived in Spokane when the temperature was fourteen degrees below zero and the air was filled with tiny particles of ice from nearby Spokane Falls. When we stepped off the well-heated Pullman car, Stuart got the full blast of the winter wind in his face. He grabbed at my hand.

"What's this, Mother? What's this?"

"This is what goes with snow," I told him. He turned and began to climb back on the sleeping car. "I am going back to California," he said.

I had a little trouble explaining to him that snow brought cold weather, and that he would get used to the wind on his face. He would wear warm clothes, a wool cap on his head, and mittens on his hands. Wearing a cap (he had never had a hat on his head) and mittens (which he had never heard of) intrigued him.

The Pullman car porter finished it off by telling him that to-

163

morrow he could go out and have a snow fight. By this time he was interested again in the new adventure and got into the taxi without any more discussion. We drove off to the beautiful Davenport Hotel, Stuart pleasantly anticipating the impending snow fight, when he could throw snowballs at his father and perhaps hit him a whack.

Stuart was not the only one to make an adjustment from a warm climate to below zero, from windows and doors open to the air and sun to a steam-heated hotel apartment, and from summer sport clothes to fur coats.

Jack had the heaviest adjustment to make. He traveled out of the Spokane office through the great rolling hills of the Palouse. His field included southeastern Washington, east of the Idaho border, one of the great wheat belts of the United States. In spring and early summer, it was a rippling blanket of green. At harvest time it was a golden sea, moving with every breeze. But in winter . . . !

In the sixty towns in his field, two had hotels with steam heat and rooms with bath. He needed all the resources he had acquired during our frontier mining days in Colorado, Nevada, and Oregon, where winter hardship was routine. During the winter months visiting two or three towns a day by a railroad of uncertain schedule and driving a sleigh into remote villages far from rail required stamina. When the "roads" opened in late spring, it was a "Model T" bouncing first through mud, then dust. Long drives and long hours, working with village merchants and through them meeting wheat ranchers and discussing their yearly need for petroleum products.

In Spokane, I was busy, for soon the United States was in World War I. Instead of Belgian Relief, we were selling Liberty Bonds. Soon, we had to do more than sell bonds, we had Red Cross work to do.

We were living in a five-room apartment in "Brown's Addition." Jack was away five days each week, Stuart was in school, so I was free to work. I volunteered at the Red Cross and found plenty to do. Everything was in confusion. Many women wanted to work but the work had not been organized. The Red Cross in Washington had not set up a plan and everything was at sixes and sevens.

Our first major assignment was to have a parade to promote the sale of Liberty Bonds. The National Red Cross office sent out instructions for organizing it. I was one of four women asked to plan the parade—Mrs. William D. Vincent, whose husband was president of The First National Bank; Mrs. George Hardgrove, whose husband was in stocks and bonds; and Mrs. Louis Davenport, whose husband owned the Davenport Hotel.

We had previously managed a big ball at the Davenport to raise money to buy wool for the knitting department. We had sold so many tickets that hundreds were unable to get into the hotel! I recall that we made over seven thousand dollars, enough to buy a considerable amount of wool for knitting socks, sweaters, and helmets.

We four were a team. We worked well together and we had fun organizing projects. It was natural that our little foursome should be invited to put on the Red Cross Parade.

We talked it over and decided that this should be no ordinary parade. We would have only women; and everyone, with the exception of the grand marshal, should march on foot. It was our thought that the sight of so many women doing voluntary work for the Red Cross would so surprise the people of Spokane that they would open their purse strings to buy Liberty Bonds.

We knew that to be a success, it must be perfectly organized. So we disregarded the plan sent from the National Red Cross, and instead consulted the commanding officer of Fort George Wright, an Army post nearby. He assigned to us a group of officers who took great interest in setting up our parade according to Army plan and even made blueprints for us to follow.

The line of march started at Brown's Addition, with the first division. The grand marshal on a beautiful black horse, and the color guard from Fort George Wright were the only men in the parade. Our *one* float consisted of a beautiful woman in a Red Cross uniform, representing the American Red Cross, Mother of All. The other divisions lined up in side streets, each with its own marshal. They fell into line, one after another.

The women were wonderful; every one of the leaders was alert and waiting for the time to move her marchers into position, until all were on parade—twelve thousand Red Cross volunteers in white uniforms! Some of the papers estimated fourteen thousand, and the story, with pictures, made headlines across the continent.

The spectators went wild. No one had realized how many women were working. Emotions were close to the surface. Tears streamed down faces, as group after group of marching women passed by.

A near misadventure was averted, a misadventure for which I would have been responsible. I had insisted that all downtown streets where the parade was to pass should be cleared. Not an automobile, not a vehicle, nor a streetcar, was to move. We had difficulty getting permission. Dozens of officials were interviewed—the Council, the mayor, the police—and we finally had our way.

As we were assembling, one of the scout riders dashed up to me. "North Central High School is cut off! No cars running to bring them to their meeting place."

This was really a calamity. We needed the high school girls to bring up our numbers. We rushed to the end of the bridge that spanned Spokane Falls. Someone shouted, "Look! Here they come! They are marching!" So they were. They had marched all the way from the school, and now, in perfect military order, they marched across the bridge just in time to take their positions in the parade.

Our committee of four fell in last. I think none of us will ever forget the burst of applause that greeted us as we moved down the line of march.

The parade of Red Cross women was far more successful than anyone dreamed. Before the last marcher had disbanded, people poured in to buy Liberty Bonds and express their appreciation of the work the women were doing. Later, we heard that it was the largest parade of women ever held in the United States, and we were very proud.

I was on the board of the knitting department and went to the office every day. We had ten thousand knitters, for we took in eastern Washington and northern Idaho.

The assistant librarian, Miss Ora Maxwell, set up a card index system, and librarians took turns in issuing wool and receiving the finished products. We had a splendidly organized packing department and a professional knitter to assist beginners to "heel and toe" the innumerable pairs of socks that were knitted by loving hands.

I was the only one in the organization who couldn't knit. One knitter always had a partially knitted sock on my desk, which she changed frequently. "For scenery," she said. "You have all these women knitting, and I don't want them to know that you can't!"

My real job was publicity. I wrote news items, but more frequently gave out human interest stories to the reporters, and they were certainly good to our knitting department when it came to publicity in the papers. Writing these news bits was good for me, and I began to try my hand at short stories. As I finished a story, I put it into a drawer and forgot it.

They would have been there forever if it had not been for two friends, Ben and Helen Kizer. Helen wrote good poetry. She also did book reviews for the New York *Times*. Ben was a brilliant lawyer, a tremendous reader. When he was a young lad, making his way, he resolved to buy a book a week. This resolve he carried on through the years, so that he had a very fine library. Ben was active in local affairs; state affairs also, as time went on. I think now, largely through Helen's influence, he has extended his interests to world affairs.

They were both interested in my desire to write and encouraged me. But I still lacked the courage to send a story to a publisher.

167

There were quite a number of Spokane people interested in the arts. We had a little club which someone facetiously dubbed, "The serious group of little thinkers."

George and Victoria Greenwood were members. She had a charming voice and sang *lieder* with verve. But George was our prize. He was a magnificent pianist. He could have been a ranking concert pianist if he had not been a banker. (He was as good at banking as he was at the piano.)

George was so advanced that some of the most famous pianists in the country came to Spokane just to hear him play and to play with him. Percy Grainger used to visit for weeks. George would have a second Concert Steinway brought into the drawing room, and the two would play duets, night after night.

The Will Vincents were members of the group. Mr. Vincent knew everybody. Every famous person who came to the Northwest sought him out and he entertained them all.

I knew many literary figures and all of the explorers.

Hannah and Harry Hawkins knew all of the newspaper people. Hannah was a star reporter with the *Spokesman-Review*, and interviewed visiting celebrities. Harry came from an acting family and was one of the pioneers in the little theater group. Hannah also wrote plays which the group put on with great success. Having no acting ability, I often did menial backstage work.

There was a fine professional actress, Sarah Truax, living in Spokane, the wife of Colonel Charles Albert; and she sometimes helped with a play, although she had retired from the stage.

Margaret Bean was another reporter on the *Spokesman-Review*. Stoddard King, who wrote the lyrics for the wartime hit song "The Long, Long Trail," had a humorous poem in the paper every day. At the instigation of Ben Kizer, Vachel Lindsay, the poet, came to live in Spokane. He fell in love and married a Spokane girl. Russell Davenport, who later became one of the editors of *Fortune*, was there "looking around."

Vilhjalmur Stefansson came to lecture on the Arctic. We met

him at a dinner party, and for some reason, he took an interest in my attempts to write. I told him, "I would like to write a book, but I don't think I have the ability."

His answer was, "Every novelist has had to write his *first* book."

This was unanswerable. It was logical. It was just writing that first book.

Stefansson knew I was tremendously interested in the Arctic. "Why don't you write a book about the Arctic? About an explorer?" he asked, his eyes twinkling.

After he left, I thought about the idea, and that was the extent of it. But "Stef" kept writing, trying to encourage me. I finally decided to see what I could do with my pen.

I got the notion that I would write about timber. We were close to the Idaho timber country. We knew Huntington Taylor, manager of the Weyerhouser Company in Coeur d'Alene, Idaho. I talked with him about it. He was interested at once and said he would arrange for a timber cruiser (an expert who estimates timber) to take me through the white pine country. He suggested that I ask Margaret Bean, who worked on the *Spokesman-Review*, to go with me.

For some time, I had employed a lady to stay with Stuart after school when my work kept me until dinnertime. Miss Scott was a very competent and reliable woman and she came to take care of Stuart, while Margaret and I were away with the timber cruiser in the deep woods of Idaho.

"Hunt" Taylor had everything arranged for us. The horses were ready when we arrived at the Taylor home in Coeur d'Alene. The timber cruiser was waiting there for us also, a tall, lean, rangy man, who looked at us with contempt.

Hunt had sent for him to come down from the woods. When he learned that he was to escort two women, he blew up. With a woodsman's special ability, he "cussed us out."

"To take two tenderfeet into the woods was bad enough, but women!"

He was finally calmed down and we started off on a narrow trail into the woods. We had two good, fast-walking, sure-footed horses. We had all our clothes squeezed into saddlebags.

The cruiser, followed by a pack mule with our camping equipment and "grub," rode ahead of us. Blanket rolls were on the back of our saddles, and we were on a great adventure.

Our guide rode along, grumpily, never speaking. He stopped at stated intervals, motioned to us to dismount, and waved his arm in the general direction of the deep woods. This we took to mean that it was our opportunity to attend to the wants of nature. We dismounted and meekly went off into the bush.

His attitude of contempt was a little hard on two women who wanted to learn something about this magnificent country; in fact, we wanted to learn everything about it.

My experience in the mining camps came to our rescue. I had learned when I traveled with men to ask no favors. I looked after myself—cooked my food, saddled and unsaddled my horse, took my bedroll from the back of my saddle and made up my bed, in the manner Jack had taught me.

The first night, when our guide announced that we had come to our camp, we dismounted, unsaddled our horses, led them to a little stream for water, and hobbled them for grazing.

This was the silent gage of battle that we had thrown before our guide's feet. He was obliged to notice us. He said that he didn't know that ladies knew how to care for horses. We said he probably didn't know much about women. He admitted that he wasn't married.

After that things went better; he cooked good meals over the campfire and began to talk about trees. The latter was indeed an illuminating experience. I have never known anyone who loved trees as he did. To him, they were friends, living people. He would point to a big tree and say, "Know how much she'd scale?" When he first asked the question, I had not the foggiest idea what he meant. After a time I realized that he wanted us to estimate how many board feet the tree would contain when it was felled and cut up at the mill.

We learned about the life of a pine tree, from a seed to a giant of the forest, how the trees were protected and scrub brush cut out; how firebreaks were made. Fire was the greatest enemy of a forest. Careless people might set a fire, but the greatest danger was from lightning.

Deeper and deeper we went into the woods. We saw no one. We were told not to wander off, we might get lost. (Each of us carried a compass.) We were so deep in the forest that we glimpsed the sky only occasionally through the tall trees. Aside from getting lost, there was danger from wild beasts—wolves and cougars, the "mountain lions" which had so terrified me at Mammoth Mine.

We were cautioned to stay close to the trails. I did not tell our guide that I could shoot, for he was now at the stage where he wanted to protect us. We thought we would be "a little bit helpless." Sometimes it pays for a woman not to be too independent.

After several days' travel through the immense white pine forest, we came to a lumbering camp, high in the hills.

Hunt Taylor had warned us to take what came and not to ask for favors in the woods camps. "Cooks are temperamental and I don't want them disturbed."

With that in mind, we praised the cooking. We ate heartily and enjoyed everything including the breakfast "stack of wheats." It reminded me of my mining camp days.

I often think of that delightful trip through the pine forest. Sometimes, when I am tired from long hours at my desk, I think of the cool green of the forest and the serenity of the great woods and I am glad that I had that satisfying experience in the mountain country of Idaho.

While we lived in Spokane, Stuart and I made two trips to California to visit my family. Father and Mother had moved from Denver and were visiting Jean and Lloyd in Los Angeles.

On one of these occasions, remembering my experience with the Dan Haskell story, I approached a studio with another story for the movies, this time about the wheat country of the Palouse, which had fascinated me. *The Western Gate* told of the changing of a great cattle country into an equally great wheat-raising area.

Allen Boone was the manager of the Robertson Cole Company studios. He bought the story for Pauline Frederick. They never filmed the story but I got a check for a thousand dollars and a trip to California out of it, and I had the excitement of going to the studio every day and working with the script writer. I felt rather set up, to have a part in the film world of Hollywood. But I was soon tired of it. It was all so artificial, and I was glad to go back to Spokane where people were normal and the world revolved about such things as mines and timber and water power.

Stuart was in the Washington School. One day his teacher telephoned to ask if she could come to see me. I couldn't imagine what she wanted, but I soon found out. They were giving intelligence tests, and Stuart had tested in the genius class. She was very excited about it.

"What will we do? What will we do?" she kept repeating.

"Nothing," I said. "We will do nothing. First of all, we will not tell Stuart anything about it. I want him to have a simple, normal life. If he begins to think he is a genius, we will be in trouble."

The teacher agreed with me. I think Stuart was in Annapolis, at the Naval Academy (by competitive examination) before we told him about being a genius. I don't know what there is in this genius business. As far as I know, he hasn't developed into an Einstein. He is an intelligent officer in the United States Navy, and I am very proud of him.

The company transferred Jack out of the Palouse country into the Spokane area, and we moved out of the apartment into a big, rambling old house on the very brink of the gorge.

Spokane has a magnificent natural setting. Hills, hollows, high places, and a tumultuous river that cuts a great gorge into the rock. In a way, it is a miniature Grand Canyon, and it must be three miles across from the Spokane side to the rimrock on the opposite bank.

Jack became interested in Boy Scout work. He thought it would bring him closer to his son. I don't know which one enjoyed it more, the lad or his father. The Scouts had so many younger brothers (too young for scouting) that they became a problem at meetings. Stuart himself was still under Scout age, and his father hit on a plan to have Stuart take the youngsters into another room and help them learn the tenderfoot work and tests. The idea took hold, and Stuart called his group "Cubs." This was long before the cub program became nation-wide.

Soon Jack was asked to take charge of the Banner Troop of the Northwest District. Realizing that this troop had a record to maintain and that his own Scouting knowledge was limited, Jack felt he must give the boys a new incentive. A fortunate choice was offering to help them earn the Horsemanship Merit Badge. He made an arrangement with a nearby livery stable to hold night classes in its indoor arena, where he could teach the boys the elementary things they needed to know in order to form a group outside. The program was immediately a huge success. The troop advanced rapidly that year, and by the time we left Spokane, there were more than eighty Scout Horsemen. This was the start of Jack's more than twenty years as an active Scouter, during which time he declined a flattering offer to become a professional regional executive.

It was during this time that Rodney Wood came to Spokane from Canada to talk to Scouters. At a recent meeting of Scouters in London he had attracted the interest of Lord Baden-Powell, the founder of the Scout movement, by his speech on big game tracking in Africa.

Rodney Wood had been in Nyasaland, British Central Africa, for some years, experimenting in planting. He was one of a group of young men, facetiously called "Mud Pups," sent out by the

British Government. They went into outlying districts and established experimental farms to show the natives improved methods so that they could earn more money from their crops.

He became a fine marksman. He shot only for safety and for specimens, but some of the game he shot is recorded in *Ward's Book of Animals.*

Lord Baden-Powell was so intrigued by the tales Wood told that he persuaded him to give two years to Scouting work, in particular, to the training of Scout leaders around the world.

Jack was as fascinated as every Scouter with Rodney's talk at their weekly luncheon and invited him home for dinner, and then to his Scout Troop meeting that evening.

All who heard him speak fell under Rodney's spell. I always thought of him as living out of his century. He belonged to medieval times, like the old minstrels, except that he talked instead of singing. When we found that he had three weeks' holiday coming to him, we prevailed on him to spend it with us.

He was the idol of all the lads in the neighborhood. They followed him day and night. Every lad wanted to go to Africa, to live in the wilds, to shoot elephants and lions. Every lad vowed he would go when he grew older.

But I was the one who later went to Africa. My object was to get material for a book on witchcraft. That African journey, as Kipling says, "Is another story"! But the seed was planted when Rodney told his stories to me during those days in Spokane, and I wrote them down. Nothing came of them then but a mass of material. After my trip to Africa, in 1928, Rodney's stories became the core of my first book.

Our house was directly on the bank of the canyon in a setting of great pine trees. Directly behind us the Hawkinses lived. As I said before, Hannah worked on the *Spokesman-Review.* She was a skilled newspaper woman with a genius for interviews.

The Hawkinses had seven children, one daughter and six sons, of various ages up to fifteen. They were ruled by an old Negro woman, who was overweight and did not like to make the effort to get up out of her chair. She had her cane and she used to lay about with it. The little ones learned early to skip out of Lessie's reach.

The townspeople predicted that the children would come to a bad end because Hannah worked instead of staying at home with them. One of them recently retired as Rear Admiral of the Navy and became head of the mathematics department of a northern California college; the only girl writes successful children's books; and the others have profitable businesses. It was a wonderful family; they were close, and they had fun, laughter, and a happy life.

On the other side of us, the Corrigans had two boys. The children put on plays and charged ten pins admission. They called themselves "The Cellar Steppers." William Corrigan is now a director in television. He put on some of Sarah Churchill's plays.

I have one more happy remembrance of Spokane. A group of us were taken into the Colville Indian tribe and given Indian names in an impressive ceremony among the trees on our place overlooking the canyon.

It came about in this way. Hannah Hawkins found out that there were more than a hundred thousand dollars in the Bureau of Indian Affairs in Washington that had been designated years ago for the Colville tribe in northern Washington State. We became interested in this because Mary, our cleaning woman, was a Colville Indian, a princess of the tribe and a fine woman.

We decided that the Colvilles should have their money; first, because they were very poor, living on a small, rocky reservation, and secondly, because they were the only known Indian tribe that had never shed the blood of white men.

We set about pulling political strings through congressmen and senators, and eventually the Colvilles received their money.

The tribe was very pleased, and to honor Hannah and me, they decided to make us one of them, with a real tribal ceremony. Adopting us, though, posed a problem. If we, as women, were made members of the tribe, our husbands would then become "squaw men." This was unthinkable, for squaw men were far down the totem pole; so they must also make the husbands members of the tribe. Rodney Wood was our house guest at the time, so he must be included, and there were one or two others.

We all thought it would be an amusing experience. But we were very wrong. It was a beautiful, moving ceremony.

A number of Indians came down from the reservation, including the reigning princess. First we women were required to gather faggots, build a fire, and bake a little round of bannock bread. Then the headband was placed around our forehead and a bundle of sticks on our backs. This was symbolic of our position in the tribe. The princess gave a beautiful speech (Indians are great orators) telling why the Colvilles had never shed the blood of white men when their neighbors, the Nez Percé, were always at war.

In early times, several white men came into the territory, the first the Indians had ever seen. Men, women, and children were curious about the pale faces. The chief warned his people not to touch any of the white men's belongings, but two little boys found a pair of boots by the river bank. They carried them off, to find out what they were.

The trappers, for they were French voyageurs from Canada, were angry and followed the boys to the wigwams of the Indians. They shot the chief at the door of his tepee, when he came to explain what the children had done. On his deathbed, the chief extracted an oath from his people never to shed the blood of white men. He looked into the future and saw these men as the first of many white men who would come to this country, and his tribe must live in peace with them.

Each year at their harvest festival, *Yep Canum*, September Ninth, the Colvilles repeat their chief's dying oath.

When the Indian princess finished her story, I was in tears; and I think everyone present felt as I did, proud that we had become adopted members of the Colville tribe.

They gave me a beautiful name, "Ki kitch ina," which means

"The bird that comes first in the spring to tell that the other birds are coming." Jack was named "Quo iss la kin," or "Three Mountains-High Horse," after a chieftain noted for horsemanship. I do not remember the other Indian names, but Harry Hawkins' meant "Father of Many," and Rodney Wood was "The Whirlwind," which suited him perfectly.

We had been in Spokane for some years when Standard Oil began shuffling people about. Jack was ordered to San Francisco.

It was "Pay, Pack, and Follow" again.

Our years in San Francisco I number among the most pleasant years of our lives. It is, I think, the most beautiful, the most fascinating city in America; perhaps in the world. Capetown, Venice, Stockholm, Edinburgh, Paris, London, these places all rank high, but to me San Francisco is the queen of them all.

We stayed in San Francisco until Jack retired in 1938.

15

From San Francisco to Africa is a tremendous leap, not only in space but in ways of thinking. Rodney Wood's stories had, of course, initiated my interest in Africa, and in San Francisco I found a means whereby I could see the country for myself. How this came about I shall tell you later, but that trip was the doorway to my career in writing. Something happened in Africa that brought to the surface my latent creative impulse.

Whether Africa is, as the saying goes, "the mother of all living," I know that the months I spent in British Central Africa stirred the talent lying dormant within me. I made sketches. I wrote poetry. I recorded daily accounts of my experiences and observations. I collected material about witchcraft, or "mankawala," as the natives call it. I wanted to sculpt and I wanted to write a book.

You know from the earlier parts of my story that I had played with the idea of writing for years. Like thousands of others, I said I wanted to be a writer, but I myself do not know whether I was serious about it. Except for the two stories I had sold to the movies, I had only bits of newspaper pieces and verse to show for my lackadaisical efforts. Even in San Francisco, where I was in contact with writers, playwrights, and sculptors, I didn't get beyond the talking stage.

Perhaps this is the place where I should give a bit of advice to would-be writers. Don't talk about it. Write. Don't write a few pages, then run to your friends and ask them to listen while you read what you have written. Don't take too seriously the opinions of your friends. There is just one person to listen to and that is the editor who is going to publish what you have written.

Write every day, if only a few lines. You will develop the habit of writing and that is the most important thing. For writing is a habit and the sooner you recognize that fact, the sooner you will develop your talents.

The sound of your own voice, reading a bit of verse, a few pages of a story, is a trap to keep you from serious work. More often than not, your efforts will end there.

"They say" writing is a lonely job. But you are never lonely when you are writing. You are carried along an exciting path by the people you are creating. Sometimes I wonder if one has the right to create so many people, and throw them out into the world. Where will they go? What influence will they have?

I have created, out of my subconscious, hundreds of characters. They roam about, leaping from the pages of the eleven novels I have written. Will they be Frankensteins to return and rend me for giving them life? Or will they be grateful for that life? I don't know the answer. I only know that they appear to me from somewhere. They become as real, perhaps more real, than the live people about me. One thing is true, to me they are human.

If a character I create ceases to have life, does not move about and talk and express his views, there is only one thing to do—kill him off.

If one has the creative impulse to write, one must write; whether or not one sells is not important. The act of creating is the vital thing. Of course one does want to sell, for that is the applause and the appreciation, the recognition of shared experience between author and reader.

Often I am asked by beginning writers, "Do you wait for an inspiration?" The answer is no. No. No.

I think there is only one real inspiration and that is the original idea. You wake up in the middle of the night. You have an idea. You will write a book about a journey to the moon, or around the corner. You live with the idea for days. It illuminates all of your waking moments.

Or perhaps the great idea comes when you are working furiously to meet a deadline. A publisher is tromping on your heels to get the last chapter in. But here is this new idea, hounding you day and night. This is inspiration to the nth degree. I must say that in my experience this noble inspiration frequently expires by the time I have finished the current book.

When the dream persists, it is true inspiration.

I remember a story Hugh Walpole told me as we lunched at the Fairmont in San Francisco. He was engaged in writing one of the Cathedral Series when suddenly he saw in his mind a little cottage on a lonely moor. Two women were peering out of a small window. They were frightened, looking for some unknown danger. These frightened women kept returning to his mind, shutting out the story on which he was engaged. Who were they? Why were they hiding in a wretched cottage on a lonely moor? What danger was menacing them? The upshot was that Walpole had to lay aside his work and write *The House on the Moor*.

That was inspiration. Mr. Walpole was too much of a man of letters to ignore it.

When I returned from Africa, I brought with me several short stories. Some I wrote while out on *ulendo* (the Portuguese word for the more common safari); several were rewrites of the stories told me by Rodney Wood; others were drawn from tales of the District Commissioner of Nyasaland, W. Kirby Green; and one I had from Colonel S. M. Prichard of South Africa.

These men had all lived in Africa for many years. They opened my eyes to the Africa that travelers seldom see. Witchcraft they knew as the natives knew it. They did not minimize the effect it has on the life of the people, any more than I minimize the effect on our lives of early witchcraft in this country.

I brought home a tin trunkful of material on witchcraft. It was my intention to trace the beliefs from Africa through the Caribbean islands to America. The book was never written, but I still have the material.

Instead, I wrote short stories. Some I sold to *Boys' Life*, among them "Here are Elephants" and "The Man who Comes and Goes in Silence."

One or two others I sold to *Munsey* magazine. This magazine was owned by our friend, William Dewart, who at that time also owned the New York *Sun*. Bob Davis made the sale. I well remember that he struggled up three flights of stairs to our San Francisco flat to talk to me about writing.

"You have a million dollars worth of material in your head. Get to work."

I was flattered. Bob Davis had the reputation of having helped more young writers than anyone in America. But in this instance he overestimated, for if I had a million dollars of material in my head, much of it must still be there. Over the years, my books have brought me a not inconsiderable amount, but far from a million.

But before I write about my acceptance as an author, I must tell you how I came to be one and this starts with my venture into the lecture field in San Francisco, with a well-known and experienced musical impresario, Alice Seckles.

When I had made up my mind that I wanted to go to Africa to get material for a book on witchcraft, I didn't have enough money for the journey, so with Miss Seckles I organized the Seckles-Fletcher Lecture Bureau, which I hoped would supply the additional funds I needed.

There had been no important lectures or lecturers in San Francisco. The few that had been available were held in churches or small halls, free, or for an admittance fee of fifty cents. We were going to change all this. We would have season subscribers at theater prices and give our patrons the great names in the lecture field.

Miss Seckles would attend to the details of hiring halls, printing tickets and programs, and putting on the show. She was well-equipped for this, having had years of experience with "Matinee Musicals."

My part was to engage the lecturers and get publicity. I wanted front page stories, not small notices among club and church items.

I understood newspaper editors. I knew that to get people on the front page I had to have newsworthy people, people whose visits to San Francisco were important enough for interviews and news stories. I went to the city editors of various papers. I showed them my list of available lecturers and asked them which names they considered news. This turned out to be a wise beginning, for the editors showed great interest in the idea and were very frank in telling me who was news and who was not.

The next step was to visit our old friend, Roy Bishop, formerly of the Balakalala Mine, whom I considered a number one business man, and ask his advice.

He was interested, but, "It's a gamble," he said. "How much money can you afford to lose?"

"I hadn't considered losing any," I said. "I count on making enough money to go to Africa."

He laughed immoderately. "Maybe you're right. Maybe it is better not to think of losing but of winning."

Then he worked out a plan. I should have sponsors, the foremost men in San Francisco should get behind the Lecture Bureau.

"I'll write some letters for you to present, and we'll see what happens."

With Roy's letters and my story, I called on some of the most important men in San Francisco. No one refused me. Naturally,

I told them there was no financial obligation, that I wanted the prestige of their names to ensure success of the lectures.

Our list of sponsors included Mr. William H. Crocker, President of the Crocker National Bank; Mr. A. P. Gianini, President of The Bank of America; United States Senator Phelan; and a number of other impressive names.

Roy was delighted. Repeatedly, he told me, "You have the answer. Don't give a thought to possible failure, think only of success."

The names of our speakers were selected with great care, because those names would sell the season tickets. It was a year when illustrated lectures on exploration were in vogue. We selected all the great travelers and explorers: Roy Chapman Andrews, Vilhjalmur Stefansson, Carl Akeley, Lowell Thomas with his sensational pictures of Lawrence of Arabia, and Sir Hubert Wilkins. Prince William of Sweden was our greatest attraction, with his pictures of unknown pygmies in a remote part of Africa.

Before Prince William's lecture, the P. E. N. Club, of which he was a member, gave a dinner for him at the Mark Hopkins Hotel. Gertrude Atherton (San Francisco's most famous and beloved novelist) was president of the club then and remained so until her death in 1948. She was well-acquainted with the Swedish Royal Family, and she wanted the dinner to be perfect.

She seated the Prince between herself and Helen Wills, the World Tennis Champion. Nothing could have pleased him more. He belonged to a great tennis-playing family. He had said that he wanted nothing so much as to meet the charming lady.

Every one of our lecturers was a success. Roy Chapman Andrews had wonderful pictures of China, the Gobi Desert, and his dinosaur eggs. He confessed to me that there had been so much publicity about the eggs that it made him ill, but the public loved his lectures. Roy Andrews is one of my favorite people.

Stefansson is certainly one of the greatest thinkers of our age. I am sorry that he has buried himself at Dartmouth, writing that mammoth book on the history of polar exploration. He is literate, scientific, extremely witty, and adventurous—an extraordinary combination. There is a story told of him that when he was questioned about a so-called scientific theory of the Englishman, Markham, that there were no fish in the polar sea beyond five miles from shore, Stefansson's reply was that it was a fine theory, "But do the fish know it?"

He has written many books on the Arctic. *The Friendly Arctic* was perhaps the greatest. But he wrote another, perhaps more important, called *Northward the Course of Empire,* in which he foretold flying over the North Pole as the short route to Europe. This, more than thirty years ago. Unlike most men of far vision, he has lived to see his prophesies fulfilled.

One of my favorite lecturers was Lowell Thomas. We invited him several times and he always filled the auditorium. He was a pleasant person, with an extraordinarily fine speaking voice. The whole world knows that voice, and the whole world knows of his extraordinary travels in out-of-the-way places.

Sir Hubert Wilkins, who was one of Stefansson's companions on Arctic expeditions, was another fine speaker. I am reminded of him today as I read of the Navy's magnificent achievement with the atomic submarine *Nautilus* under the polar ice cap. Nearly thirty years ago, Sir Hubert stood in our drawing room, leaning against the mantel, and astonished the company by saying, "Does anyone know where I can get a second-hand submarine? I want to try a journey under the Arctic ice."

This was an astounding idea, and there was instantly an avalanche of questions.

One of the guests was George Douglas, an editorial writer on the San Francisco *Examiner.* He was very interested in Sir Hubert's conviction and wrote an editorial about it. As far as I know, that was the first announcement of Wilkins', or anyone else's, under the ice idea.

Later, he got a submarine and did make a successful try, but not a real journey of such tremendous importance as the one made by the *Nautilus.*

Carl Akeley, another lecturer, was one of the most interesting men I have ever known. People remember him as a successful explorer in Africa and as former President Theodore Roosevelt's guide and companion on his big game hunt; but he accomplished many other things of importance. He invented the first stop-and-go traffic signals and the modern method of taxidermy. In the old days, skins of animals were stuffed with straw. They bulged in the wrong places and were often ridiculous looking. Akeley was the first to measure the fresh skins carefully and build a framework to fit the actual size, mount the wild game in a proper background of trees and bushes, and paint in a scene of the actual country. His method is now used all over the world. During World War I, he planned the concrete ships and participated in the development of the modern method of spray painting concrete buildings.

From this list of speakers, you can see why our lecture bureau was a success. I withdrew at the end of two years. I had the money for my trip to Africa and other ideas in my head.

I did think it rather amusing that I had contrived to have all these great explorers pay my way to the Dark Continent! Of course they never knew that their talks provided the cash for steamer tickets and travel which eventually led to a writing career for me.

So it was after Africa that I settled down to write.

It is amazing how one forgets. If I had been asked about the publication of my books, I would have said that the first book that I wrote was taken by a publisher and every book thereafter, up to the present number of thirteen; that my whole writing life was a series of acceptances.

But as I read over a series of letters taken from dusty files, I find that I had a number of setbacks, and several books were not immediately accepted. In fact, one or two have not been published to this day.

The first writing I did after returning to San Francisco from Africa was an article on native dances that I had seen there. I called it "The Hidden Dances." It was accepted by *Asia*, a travel magazine, and published under the title of "A Bootleg Dance among the Ma-Nganya," or some such distortion.

The fact that an editor would change a title was a complete surprise to me. I did not know, as I now know, that editors love to change titles. Not only the editors, but the entire editorial staff and the salesmen have conferences in which your carefully selected title is tossed about until finally, from complete inertia and weariness, a title is chosen.

Later, I found that by giving an editor a number of titles, burying my choice in the middle of the list, I would later have another chance to voice an opinion and get the title I really wanted.

On the *Asia* material, I was not consulted. I was horrified when *The Hidden Dances* came out with such a frivolous, even comic title, but they had paid me a hundred dollars and I swallowed my disappointment. I received a great many letters about the article. Many said what I felt, that the title had nothing to do with the story. The only peg they had to hang the title on was that I had given a chief some money to make native beer. On the beer the dancers would work themselves up to a high pitch. Only then would they dance some of the hidden dances that Europeans had seldom, if ever, witnessed. However, there it was, I did give the chief the beer money.

Several of these African stories were bought by *Boys' Life*. They were magnificently illustrated by Manning deV. Lee. They had an immediate success because they had an unusual African setting. Mr. George F. Pierrot, managing editor of *Boys' Life*, wrote me an enthusiastic letter, and I was happy because boys liked the stories.

Earlier, as each story was finished, I had asked Jack to read them at his Boy Scout meetings. They were so well received there that we were sure they would be liked by other boys.

Three of the African stories had now been sold and published, but I still had a number of others. They had a central character, a young English commissioner in the lake district of Central Africa. Each tale told of his experiences with the natives he had been sent to govern. Some were worked around native customs and witchcraft.

I don't remember how I first had the idea of a book to be made up of these stories, but in 1930, I sent them to the Bobbs-Merrill Company in Indianapolis.

I had a reason for this. One of the speakers on our lecture bureau was Richard Halliburton, whose *The Royal Road to Romance* had taken the country by storm. Crowds came to the lectures and bought hundreds of his books, which Paul Elder's bookstore sold at the lecture hall. We extended this courtesy to all the lecturers. (We did not get a percentage.)

Of all the publishers represented on our programs, Bobbs-Merrill did the most to help its authors. It advertised extensively and gave a luncheon for book dealers and reviewers, with a splendid tie-in promotion program. I said at the time, "When I have a book to publish, I will send it to Bobbs-Merrill."

And I did. Bobbs-Merrill accepted the African stories. I did not realize it, but I was launched as a writer. It was one of the times in my life that the gods were on my side. Not only was my first book to be published, but I had David Laurence Chambers as my editor, and so he continued to be for nearly twenty-five years.

Mr. Chambers is one of the great editors of America. Although he is not as well-known, perhaps, as Maxwell Perkins for his work with Thomas Wolfe, I am sure the number of young writers Laurence Chambers has taken by the hand and led through the maze of the literary world will surpass that of any other editor.

Unfortunately, some of the writers left when they got over that early hurdle. That always seemed to me poor sportsmanship. A publisher invests a good deal of money in a new writer. It costs to produce a book. The editor has nothing to go on except his faith in the author. The first, second, and even third book may bring in little profit. If the publisher just gets by, he is lucky.

Publishing is one of the greatest gambles in the world, and that gamble is taken every spring and fall by dozens of publishers. Sometimes there is a "runaway book," such as Hervey Allen's *Anthony Adverse*. When this book appeared, there was a strong prejudice against the historical novel. I think all writers of historical fiction should say a prayer to Hervey Allen, for he opened the way after long years during which no publisher would look at a novel based on history.

Mr. Chambers led me along the path. What success I have had I owe to him. I stayed with him from 1930 to 1957, until his retirement. He is a man of great erudition and he knows all aspects of the publishing business thoroughly, both business and editorial. I wish he had not retired. I hope one day he will write about the authors he has led to success. The list will surprise many people.

Here is, I think, the earliest letter I had from Laurence Chambers. It concerns my first book, *The White Leopard*, which was published in 1931.

August 26, 1930

Dear Mrs. Fletcher:

It is with the greatest of pleasure that I tell you that we are eager to publish your manuscript, *Adventures in Africa*. We are all most enthusiastic about it.

. . . We have something of a problem to work out with this book, because if it is published as a boys' book, adults will not read it. And if it is published using the title *Adventures in Africa*, that will accentuate the fact that it is a collection of short stories and a book of short stories is seldom popular and difficult to sell. We wish to reduce this short story element as far as possible. What would you think of calling the book *The Leopard* and making each story a chapter? This is really essential, in my estimation, to the success of the volume. . . . In this way, with just a little more work, you will have a splendid, unified book, much more desirable than a mere group of adventures.

There is one story, "The Snake God," which I do not think should be included here. It does not seem at all fitting for a boys' book and even if it were rewritten I do not believe it would meet with the approval of the librarians over the country . . . I'm sure they would frown upon too much black magic and I am inclined to think myself that it isn't a good thing for young minds to dwell upon. Your stories have so many superior qualities that I am sure the book will not suffer from the omission of "The Snake God."

And now as to the illustrations . . . We generally limit ourselves to four or five full page illustrations, for to exceed
that number, the book would have to be priced higher than
the usual $2.00. And just now with the price-cutting move-
ment of some publishers creating havoc with the market, it
would be fatal to price the book at more than $2.00. . . .
I shall be glad to have your opinion in regard to this matter.

I am returning the manuscript to you today and shall
await your comment with impatience, for I am eager to get
that contract ready for your signature.

With heartiest congratulations on your achievement and
very best wishes, I am,

Cordiallly yours,

D. L. Chambers

This letter is included because it is the first letter I had from
an editor accepting a book I had written and because I think it
is a model letter from editor to author. Notice the technique:
first praise, to put the author into a happy, jubilant mood, then
the suggestion of changes. After the impact of success, the idea
of a few changes amounts to nothing in the mind of the writer.

Mr. Chambers always used this method during the whole of my
long association with him. I would send in a manuscript of a new
book. He would write or wire, "This book is probably the best you
have ever written." I was then so joyous that the three-page telegram suggesting innumerable changes, which came the following
day, never dampened my spirits in the least. Always, after these
suggested changes, he would write, "But after all, you are the
author." This was the master stroke which restored spirits beginning to droop and confidence in my ability to write.

In my first book I knew there was much work to be done. I
had to take a series of stories and give them narrative unity. Inexperienced as I was, I accomplished it only under Laurence
Chambers' patient guidance, but eventually we had a book.

There were numerous changes of title before we decided on
The White Leopard, with the subtitle, *A Tale of the African
Bush*. It was published by Bobbs-Merrill, August 25, 1931.

An English novelist, I think it was Arnold Bennett, once commented that a writer never felt that he had reached ultimate success until he had seen his name on the title page of a book. I subscribe to that. I well remember when the postman left *The White Leopard* at our flat at 2442 Leavenworth Street, San Francisco. It was a morning of heavy fog. The foghorn was wailing on Alcatraz, directly across from our windows. We could not see the island because of the density of the mist.

The postman rang. I rushed to pull the lever that opened the front door, two flights below.

"Got you some books." The postman's voice was cheery. "They weigh heavy."

I ran down the steps and took the package. I could scarcely wait to tear off the wrappings. There was *The White Leopard* and my name across the title page, Inglis Fletcher. I sat down abruptly, for my knees were giving way. I had written a book! It was in my hand! The miracle had happened.

No one was there to share my happiness. Jack was at work, Stuart in Annapolis at the Naval Academy. I was alone!

Perhaps it was best that way. It was a sublime experience for me. I turned the pages slowly, looking at the superb woodcuts by Kurt Wiese, the action pictures that Mr. Chambers said were necessary for a juvenile book.

All day I was alone with my happiness. I looked at the book again and again. I enjoyed the book itself, its fine printing and general make-up.

Two exciting things had happened to the Fletcher family that year. Stuart had won three competitive examinations for Annapolis: the Naval Reserve, the Senatorial, and the Congressional. He had also stood first in competitive examination for the new California State Nautical School. He was on his way to a life that he had talked about since he was five years old and had made friends with a retired naval officer across the street.

And I had written a book.

Both of us had started long dreamed of careers. Mother and

son had both entered on a course that was to carry us to far places of the earth, Stuart on ships and I with my books.

Telegrams and letters of congratulations poured in, from old friends, from librarians, from booksellers, and from lads in almost every state of the Union.

Newspaper reviews were splendid. One in particular, by Charles F. Finger, in the *Herald-Tribune*, said: "It is very real, the way in which *Mr.* Fletcher handles the conjuration scenes." I was called Mr. Fletcher many times after that, partly because of my name and partly because, as some reviewers indicated, of the way I wrote battle scenes.

I immediately wrote letters of appreciation to Rodney Wood, W. Kirby Green, and to Colonel S. M. Prichard, the three men who had helped me with my plots for the stories by telling me their actual experiences.

One letter I received that pleased me very much was from the late Colonel, the Honorable L. S. Amory, Secretary of the Colonies and Dominions of Britain. Stefansson had given me a letter of introduction to Colonel Amery, and when I was in London on my way to Africa I visited him at the Colonial Office. He was very interested in the fact that an American woman was going out to British Central Africa to study native witchcraft.

Before I left, Colonel Amery asked if I would like to have "a line" to the various colonial governors in East Africa. I said I thought it would be nice. I was so inexperienced that I did not know that a letter from the Secretary of the Colonies and Dominions was almost as important as a letter from the king. Nor had I any idea of the doors this letter would open magically through all of my journey in Central Africa.

I have seen Colonel Amery a number of times since, whenever I visited London. I have met his charming wife and his son, Julian. Julian had a fantastic career in middle Europe, during the war. He is now an M.P., married to Lady Caroline Macmillan, daughter of the present prime minister.

Here is Colonel Amery's letter about the book for which he had helped me collect material:

112 Eaton Square SW1
21st Septr. 1931.

Dear Mrs. Fletcher:

I took *The White Leopard* with me for the last weekend and thoroughly enjoyed it. You seem, if I may say so, to have got a remarkably good grip of the setting, both physical and psychological, of the work of administration in Central Africa, and I quite agree with you that your method of presentation is far more effective than would be a series of more or less propaganda articles.

Certainly for myself. I not only greatly enjoyed the story but appreciated the spirit in which it was written.

Yours sincerely,

L. S. Amery

Mr. Shively, of the Bobbs-Merrill New York office, wrote that he had placed *The White Leopard* with the Junior Literary Guild. This was followed by an enthusiastic letter from Helen Ferris, Editor of the Guild, who said they were proud to publish such a fine book. Mr. Chambers wrote that this was "top honors, but the book deserved it; you have presented a different Africa and an authentic one."

English publication followed; later, it appeared in the Scandinavian countries.

The London *Times Literary Supplement*, printed the following over the signature of Admiral Gordon Campbell, the Naval hero:

It is more than a thrilling tale of adventure, for it reveals the indomitable spirit of those servants of the Crown, who in various parts of the British Empire, bring justice and good government to native races, that a little while ago were sunk in savagery.

One of the early letters I wrote after *The White Leopard* was published was to the distinguished artist, Kurt Wiese, to express my appreciation of the extraordinary sensitivity he had shown in depicting the native African as he really is.

All editions went well. In fact, in 1958, twenty-seven years from the date of the first issue, I received a royalty check from a Canadian publisher, and, in the same mail, a copy of a German edition.

So it is with juveniles.

Red Jasmine followed *The White Leopard*. I wanted so much to write an adult book that I hurried into this one without giving it the framework of the type of novel I really wanted it to be. Just why I do not understand. I had background material in plenty, but somehow I couldn't get the book to "jell." Perhaps I had been reading too many African novels, the old summer type of light reading. I didn't want it to be that kind of book. I was strong for a political novel with an exotic background. As I try to think of the book from this distance, objectively, I believe my mind was too crowded with ideas for too many books for me to be able to concentrate fully on any one of them.

Red Jasmine! The title was wrong. I had called it *Burnished Sun*, a quotation from the Prince of Morocco's speech to Portia: Mislike me not for my complexion, The shadow'd livery of the burnish'd sun." That title was cast out; a dozen others were offered, but *Red Jasmine* was chosen. Why, I did not know. White, the jasmine flower grows in Africa; I have never heard of a red one. But there it was. I was too new a writer to fight for a title so I let it go.

I can't say that the title was the reason the novel did not have the depth I wanted it to have. It was a serious subject really, the political problems that are ever present in a colonial government. Perhaps I was ahead of the times with the story. Nyasaland, the background, was a Crown Colony. The British objective was to rule for the native, the real owner of the land. I thought the governor and his officials did this job superbly, and that is the story I wanted to tell, honestly as I saw it without giving it the onus of propaganda.

Somehow I failed. With my light presentation, along with the frivolous title, it became just a novel for summer reading. It had favorable comment from the reviewers and it made the best-seller lists, but even now, I don't like to think of that book. I have a feeling for the man who writes a serious play which turns out to be a successful comedy.

So I'll pass *Red Jasmine* by and move on to my more serious work, the historical novels of Colonial and Revolutionary America which came to be called "the Carolina Series."

The idea of an American novel with a background of rivers had been running around in my mind long before I wrote the African books, *The White Leopard* and *Red Jasmine*. I had even done some of the research, but no writing. It was one of those "head novels" with not a scratch of pen on paper.

I was trying to write a biography of Sir Richard Burton, the great English explorer and traveler who had discovered the African lakes, Tanganyika, Victoria, and Nyasa. Sir Richard had led a thrilling life, exploring wild places. He spoke perfect Arabic in many dialects. His most dangerous feat, perhaps, was to enter Mecca, the holy city of the Arabs, as a pilgrim. At this time he was the only European ever to have visited Mecca. He made the journey at the risk of his life, for the fanatic people would have torn him to pieces if they had known their holy place had been polluted by an unbeliever.

I had visited many of the places Sir Richard explored in Africa and Egypt when they were little known to Europeans (not, of course, Mecca). I wanted to write his biography but I was running into difficulties. Once I wrote to my publisher:

> I find the Burton biography goes so slowly that I think I could be working on something else as well. There is so much research to be done on the biography, and I am constantly stopped for want of authentic information that I must send to England to verify. . . .
>
> I think I can be doing a piece of creative writing as well. The reason I ask you this is because I do not know whether you would be interested in an historical book with an American setting, or whether you think I should stick to the African background until I am better established.

Although at the time I had no idea that this was the beginning of my thinking that later led to the Carolina Series, I find myself writing to my publisher a bit later:

> Would you be interested in a book I had started to write before I went to Africa? It is a book about rivers—the Ohio, the Mississippi, and the Missouri. It would take a typical American family who in Colonial times migrated from Virginia and North Carolina, westward, always following the rivers which were then the great thoroughfares of travel?

I still have the detailed outline of the story which I enclosed with this letter. I don't remember what my editor wrote about it, but the American family saga was never written, nor the Burton biography. Something happened to turn me toward the Carolina Series.

I went to the Sutro Library in San Francisco to look up some genealogical records of my mother's people in North Carolina. (My grandfather, Joseph Chapman, had been born in North Carolina.)

Miss Bruner, the librarian, was interested in my research and one day she said, "You are so interested in history, why don't you write a novel with an eastern North Carolina background? I've looked it up and there has been only one novel written about that section, with the exception of James Boyd's *Drums,* and that is a juvenile."

This idea was new but it attracted me. It might be the background of the saga of the American family. The more I thought about it the more I liked it. It would mean research, a great amount to get the authentic background. That posed no problem. I loved reading, I loved history, and I loved land, the essential background for such a series. Even then I was thinking in terms of more than one book.

Again I wrote to my editor. He was interested but he warned me against the panel idea. "Too often," he cautioned, "one panel is written and that is the end of it. Either the author gets tired of the whole thing, or the first book is not successful and the plan is discarded. Write a book with the Carolina background and see what happens."

With that slight encouragement, I resolved to write "the great American novel," from the Atlantic to the Pacific. I would carry my typically English folk who had migrated from England to the Jamestown Colony on through the vast reaches of America. The book would be based on land, man's desire to own land, to cultivate it, to fight for it. This, I thought, was a tremendous idea, epic in scope.

As I say, the book was never written for when I settled down to write about the typical family moving from east to west, I became so fascinated with the locale that I have never, after eleven books, been able to get my people out of North Carolina.

About this time I heard that there was a great mass of material in the Huntington Library in Pasadena. Down I went, eager to make a start. Research in the Huntington Library was one of my greatest experiences, second only to research in the British Museum. In spite of the great difference in methods there is a great similarity. The atmosphere of authentic culture in both libraries inspires one to work. The British Museum has an air of ancient culture; the Huntington is more modern. It is a rare experience to sit in the beautiful Huntington Gardens and read.

A little group under an arbor is playing folk music on reeds and lutes and other ancient instruments. A young man lies on his stomach in the grass, reading a yellowed tome that recalls the old days. A dancing class practices pantomime. They look like figures on an old Greek vase.

In this lovely garden it was easy to drift back to the beginnings of America through old documents and letters that were written even before the earliest days. I came to know the Elizabethans, the people of the sixteenth and seventeenth centuries. I knew what they wore, what they ate, what political situations interested them. I had newspapers, letters, deeds, and the vital statistics of Jamestown, Williamsburg, and Edenton in the Carolinas.

The whole panorama was spread before me and I began to absorb something of the spirit of those far-off times, to reconstruct a pattern of living which has been of service to me throughout the years. From lovely eighteenth-century paintings, such as Gainsborough's "Blue Boy" and "Pinkie," I learned about the elegance of the period. I discovered that the settlers of our Colonies lived in the shadow of England; in speech, in dress, and in their manner of living.

There is a great difference in the methods used by writers of historical fiction. Some first think up a plot, to be built around, usually, a wild female, a nymphomaniac who jumps in and out of bed with all manner of men from the footman to the lord of the manor. What period to use? The time of Charles the Second will suit admirably. Speech then was broad, morals broader. As for research, a book or two will do. Defoe and Pepys' *Diary* will give the background. There you have a formula for a successful novel, perhaps even a "runaway bestseller," in publishers' parlance. There, too, you have a synthetic historical novel, good for a season or two, perhaps, before it is forgotten.

Another method is to write a fictional story around a few characters who are modeled from real persons. In this type of novel, the story is the thing. I think Sir Walter Scott comes under this category. He never let history interfere with the progress of the story, but he used enough authentic background to give reality to the action and a true picture of the times. I think this is the ideal procedure to follow in writing an historical novel. It was Dumas' practice as well as Scott's. As we know, their novels have endured.

A great deal of information about the early days in America I obtained from the diaries of William Byrd (1674-1744), several of which were deciphered from his archaic shorthand. I am sure that when this Virginia gentleman was recording such things as the day's weather he had no thought that he was helping future novelists. William Byrd was an intellectual with many interests and his diaries are invaluable for source material for books of the period.

The background of *Raleigh's Eden* is not too far from Byrd's home, Westover, in Virginia, so his weather must have been the weather of Albemarle. In North Carolina, where my novel is placed, even today we listen to the radio every morning to get the weather report. Give a little, take a little, Virginia weather is our weather.

Back in San Francisco, I finally settled down to write. For one of the characters I chose an ancestor of mine, Roger Mainwaring (pronounced Mannering). "Duke Roger," as he was called, was shipped out to the West Indies as a bondsman, along with a few hundred other eager young men of the West Country who had formed the core of the Monmouth Rebellion in England. After he had served out the period of his bondage (seven years), he came to the Carolinas and became the head of a family. I believe he is the most popular character I have ever created. People visit us here at Bandon just to inquire about him and to learn his fate.

Roger entered into several of my books. Whether I planned him to or not, suddenly there he was, becoming more and more important as the book progressed.

In *Raleigh's Eden*, Roger was the springboard, other people came alive just to support him. His granddaughter, Mary Mainwaring, became one of the characters. He married and had love affairs. But he has never died.

Once, in a subsequent book, for some unknown reason, I inserted a sentence, "In the Leeward Islands where Roger Mainwaring came to his tragic death, etc." This line brought countless letters and many visitors, all alarmed because they thought they had missed a book that described Roger's death.

"Don't let him die!" wrote a schoolgirl. "I think he is my very favorite human being. I don't want him to die. Can't he live on and on?"

I'm fond of Roger myself. Perhaps one day I'll write about him, living and dying down on Antigua. I could work it out that way because I've always dreamed of going to Antigua, a fabulous island I've never seen.

The characters in *Raleigh's Eden* all developed from the theme of the book, that of a group of people who loved and cherished the land. They developed the land, they planted the land, they traded the produce of the land and of the forest. Tar, pitch, and turpentine, along with hogs, cotton, and cattle were the early sources of wealth in the new country.

I saw the Albemarle country in my mind. Presently, another group came to join my characters from England—the men who fought the Revolution, the signers of the Declaration and the Constitution, governors, senators.

"Never lose your story," my editor, Mr. Chambers, wrote, "particularly your love story. That is what your readers want."

I found that it was more difficult to make fact sound like fiction than to make fiction into fact, but that is what I had to do. And did—until the novel was twelve-hundred pages long!

While I was struggling with my mass of material *Anthony Adverse* was published. Its enthusiastic reception was an encouraging sign to writers of historical fiction, for it was indicative of the fact that the true historical in the pattern of Scott and Dumas had found a place once more. The "costume piece" was being crowded out in favor of the novel of substance.

I sent my novel to my publisher with some trepidation. A great mass of manuscript; a sprawling, unwieldy story. I had yet to learn that one of the tests of the professional writer lies in his ability to select his material. I just wrote and wrote and wrote and deleted nothing. I am sure the manuscript readers must have cringed when they saw twelve hundred pages.

Jack and I visited Washington in 1937, the year I sent my attempt at the "great American," which I had finally named *Raleigh's Eden* (because it was about the land that Raleigh's adventurers had called Eden), to the publisher. On our way home, we stopped at Indianapolis to learn my fate. There was a new (to me) editor. When I saw her, my heart sank. I knew I could never write anything that she would like. She told me the answer was "No," an unequivocal "No."

Jessica Mannon, the assistant editor with whom I had corresponded during *The White Leopard—Red Jasmine* period, tried to soften the blow. She took me to Mr. Chambers, president and editor-in-chief of Bobbs-Merrill. This was our first meeting. It was a dreary interview. He talked enthusiastically about the two African books and avoided discussion of *Raleigh's Eden*.

"We have decided not to accept the book. It is too long, too involved, too many characters."

"Do you think I could rewrite the story?"

He gave me no hope. "Perhaps you can improve it, but we promise nothing. Nothing at all."

I left the office. Jessica was waiting for me. She was kind, but I could see that she, too, didn't think I could ever do anything with the book. But we were never more wrong, as it turned out.

I went back to the hotel where Jack was waiting for me. He didn't need to ask any questions. "When can we get out of here?" I asked.

While we waited for the train Jack ordered sandwiches. I ate them glumly. I have never before or since been in such a foul humor. All the work I had done on that book! I knew it was good. I knew the theme behind it was good. It might be that there *was* too much story, but it couldn't be all bad. I had criticized too many books for newspapers and magazines, to be completely blind to faults, but the locale was right, new and fresh. The theme of the land and its development was right. The main story was the Biblical story of Sara, the barren woman, and the slave girl. I knew with everything that was in me that it was an excellent story. But what good did it do for me to know it if the editor didn't?

The train came at midnight. It was a milk train, without a sleeper, just huge tin cans of fresh milk. We sat in an uncomfortable red plush seat car and tried to sleep.

I mulled it over all night and by the time we arrived at the Statler in St. Louis, had hot baths and breakfast, I had regained my equanimity and had begun to plan a new story.

This time I would seek a new publisher.

We visited my family and the old Chapman Place briefly, and soon were on our way to San Francisco. In those three days I had completely rewritten *Raleigh's Eden* in my mind, and now I was eager to get to work. That is one thing that has always helped me, I love to write. Good or bad, I always want to begin another book even before I finish the current one.

It was some months after this that Jessica Mannon wrote me a short note, "Where is Adam Rutledge, and his family and his friends? I am now his editor and I want to renew my acquaintance with him."

I was certainly pleased to have that letter. Some work had been done on the script, but it was still over a thousand pages. However, I bundled it up and sent it, with joy, to Jessica.

I had a high opinion of her critical faculties. She could see beyond the difficulties into the heart of a book. She seemed to have an instinct for books, perhaps inherited from her father who was for many years editor of an Indianapolis newspaper. It was about this time that she discovered that classic among cookbooks, *The Joy of Cooking*, and put it through to its success over the years.

After a time, it seemed months to us, a contract came for

Raleigh's Eden and with it a long letter from Jessica. It was one of the kindest, most understanding letters that an editor ever sent to a writer. She explained that they would, if I wished, work with me to help get the book in shape.

> An author never wants to delete his own words. It is best to have someone who can see it as a whole, and cut where it is most effective. You must not feel that this procedure is unusual. It happens frequently.

I was reluctant for I thought I could do the work myself, but Jack convinced me that Jessica was right, so I signed the Bobbs-Merrill contract and was on my way to an association that lasted through eleven books and twenty-five years of publishing.

I am sure I would be with them yet if Mr. Chambers had not retired. I soon found that my impression of him, at the time he turned down *Raleigh's Eden,* was entirely wrong. He is a thoughtful, sensitive man. He loathed to tell anyone that he was not going to publish his work. He had not only a mind of heroic proportions but a wonderful and delightful sense of humor, something that everyone who deals with temperamental authors needs to carry him through the storms.

I have been accused of not being a real author because I did not show an uneven temperament. After I got to know all the delightful people in the office they gave me a nickname. I was F. A. (favorite author) to half the staff.

I am one of those writers who has such a mass of material in mind that it comes gushing out. Often I am way ahead of my pen, leave out half a sentence, forget what I have done with my characters, or give them blue eyes in one line and brown in another. The one who has to sweep up after me has troubles.

One critic wrote to me, "What are you going to do about Lavinia? At one point, you have her announcing that she is going to have a child. A year and a half later nothing is said about the baby. How come?"

To which I replied in chagrin, "Everything was slower in Colonial times."

I have always had trouble with timing, especially when carrying several generations in a story, but I don't like *time*. I wish it would stand still and not interfere in one's business. It would be marvellous to live in a timeless world.

Raleigh's Eden was published in September, 1940. In the meantime we had made two visits to North Carolina, to be sure that the background was correct in all details. My publisher, who was most meticulous, decided that I must have the galley proofs read by an authority at the University of North Carolina to avoid any historical errors.

So we journeyed again to Chapel Hill and inquired at the University Library about an historian to read the novel. Dr. Hugh Lefler, whose field is North Carolina Colonial history, was suggested. At first he said he was too busy, but he finally gave way and took the galleys. When we kept our appointment to see him the next morning, we found him hollow-eyed and sleepy.

"I sat up all night, reading," he said with annoyance. "I got into the book and I couldn't put it down." He turned to a list of questions, but first he said, "What references did you use? What source books?"

I gave him a list of forty-nine or fifty books I had used, plus original documents I had consulted at the Huntington Library and the courthouse records in Chowan County.

The Lord certainly had His arms around me when I was sent to Hugh Lefler. He is a most knowledgeable man on North Carolina Colonial history, and he was deeply interested that I, an outsider, should write a book about North Carolina.

"You'll have plenty of criticism," he remarked. "We don't like people from out of the state to write about us. We are proud of our history, but we are inclined to keep it to ourselves. We know it. It isn't necessary for anyone else to know it."

I knew well enough what he meant! Virginia and South Carolina, and the old saying, "The valley of humiliation between two mountains of conceit."

"My grandfather was born in Tyrrell County. Won't that help?"

He laughed. "Perhaps, perhaps. But you're going to run into a whirlwind of criticism. Some of your statements will be new to your readers and, as I said, you are an outlander. I think it is a good book. Eastern North Carolina history has been sadly neglected. Good luck to you."

I had no idea, then, of the extent of the criticism that was to follow or of the sensation the novel was to cause when it hit the book dealers' shelves.

My publisher had planned a special limited edition to be autographed by the Honorable Clyde Hoey, Governor of North Carolina. I well remember the day we went to the Governor's office for the signing of those hundreds of pages. It was hot. I wore a cool white linen dress, but the Governor was dressed as he always was, in a worsted cutaway coat and waistcoat, striped gray trousers, and a high wing collar with an ascot tie. The Governor was of the old school, and a great orator. Later, when he was in the United States Senate, the press constantly referred to him as being the prototype of the traditional senator of the old days.

That summer's day, however, after the photographers had departed, he sat and signed the three thousand pages with an easy flowing movement, undisturbed by the weather or the boredom of writing his name over and over again. Although his interest was in North Carolina, I shall always be grateful for his courtesy to an unknown writer.

The first criticism came from Edenton before the book was published. I had given a set of galleys to Mrs. Sydney McMullan, Librarian of Cupola House Library, to read for corrections in local history. She knew more folklore and more local history than anyone in Chowan County. Somehow some of the disseminators of local history got a glance at a galley or two, just enough to whet the appetite for more. One group was exceedingly critical and they communicated with a group in Raleigh.

It seemed that my interpretation of portions of the history of Edenton differed from local beliefs. Some of my statements did not conform to their word-of-mouth traditional stories. That I had found my sources in California instead of North Carolina was something not to be borne.

They did not realize that my facts were from authentic documents, not from local histories or folk tales. Later, changes were made in some of the locally written books. One school history was found to have almost a hundred errors. It was not the mistakes that worried me so much but the fact that exceedingly vital and important data had been left out. Those that were written about the time of the Civil War were slanted. Later volumes continued omissions of earlier ones. Fortunately for North Carolina, new and excellent histories are now available.

So my book was violently criticized. One of the Raleigh papers carried a review which listed as many as eighteen or more mistakes. Of course I wanted to answer the reviewer and point out the sources from which I took my facts, but my publisher said, "No, do not get into a controversy. These accusations will cause people to think; perhaps they will even look up the controversial item."

But there were several real mistakes, mostly in location. The outstanding one resulted from the extensive cuts made in the manuscript. Once, in the later stages of my book, I was asked to cut several more chapters. I wrote back to the publisher and said if there was any more cutting done, they would do it.

They did. They took out two chapters. The result was that my hero, Adam Rutledge, journeyed down from the Western Mountains and arrived at his plantation, Rutledge Riding, the following morning. It was a matter of some three hundred miles. This was easily corrected in subsequent editions. I merely wrote another line, "After a journey of three weeks, Adam arrived at his plantation on the Roanoke River." And since I am a frugal person, I used the two chapters in a later book—they fitted perfectly!

Most of the criticism was to the effect that I had made the story too romantic, "North Carolina was settled by ordinary folk, even people from the London gaols."

This was a totally wrong conception, although it had persisted down the years. The truth is that it was settled by men of all classes, but the Albemarle Sound section was settled by cadets of the great county families of Devon and Cornwall. Almost every old family in Edenton has the right to a coat of arms or a crest. Replicas hang on the walls of most of the old homes; the people trace their ancestry directly back to the maritime counties of England, Devon and Cornwall. These county families had furnished the ships that brought the young adventurers who attempted to settle Roanoke Island in the days of Queen Elizabeth, and many of them were a part of the permanent settlement of Jamestown.

However, I had my defenders and I was astonished at the number of them. Many of the Edenton people, of course, supported me, for they know the facts.

I should say also that many of my critics gave way after a time. Some even went so far as to say in print that they had been wrong in their criticism and that a check into Colonial records revealed the facts I had used to be correct.

My publisher had arranged a tour of a number of cities in the interest of *Raleigh's Eden*. Chicago was among the first. A luncheon for book critics was arranged by Rose Oller of Marshall Field's book department. It was very successful and I formed friendships there which have lasted through the years.

I remember my astonishment when a large canvas bin filled with copies of *Raleigh's Eden* was rolled up before me. It was my first autographing party and I signed every copy, three hundred in all. Afterward, I signed books in North Carolina—Raleigh, Charlotte, Chapel Hill, Winston-Salem, Greensboro, and Durham.

Then came Richmond, where Peggy O'Neil, one of the very fine book women of the country, had the department in Miller and Rhoads' store. Norfolk and Washington followed. On our way west to San Francisco we visited Atlanta, where we found another outstanding book woman, Luise Sims, then of Davison, Paxon. We visited Houston, Dallas, San Antonio, and Denver, my husband's old home. Here we were entertained day and night. Then Salt Lake, Reno, and finally San Francisco where there was a big "home-coming" party at Paul Elder's bookshop.

I've forgotten how far we traveled but we piled up a formidable mileage on the old Packard, and I signed many hundreds of books. When we arrived home there was a note from my publisher saying that *Raleigh's Eden* had been sold to *Omnibook* for a condensation.

We made long tours for several later books, but the one for *Raleigh's Eden* was my first and most exciting.

My feminine vanity will not permit me to omit mention of the fact that I had two charming suits made by Anthony Blotto for my tour. As for hats, I had eight or ten by Lili Daché, John Frederick, and Reine. It took quite a few autographed books to pay for my costumes but I always felt in the height of fashion when I stood on a platform to speak.

I was amazed, and I'm sure my publisher was delighted, with the fine reviews and the hundreds and hundreds of letters from all over the country which we received on *Raleigh's Eden*. I answered all letters (I still do). In the San Francisco days I had a wonderful secretary, Gladys Miilu. She was Canadian-born and one of the most sensitive, responsive secretaries I have ever had. She spent days answering letters and writing thank you notes to the critics.

For an historical novel, the reception was remarkable. For some unknown reason the author of historical fiction has no real position in the writing world. Like Kipling's Tomlinson, he is not "good enough for heaven or bad enough for hell," so he wanders about aimlessly somewhere in the middle. I could never understand this. Surely there is as much imagination needed as in straight fiction, plus a depth of research often comparable to that of the writer of history.

I am reminded of a reviewer (I say reviewer, not critic) who wrote a long article about *Raleigh's Eden* in which he gave a complete synopsis of the story. At the end he made this comment: "This is a good enough historical romance if you like historical romances, which I don't!"

Raleigh's Eden went well for a number of years. Eventually it was reprinted in a Permabook paperback edition and translated into fourteen languages. In Sweden its title was changed to *Thus Was Born a Nation*. It seemed to me the greatest compliment that could be paid me, for it showed a depth of appreciation of what I was trying to say: that the land is basic to the progress of any nation, and that this progress depends upon the people who must not only develop the land and make it productive, but must also hold it, even at the price of waging war. Freedom to develop the land must include the freedom of the people as individuals. The two freedoms are inseparable.

While I have never had a runaway best-selling novel, all of my books have had a good steady sale that continued for many years. Of course, some of them are now out of print, but we still receive letters after twenty-odd years of publishing asking where they can be purchased.

Raleigh's Eden set the pattern for all the books that followed.

18

The next book, *Men of Albemarle*, was inevitable. All through my research for *Raleigh's Eden*, I kept running across a group of men, leaders in the Albemarle, before and during the Revolution. The Iron Men of Albemarle they were called.

These men lived in Pasquotank, Perquimans, Chowan, and Tyrrell precincts. They were lawyers, doctors, and planters, and they represented the people who lived around Albemarle Sound, in the country that was designated as Albemarle, after the Duke of Albemarle, one of the eight original proprietors. The precincts have long given way to individual counties, but the area is still designated the Albemarle and it is unified in its interests.

The novel takes place in 1710-12, during the time of Queen Anne's wars when the name of another Churchill, John, Duke of Marlborough, was on everyone's lips in England. It was also frequently heard in America, since the English men and women who lived on our side of the ocean looked to the Mother Country for their political thought as well as for their creature comforts.

I read the *Colonial Records of North Carolina* assiduously. Like most novelists, I was not so interested in facts and figures as I was in small, obscure items that gave a hint of the character of the people about whom I was writing.

I spent at least a year on research, another on writing *Men of Albemarle*. After the six years it took to write and rewrite *Raleigh's Eden*, I settled down to the routine I have followed ever since, a novel sent to the publisher every two years. I understand that I have been called a publisher's delight because of the regularity with which I write my books, so that the publisher can always count on a book from me on May first every two years. Through nine books I met that self-imposed deadline.

After the research has ended I must find characters. In *Men of Albemarle* I had the historical "Iron Men" so that was easy. During the period there was the continual strained relation between the Quakers and the government which led to what was called Cary's Rebellion. Over and above these differences was the Tuscarora Indian War. I had the backbone of a story through research, but the fictional characters bothered me. In Colonial Records I came on an obscure item:

> Mad^m Catha Hyde Came before this Board and was admitted to prove upon oath ye Importation of Eight person into this Governm^t (Viz^t) Edwd Hyde Esqr Mrs Penelope Hyde Wm Clayton, Jno Lovick Mary Tudo James Gregory, Andrew Stephenson & herself^e.

Now this is the sort of thing that pleases a novelist. A group of people who came into a new government, to settle. Who were they and why did they come? Some of the names I knew. Edward Hyde, a cousin of Queen Anne, was the governor sent over to untangle the muddle occasioned by three men who each claimed to be governor of the province of North Carolina.

Madam Catha Hyde was the governor's wife, Edward Hyde and Penelope Hyde were their young children. John Lovick was the governor's secretary; James Gregory and Wm. Clayton, members of governor's staff. That left Andrew Stephenson, whom I made tutor to the children, and Mary Tudo. Who was Mary Tudo? It took very little imagination to add an "R" to the name. But who was Mary Tudor?

The royal family of Tudor came to mind. How could I place the woman who came with Madam Catha to the little village of Edenton and connect her with the English royal family?

I was working in the Library of Congress one day. Jack was with me. He researches by taking a book, turning pages idly, reading a little here and there, then saying libraries give him a headache and going out for a walk.

This day it was different and he inadvertently came upon the solution of my number one problem. What he found was that Lady Mary Tudor was the illegitimate daughter of Charles the Second, brother of the ill-fated, also illegitimate, Duke of Monmouth.

After that, it was simple to look her up. I found she had disappeared from England for a time because of her political activities. It was easy to believe that she came to America with Madam Catha Hyde. Since Governor Edward Hyde was a cousin of Queen Anne's, he was also a cousin of Lady Mary Tudor. America was a vast country. It was easy to be out of reach of the Queen in this new country. So Lady Mary became one of the characters in *Men of Albemarle*.

The principal character, as I mentioned earlier perhaps my favorite of all the men I have created, was my ancestor, Roger Mainwaring, the former bondsman who took ship for North Carolina and landed at "the little town on Queen Anne's Creek." Roger was filled with the idea of man's dignity and freedom, something he had gained in his years of servitude. He loved land, a Devon inheritance, and he realized that land itself did something for people; the fight against the wilderness all about them gave strength to the weak and added stamina to the strong.

He was a strong man who believed firmly in the Englishman's freedom granted by the Magna Charta. He believed in the enforcement of the Common Law. But his great interest was in the fundamental rights of the common man, as set down in the Great

Charter granted by the Lords Proprietors to the Carolinas through Locke's Fundamental Constitution, a document that gave more freedom to man than had ever been granted by law.

Men of Albemarle was written after *Raleigh's Eden*, but the historical events on which it was based took place a number of years earlier.

It was the day of the pirates along the Outer Banks, and the young girl, Anne Bonney, lived in the Albemarle before she joined pirates and freebooters and became the partner and woman of notorious Calico Jack.

One character that got away from me was Stephenson, the tutor to the Hyde children. He was often in the taverns drinking and cavorting, not acting as a tutor should. He was, I think, the first of my characters who got out of hand. I couldn't contol him. I didn't want to kill him, so I sent him up to Virginia to teach Latin at William and Mary College. For all I know, he is there to this day.

Out of the large group of fictional characters in *Men of Albemarle*, probably the two outstanding are Mary Tudor and Roger Mainwaring.

Roger had in him some of the qualities of the reckless adventurers, the unafraid men who roamed Elizabethan seas and later settled the West Indies and America. They had broad ideas and ventured greatly, yet they believed firmly in law. They also believed that the wealth of nations lay in the land. In a measure their beliefs followed those expressed in Adam Smith's book, *The Wealth of Nations*, which was published about that time.

The planters, many of whom were also politicians, were followers of Adam Smith, and they tried to establish law and order patterned after the Old World's Common Law.

Men of Albemarle was written in several places, California first, then in Edenton ("Queen Anne's Town" of the book), and was finished in Indianapolis.

In Edenton, the George Woods offered us a vacant house on Greenfield Plantation, an old fishery on Albemarle Sound, twenty or thirty feet from the water, in a grove of pine trees. We made the place habitable by fixing up a kitchen, partially renovating the upstairs bedroom, and painting the ceiling of the "great" room to contrast with the natural pine-paneled walls. We had breakfast and lunch in our kitchen and dinner with the Woods at the plantation house.

The "great" room had two arches into the hall, on either side of the fireplace. The little stairway that went from the hall to the second floor gave the downstairs a quaint Old World look, reminiscent of the old tavern at Broadway, in the Midlands of England. We discovered an old English pier table (of carved black oak) in a second-hand store along the waterfront of Elizabeth City. Edenton friends donated chairs and an antique "falling leaf" table.

Here we settled down to serious work. I chewed a pencil and Jack banged the typewriter from early morning to four in the afternoon. Everything went well except for the "borers," horrid little bugs that bored into the wood in the ceiling. Wood dust constantly sifted down on my head, so I sat at my beautiful sixteenth-century table with my hat on, causing a great deal of merriment among our guests.

Speaking of guests, hundreds came through the gates when they were open. (My hostess, Fan Lamb Wood, kept them closed until four o'clock.) A novelist was a novelty in Edenton. For some reason that I have never fathomed, writers everywhere are considered something apart, certainly not quite like people. So folk from all over the state rode down to Greenfield to have a look at the Wood's guests.

Benbury, the youngest son of the Wood family (the two older boys were at Porter School in Charleston, South Carolina), would ride his little white mule down to the fishery when he heard that guests were coming. Very seriously he would ask "if I wanted any scenery." This was a secret code between us. If I said "Yes," he would drive a couple of cows down the lane and out into the water at the verge of the cypress swamp. They made a sort of Constable-like rural scene, peaceful and bucolic. The guests always commented on the serenity of the surroundings. "So suitable for a writer," they would say.

Sometimes wildfowl flew in of their own accord, ducks and white egrets; these beautiful birds certainly added to the picture.

We had many picnics at the Fishery. Once when I said I wanted to lay a brick terrace in front of the stoop, Fan Lamb gave a really big picnic. She invited people from all nearby towns for a hundred miles around. A brick was the price of admission. We received enough old bricks to make a little terrace.

My editor, Jessica Mannon, and her husband, Bud, came to see us in time for the brick picnic. They were staying in Edenton at the Hotel Joseph Hewes. Jessica was delighted when the colored waiter in the dining room tried to sell her a copy of *Raleigh's Eden*. She thought that was a high point in promotion.

The supper that night was out of doors. Several of the plantation Negroes were on hand to cook the steaks and serve drinks. Hearing everyone call the cook "Frank," Bud Mannon, Jessica's husband, asked him for something, calling him by name.

Frank drew himself up, saying, "Who *dat* calls my name and I don't know hissen?"

I hastened to make a proper introduction, so everything was all right.

When I was somewhere near the middle of *Men of Albemarle*, I got an idea for another book, one that would deal with the development of trade. To do that, we must go to Nassau, because this book would be of the period when pirates were roaming the seaways as far north as Albemarle Sound and the Outer Banks near Ocracoke.

So off we went to Nassau. I think I manufactured the idea because I was stuck; the second book was not going as smoothly as I wished and I needed a rest, or thought I did.

That is one thing about me, I can always rationalize the need for a journey. Sometimes, like the trip to the Indies, my reasoning stems from a projected book. Several times I was obliged to go to

England to research in the British Museum, and once to Scotland to find the real story of Flora Macdonald. These research missions always coincided with the yearly meeting of the P.E.N. Club at Zurich or Edinburgh or Venice or London, I might say.

We went to Nassau in the late summer. There were no tourists, and the great hotels were closed. We stayed downtown at the Hotel St. George. It was quaint, comfortable, and altogether satisfactory and reasonable. We ate outside on a terrace that gave directly on the Nassau Harbor Passage, where large ships passed to their anchorage. One could sit at a table under an arbor of huge palm trees and almost trail one's hand in the water of the channel. The mangoes for breakfast were luscious, and the fish, fresh out of the water, incomparable.

A party of six sitting near us at dinner fished between courses. There was great excitement as they caught a large "passing jack" and had it cooked while they waited. "Passing jack" appear in these waters only twice a year. Schools of them come from Africa, swim into the Gulf of Mexico, then return to their home.

I had been told that Miss Mary Moseley was an authority on the history of the Island. I asked at the desk how to find her. The clerk at once took up the phone and called Miss Moseley. I explained to a pleasant-voiced woman what I was looking for. I wanted Island history as far back as their early governor, Woodes Rogers.

"Come right over and I'll let you see my records," she said.

I have had delightful experiences when researching. Librarians everywhere have been eager to help, but never have I met with the spontaneous enthusiasm that Miss Mary Moseley showed when I inquired about the early history of New Providence.

We found her a tall, delightful woman of great charm. She immediately got out a mass of documents for me. It seemed she was gathering material for a definitive history of the islands. (She had written an excellent guide book to the Bahamas.) She turned her material over to me without a moment's hesitation.

Miss Mary was a newspaper woman. Her family had owned the

217

Nassau *Guardian* for generations. She told me that when she was a small child her father would take her to Government House when the Assembly was in session. She had a small table next to the press, where she could write her little stories. The table was almost against the high seat where the governor sat. "I could see and hear everything and I felt very proud for I was the only little girl so honored."

The next night we dined with her on a marvellous turtle dish which I can never forget, a dish that is served by the Islanders to special guests.

We did a little touring on that delightful island, and a great deal of research. Miss Mary had procured a key to the Public Library, so we came and went to and from the old octagonal building (so much like a shot tower or a lighthouse) as we pleased, before or after library hours. Our only duty was to close the heavy wooden shutters if a hurricane threatened.

From the library windows there was a magnificent view of the Island and the sea beyond. It took little imagination to see the pirate ships sailing into safe harbor, running ahead of Spanish ships or pursued by government sailing frigates.

It was a short distance from the beach, up the hill through crooked streets, to the charmingly tinted houses, behind walls of coquina and hedges of tropical flowers. But the feet of the pirates made paths along the beach to the taverns. They were unimpressed by the beautiful coral sea gardens in the blue water. Their interests were in the gold and silver from the treasure ships of Spain that sailed from South America to the Azores and Madeira. I used this later in *Lusty Wind for Carolina*.

I learned, too, that the Bahama Islands had six of the same eight Lords Proprietors who had governed the Carolinas, and also the same chief justice. I thought that this accounted, perhaps, for the many ships from the Indies that sailed into Albemarle Sound and anchored in the little bay on which Queen Anne's Town was located.

To this day in the little museum in Cupola House, Edenton,

the records of those West India trading ships are preserved. They tell a story of the old Triangular Route across the Atlantic from London to the West Indies to the sea coast cities of the Carolinas, up to Boston and back again to London. Merchandise and mail came by this route across the Western Sea to take advantage of the trade winds and fair sailing.

We returned to Edenton with a mass of research material and with twenty-four straw hats as gifts for our friends there. By autumn we were home in California, where I worked earnestly to finish a draft of *Men of Albemarle*.

In February, I was on my way to Indianapolis to consult my editors at Bobbs-Merrill. Again, I had a May first deadline and I wanted to turn in the completed manuscript on the precise day it was expected.

I was cordially received by Jessica and Mr. Chambers. *Raleigh's Eden* had been more of a success than they had expected. I felt fine. I wanted to get *Men of Albemarle* on the presses because I was eager to begin *Lusty Wind for Carolina*.

The visit to Nassau had shown me that there was a real story in a book based on trade. But my high spirits soon fell to lowest ebb. My publisher thought that *Men of Albemarle* certainly could not be finished properly by the first of May.

I walked to my hotel, sad and gloomy and forlorn. I did not eat any supper. I went to my room and sulked. Since this is not my nature, I soon thought my way out of the doldrums. I remembered St. Louis and *Raleigh's Eden*. I made up my mind that the book *would* be finished by May Day.

As soon as the office opened, I was there to talk to Jessica. I told her the book would be finished on time. I would stay right there in Indianapolis until it was accepted. Jessica cheered me on. She said she knew I could do it if I were determined.

"I *am* determined," I said, and went right up the street to the public library. They had the early volumes of Saunders' *Colonial History of North Carolina*, and I would be allowed, because I was a Bobbs-Merrill author, to take home the volume that I needed.

Looking back, I have an idea that nobody ever had even wanted to look at Saunders' *Colonial History*. I lugged the heavy volume down the street to the hotel; before noon I was at work. Some nights it was eleven o'clock before I laid down my pen.

Jessica found a typist for me. She was quick and eager and learned in no time to decipher my handwriting, which grows worse and worse the longer I work. By the end of the month, I had a complete second draft which Jessica approved. I went back to California to polish it up. I had the manuscript in Indianapolis a few days before the first of May.

I was happy. I had proved that I could, under pressure, complete a book on time. Of course there were some further changes and rewriting but it didn't amount to much.

Again, the publisher brought out a beautiful book, with a fine dust jacket by Paul Laune (who has done all my Carolina books). Walter Hurley was in charge of production. I have always considered him one of the best in the business. And Ross Baker, head of the New York office, wrote me that he had made the sale of a popular edition to Doubleday.

Through my London agent, Curtis Brown, translations were arranged in Sweden, Denmark, Belgium, Czechoslovakia, and Norway.

I was very happy when my old friend, Gertrude Atherton, wrote in a national paper:

> *Men of Albemarle* is magnificent. It opens with a bang; and the pace never drops. In the very first chapter one becomes deeply interested in the characters, the locale, and the promise of great things to come. Mrs. Fletcher is in the top rank of America's historical novelists.

Like the two African books and *Raleigh's Eden*, *Men of Albemarle* was on the best-seller list. I was in demand for talks at clubs and colleges and made a tour of bookstores to autograph books. Since the limitation-page books were sold only in the Carolinas, people in large numbers wanted autographed books for their permanent collections, and of course an author is always happy to oblige.

With *Men of Albemarle*, my historical series was on its way. I had passed another hurdle. But I knew well enough that a second book might ride on the success of the first. It is the third that shows the capacity of an author.

Men of Albemarle was not off the press before I was at work on *Lusty Wind for Carolina*, the third novel in the Carolina Series.

CHAPTER

19

Lusty Wind for Carolina was written during the war years. It was published October 16, 1944, two years after *Men of Albemarle.*

Jack had retired from Standard Oil of California, and the first year of the war he worked in Douglas Aircraft as an assembly mechanic (any way to get into war work), later as inspector and tester. After a year, he received an offer as shipyard training director with the U. S. Maritime Commission. He was given his choice of three yards, and naturally chose North Carolina, at Wilmington (a wartime subsidiary of Newport News Shipbuilding Co., and probably the most successful of the "war babies").

The Wilmington venture was a happy one for me as it turned out, but for a time it looked as though we could not find a place to lay our heads. We had two offers of housing: one in the attic apartment of a friend; the other, Clarendon Plantation on Cape Fear River, a few miles north of Laurence Sprunt's famous Orton Plantation. In fact, it was Mrs. Sprunt who suggested to Mrs. Devereaux Lippitt, owner of Clarendon, that she open the house for us.

"Mrs. Fletcher wants some place to stay while she writes a book," she told Mrs. Lippitt. "Clarendon would be the very spot."

Mrs. Lippitt was intrigued by the idea of having a book written in her country house, so she telephoned and asked us to go down to the plantation. "If you like it," she told me, "I'll get it ready for you, although we have not had it opened for eight or nine years. It is completely furnished and in good order. We have a caretaker who lives on the place."

We motored down the west side of the Cape Fear River, through beautiful woodland country. As we came to Clarendon, we drove into the grounds along a curving driveway, lined with maples. The plantation itself was in the midst of a pine forest.

When the house came in view, my heart sank. I looked at Jack— it couldn't be possible that we would live in such a beautiful home!—there must be some catch to it.

When we went in, I was even more disconsolate. The house was completely furnished with European furniture—great overstuffed tapestry sofas and chairs, mahogany chests and bookcases, all sorts of tables, little and big, heavy brasses at fireplaces. A long drawing room gave on a wide piazza with tall white columns. This looked out on a canal that ran down through old rice fields to the Cape Fear River. There were gardens on either side and a magnificent grove of untouched pines to the south. On the other side there was a quaint old Colonial house that had been made over for the caretaker. There were boxwood walks, sunken rose gardens, and a large kitchen garden.

The house was of red brick, with copper roof and trim, and growing all about the house and gardens were camellia bushes, some reaching to the second story. The camellias were coming into early bloom, red and pink and white. It was breathtakingly beautiful.

The right-hand wing was a glassed-in sunroom, at least twenty by thirty feet, with a large fireplace. There was a dining room with a great mahogany table, cupboards filled with china, even flat silver, kitchen pantries, and a buttery beyond.

223

We climbed to the second and third floors. The third had a large studio. (Mrs. Lippitt is an artist.) The bedrooms were complete with linens. All in all, we could, and later did, sleep as many as eighteen people.

We went downstairs. Mrs. Lippitt said she had forgotten to show me the library. When I saw the library I knew I had to have that house. It was back of the main entrance hall and its glass doors opened onto the long gallery on the river side of the house. On one side from floor to ceiling were bookshelves filled with eighteenth-century histories, novels, plays, and poetry, exactly the books I would need for *Lusty Wind*.

Only one thing remained—the rental. I was sure it must be tremendous, but I intended to write my book there if I didn't have any money left for food.

Hesitatingly, Mrs. Lippitt told my husband that she could not think of charging any rent. She would be happy just to have an Inglis Fletcher book written in her house.

He, of course, protested. Finally, it was arranged that we would take over the charges for the caretaker, water, and lighting plant, in lieu of rent. We agreed on the spot, and the next day we were in Clarendon, bag and baggage.

We could see the lights of the shipyard at night, and found that we were only about five miles across the water, although it was a fifteen-mile drive by the road and bridges. But Jack said that the journey back and forth down the tree-lined road, the old river road of Colonial days, would not be too tiring for him.

We had not been at the plantation long before I found that everything I wanted for the beginning of my book was right at my door. For instance, the ancient village of Old Town Creek, long gone, was said to be just beyond Clarendon Plantation, at the edge of the pine woods. ("Piney woods," the Negroes called it.) Old Town Creek was where the Yeomans had first settled, and where a few years later they were joined by the New Englander, Henry Vassal, and his group.

I came across this information through my little Negro cook,

Hannah. She lived not far beyond the woods, "down the road a piece." She could have taken a short-cut through the woods, which was almost bare of undergrowth. But, no, she must trudge down the road instead. I could not understand this, and when I pressed her to tell me, her only answer was, "I am afraid of the foxes."

I insisted that foxes would not attack, they would run; but my words had no effect on her. We had been at Clarendon some weeks before I understood her answer.

The house was surrounded by great forest trees. Near the front door, in a crescent of pines, were two gigantic tulip poplars. The wind soughed through the branches and made sounds almost like people talking, a little distance away. More than once I got up from my desk and went to the door, to find no one there.

Once, Hannah was nearby and I said, "I thought I heard people talking."

She looked at me with the blank expression that comes over the face and eyes of a Negro when you speak of the supernatural, or, as the African natives call it, the spirit world, and said, "You, too, hear the voices, the voices of the long dead."

When I questioned her further, I got the full story.

Long, long ago there was a town on Old Town Creek where many people lived. Ships came from the north and from the south, to settle people on this creek. Axes rang through the deep forest. Hammers and saws were heard as the people built houses and public buildings to make a town; and there was joy and singing of hymns on the Sabbath day. All of this happened long, long ago, in the far-off past, beyond the time of many grandfathers. Hannah's people came with the settlers from the south in a big ship.

I gathered from her tale that her people had arrived with Sir John Yeomans, from Barbados via Charleston. I knew that the Huguenots had attempted a settlement on Cape Fear River about that time. Evidently they had brought slaves with them. Hannah's ancestors belonged to the group which arrived on the river in

1663, and not to Henry Vassal's northern settlers who arrived in August, 1666.

Hannah believed firmly that the voices in the piney woods were the voices of these long-gone folk who spoke to their descendants at night or in the late afternoon when the sun was setting. Sometimes, their voices could be heard in the midst of thunderstorms.

Some of the old names were Cary, Knight, Sanford, and Humphrey Davenport, names that are even now found in North Carolina.

Hannah knew that the spirits of these early settlers rode the storms, roamed through the woods at nightfall. That was the reason she wouldn't walk through the piney woods and along the paths among the turpentine trees at dusk, for she did not want to meet the spirits of the long-dead. Some people who walked through the woods never came out again, Hannah told me; then they, too, joined the voices.

She had told me she was afraid of the "foxes," she said, because it was best not to speak of spirits aloud, but since I, too, heard them, it would not harm either of us.

That summer there were many violent thunderstorms that seemed to break directly over our heads, with great crashes of thunder and violent flashes of lightning. One day, during one of these terrific storms, I went into the dining room. It was dark, all of the shutters were closed against the storm. I noticed a movement in the rug. I wondered if the wind could be blowing in through the kitchen, or perhaps the cellar. It was then that I discovered Hannah; she had taken refuge under the rug, beneath the dining room table.

I said, "Get right out from under that rug, Hannah, and stand on your feet. The Lord is going to look after you. He won't be pleased to see you groveling under the table."

She crept out and stood trembling before me. "I think you likes a storm, Mrs. Fletcher. I see you at the door looking out, 'jes like you loves it."

I felt sorry for her, she was so terrified. "Remember what I tell

226

you, Hannah. The Good Lord will look after you if you are standing on your feet. He might not see you if you are crouching under that rug."

"Yes'm, yes'm, I know. But I don't like the noise He sends with the storm, seems like He's mad at something."

All the talk about the voices sent me to the *Colonial Records*, to read about the early settlers on the land where we were now living, and it gave me a new idea about my book *Lusty Wind for Carolina*.

The title came from an old song:

> *Give me a spirit that on this life's rough sea*
> *Loves t' have his sails fill'd with a lusty wind,*
> *Even till his sail-yards tremble, his masts crack,*
> *And his rapt ship run on her side so low*
> *That she drinks water, and her keel plows air.*

> *Chorus*

> *Till the ship drinks water, and her keel plows air.*
> *Oh, heigh-ho, and a lusty wind.*

The period was exciting. During the years 1718-1725 pirates roamed the seas and made rendezvous on the Carolina Banks and at the Island of New Providence, where Woodes Rogers, the naval hero, was governor. After the Peace of Utrecht in 1713, the merchants of England began to see in the New World of America a source of wealth through trade, and with the great navigator, Woodes Rogers, to enforce the law and keep the sea lanes open, British merchants took advantage of the opportunity to send out their ships.

Woodes Rogers had the new "Law of Amnesty to Pirates" as a background for his government. The pirates might, on surrender, become freebooters and legally destroy Spanish ships that plied the Plate Route. They must, of course, keep "hands off" British ships.

The theme of the book was to be the fight of traders for freedom of the seas and the development of trade in the Colonies. Again tar, pitch, and turpentine would play their part and be sent from the New World to replenish the naval stores of the Old.

My favorite fiction character, Roger Mainwaring, appears in *Lusty Wind*. But history gave me Woodes Rogers, who to me was one of the most fascinating men of the days when pirates and freebooters roamed the Western Ocean. Perhaps some television fans will recognize Woodes Rogers in the *Buccaneer* series. He appeared in the early plays as governor of the Bahamas. His place was soon taken by Acting Governor, "Mister Bemish," who attempted to govern the islands with the help of ex-pirate Dan Tempest. I am hopeful that the English producers of this excellent and exciting series will bring back Woodes Rogers one day.

I have always thought this period of history as exciting as early Elizabethan times, when the great sea captains of England came to America: Sir Richard Grenville, Sir Francis Drake, and the Hawkins brothers.

I had already gathered considerable material in Nassau, but there was still a great deal to be found before I could begin to write more than an outline of the book. I went to Washington and the Library of Congress. I had worked at the Library before, but this time it was "in the grand manner." David Chambers Mearns, nephew of my editor, David Laurence Chambers, was in charge of the Manuscript Division of the Library of Congress. Mr. Chambers wrote a letter to his nephew, and he assigned me a large room in the main building, where I was afforded every facility for work, as well as ready access to the stacks. I went through that fine Library doing research on pirates, reading early English records on trade and plantations, state papers, and plantation records of the West Indies, Carolina, and Virginia. This material gave me a solid background for my book, and the story developed as I read.

As I have said, the Huguenots were always, to me, the most romantic of early American settlers. Their struggle for freedom of religion against almost overwhelming odds forms one of the most courageous episodes in history. So I chose a Huguenot background for some of my characters. I used the heroine to show the

French cultural background in America, which still survives in sections of the South today.

I find in looking over my notes, that in addition to the Nassau Library and the Library of Congress, I spent much time in the Wilmington North Carolina Public Library, where Miss Emma Woodward (now Mrs. Dougal MacMillan) had collected a great mass of North Carolina material.

Mrs. MacMillan gave enthusiastic assistance to my research and came upon some very useful material. I also worked in the Chowan County Courthouse, Cupola House Museum, State Historical Library at Raleigh, and the Library of the University of North Carolina at Chapel Hill. One of my most interesting experiences was working in the library at the U. S. Naval Academy in Annapolis; and my visit to the Mariners' museum at Newport News is unforgettable, because there I had an opportunity to examine models of ships of the period.

But all this is getting away from Clarendon Plantation and our pleasant life there. The Cape Fear River was teeming with ships—supply ships, new ships being tested, wartime visiting ships of many types—all visible from my library window.

The war was close to us there, because of the German submarines that harried our coast. Sometimes they were close enough to fire on our ships before our men could get them down the coast to Charleston where they would load war material for our troops overseas. We know now that more than a hundred ships were sunk off the Carolina Banks.

At Nags Head, one dark night, we saw a fight off the coast with brilliant fire and an explosion. We were never told what ship went down, but from the oil that washed up along the shore, we knew it was a tanker. The next morning, managers of hotels along the Banks, in order not to alarm the guests (or to spoil their swimming in the surf), sent men out at dawn to clean most of the oil off the beach, but enough traces remained for us to be able to reconstruct the story.

Cape Fear was a particular target for submarines. Once, they even came up as far as the Dow Chemical works, which they shelled, with poor marksmanship. That night shipyard lights were turned off and the river was in total blackness.

Since our land lay along the river we were considered to be in a danger area, as was Orton Plantation, closer to the mouth.

Shortly after we moved in, one of the Army officers of the area called to tell me not to be worried for we were being guarded— the jeep patrol came into our driveway as far as our front door four times each night. If there were any suspicious people about, we were to notify him at once. He gave me a private telephone number to call in an emergency.

The officer made quite a call. He seemed to be interested in my work so I took him into the library, showed him my books and the great supply of maps of the 1700 period which I had tacked on the wall.

He was particularly interested in the maps, and I told him about the Old Town Creek settlement about which I was writing. He even examined some of my manuscript. I was quite flattered to be the object of so much interest.

It was some time later, when he knew me better, that the officer confessed that I had been reported to him as a suspicious character who wrote all the time and had maps on the wall. The report had been made by a Negro woman who kept the store down the road. She had the information from my cook.

I was delighted when he told me this, because it showed how truly patriotic the Negro population in the district was. Afterward, I became great friends with the Negro storekeeper-postmistress and she sent me workmen whenever I needed help, such as "lightwood" for our fireplaces, wood for the stoves, or vegetables. I never mentioned her early suspicions of me, but I knew she was confident now that I was not on Cape Fear to communicate with the enemy.

Often when Jack held meetings at the shipyard at night, I was glad for my protective jeep. If there was trouble I had only to put my head out of the window and shout, or to telephone the officer at the fort.

The one time there was real excitement I was staying in Wilmington for the night and so missed the search for the German.

In front of Clarendon Plantation the old rice field, a marsh, extended far up and down the river shore. The canal from my library door to the river was wide enough for fishing boats to come up to the steps at the end of the garden.

The rice marsh had been abandoned for many years. It was a breeding ground for birds and snakes. Alligators lived there, also; they lay on the banks of the canal in the sun and callumped into the water when anyone appeared. They also bellowed loudly when it was about to rain, and frightened our guests with their raucous noise.

The canal was useful to us. Hannah's husband was a fisherman and he would bring fresh fish to our very door: croakers, bass, and flounder, right out of the water. Fish has a different taste when it is fresh caught, and during the war when food was rationed, it was "an ever present help" to our table.

One of the officials of the shipyard, Sandy MacMahon, arranged to have the ships blow a salute to us as they came back from their trial run down the river. If I remember rightly, it was two toots of the whistle for Clarendon Plantation, and one for the Sprunts at Orton.

The shipyard was running to capacity. Production had come up from five ships a month to eleven completions, and the Maritime Commission's *Bulletin* acclaimed the North Carolina Shipbuilding Company's training department the most efficient in the industry. This was, of course, very gratifying to Jack.

Unfortunately, many of those ships are now in the graveyard of ships lying side-by-side in the backwaters of rivers and streams, waiting to be reactivated for another war, to put out to sea again.

But to go back to the excitement I missed by being in Wilmington. After all the careful plans for guarding the river plantations, someone had reported that a parachute had been seen landing in the rice marsh, directly in front of Clarendon.

Immediately rescue and protective forces got into action, for this could be the long talked of German invasion from the coast, a first landing by parachute, to be followed by sending subs up-river to demolish the shipyard.

In no time armed jeeps were at Clarendon and dozens of men with rifles were searching the woods, the grounds, and the rice swamp; but no invaders were discovered.

I have often wondered how I would have reacted if I had been alone, as I often was, and had looked out of my bedroom window in the middle of the night to discover the house surrounded by an army with rifles and machine guns. Fortunately I was spared that excitement, so I'll never know whether I would have been brave or craven.

One good came of the incident. It proved that the defense of the river was excellent. It could get into high gear with no lost motion; the shipyard went right on building ships without interruption.

I, too, went on working on *Lusty Wind for Carolina* without interruption. Every day from eight-thirty to four o'clock in the afternoon, I sat at my desk, seeing those eighteenth-century folk walking about the piney woods, raising their houses, building their boats, eating, drinking, and perchance some of the young ones making love.

My editor was vastly pleased with the outline of the story. He kept writing me to send manuscript to him so he could keep pace with me.

Against my better judgment, I followed his wishes. This was a mistake, because he worried about the outcome. Particularly did he worry about the love story. He was afraid that I would become so involved with the theme of trade and ships that I would neglect my characters' emotional life. He told me again that he was strong for a good firm love story, "for that is what your readers look for."

I suppose he was right. I may say that he was almost always

right in matters concerning novel writing. Sometimes I grew weary of so much rightness and would argue a point, knowing full well that in the end I would give way to his superior judgment.

But I was beginning to feel that I knew something about writing. This was my fifth book.

Now, after eleven published books, I am beginning to wonder whether I know anything about writing at all. I have found that each book presents its own problems, and whether the books one has written help or not is a moot question.

I am asked sometimes, "What is your technique?"

I confess that I don't know that I have a technique. I have a specific period and the history of that period well-established in my mind. I know how the people dressed, what their political opinions were, what authors they read.

With real historical folk, there are usually journals or speeches to work from. I always endeavor to adhere strictly to their political opinions. As for my fictional characters, I am as free as the air, although I must always place them in their time in order to make them believable. All of the people, all of the events, must fit into the framework of the novel.

I have a few theories about writing. Writing should be simple, no extravagant phrases, words, or metaphors. If a reader stops reading to say to himself, "This is good writing," I have missed my objective, which is to tell a story. Simplicity in style and integrity in history and characterization form the backbone of an historical novel.

These thoughts came to me often as I was writing *Lusty Wind*. Perhaps the surroundings had something to do with it. I was not confined to the four walls of a library. I could, by raising my eyes from my paper, look into the very spot where my characters lived. My people were close to me.

Robert Fountaine, the Huguenot weaver, was driven from France by the revocation of the Edict of Nantes. He brought with him his invalid wife and his beautiful daughter, Gabrielle. Fountaine's grant of 8,500 acres on Cape Fear was the locale of the story.

233

Other characters walked about the forest and down to the shore.

David Moray, the Scot, who had been an officer in the army of the Pretender, was now a bondsman and a gardener.

Gay Molly Lepel, Gabrielle's friend, and Michael Cary, and a host of others form the settlement on Old Town Creek.

Then the pirates: Blackbeard, who roamed the Carolina coast; Charles Vane, deadly but quiet; Rackham, called Calico Jack, and his woman, the beautiful Anne Bonney (who had appeared in *Raleigh's Eden* as a young girl, the "leet" or bondswoman); Stede Bonnet, gentleman turned pirate. All of these were as real as the political characters, and played their various, nefarious parts.

In writing a book with a definite historical background, one must take care to keep the historical and fictional sections in balance.

Then there is the theme to consider. In *Lusty Wind* I used the freedom of the sea lanes and the development of trade in the new and sprawling Colonies in America. The theme is embedded in the warp and the woof, strong enough to hold the story together, but never bold enough to dominate the tapestry.

Yet, in the end, the story is the thing, and all of these considerations must be subordinate to it.

As I approached the completion of *Lusty Wind*, I went again to Washington to check details at the Library of Congress and the Folger Library. I consulted some experts also, but, of course, it is the writer who is responsible. He has created the situations and the people who walk through the pages of his book.

To me this is always a great responsibility. I have never yet sent off a manuscript to a publisher that I have not felt I could have done better if I had had more time. Perhaps that is not the truth. Perhaps I could not have done any better if I had had a year longer.

One thing is certain. In every story I have sent out, I have always felt a great responsibility for the people I have created. Out of thin air, out of my subconscious, or out of the earth that conceals the past, there they are on the printed page, to remain forever the responsibility of the writer who created them.

So the book progressed and the story unfolded; work every weekday, visitors every Sunday. From Camp Davis, a few miles north of Wilmington, came soldiers who found respite from the dry, brittle surroundings of the massive camp in the pleasant relief of green trees, flowers, and gentle surroundings. Sometimes we had fourteen or sixteen of these weekend visitors. The lads came, bringing with them things that were hard for a civilian to buy, chocolate and cokes. In turn, Hannah cooked fried chicken and baked beautiful cakes.

I remember well when eight officers of the British Composite Anti-Aircraft Battalion came for a weekend. When they saw the great basket of fresh eggs Hannah had for their breakfast, they almost wept. At home, they had only one egg a month, and this munificence was almost more than they could bear. Also, whole watermelons—they knew watermelons only as slices on restaurant tables.

One amusing thing happened during their visit. Knowing that the British love their early morning tea, I decided to surprise them with that delicacy. I dressed our little Negro boy, who brought in the wood, in a white jacket, told him to put the cups and saucers and Sevrès teapot on a silver tray, and carry it up to the English visitors. He was to knock at the door, and when it was opened, he was to hand the tray to the officer and say, "Gentlemen, here is your morning tea."

That was the plan. What happened was that the boy forgot what he was to say. He thrust the tray at the officer who opened the door, but the only word he could remember was "gentlemen." So he said "Gentlemen" and fled. One of the men grabbed the tray, while a young "Left'nant" fell over backward on the bed in complete surprise. It was the first time he had seen a Negro boy close at hand, and afterward he said that he was thoroughly frightened.

I believe that *Lusty Wind,* written under the stress of war, took on some of the anxiety, the worry, and sadness of the times. I do not believe that one can be surrounded by thoughts of war and world strife without anxiety showing in some way. And after all, our son was a gunnery officer somewhere in the Atlantic Fleet.

All of my books have had their followers who write to me saying, "This book is the best." Many still cling to *Lusty Wind* as their favorite.

The press on *Lusty* was very good. I liked well Jonathan Daniels' comment in the *Book-of-the-Month-Club News* for October, 1944:

> It is not only her best book, but one of the liveliest and best informed novels recently written about this period of American settlement. She has stuck close to history. Her book is no costume pageant, but a dramatic story of credible human beings in a convincingly human colony.

The book was published in England and translated in Scandinavia, Brazil, Spain, Czechoslovakia, and several other countries. It was a selection of the Literary Guild, Dollar Book Club, and Book League of America, with popular editions by Sun Dial and Blakiston. There was a special Clarendon Edition.

Lusty Wind is the only book I have written that sold over a million copies. I do not think it was because it is my best book, but more likely because it was published during the war years when people had little time or gasoline for travel. They stayed at home and found relief from the pressures of wartime living in books.

May I say that *Lusty Wind for Carolina* swept into the million class on the lusty wind of war?

The long toil of the brave
Is not quenched in
Darkness nor hath counting
The cost fretted away
The zeal of their hopes.

O'er the fruitful earth
And athwart the sea hath passed
The light of noble deeds
Unquenchable forever.

This verse from Pindar's *Isthmian Odes*, as translated by Sir
John Sandys, I encountered first on the Wright Brothers National
tional Memorial at Kill Devil Hills on the Outer Banks off the
North Carolina coast. I copied it down and over the years read it
from time to time, enchanted by its beauty and the thought behind it.

There is something intriguing and soul-satisfying in the thought
that the long toil of the brave is not quenched in darkness, but goes
on forever. Those great men, who with imagination and courage
conquered the sea and the land and the sky, are never forgotten.

237

They have given to the world an example of high courage that is boundless in scope. It is comforting to believe that their noble deeds remain a part of the history of mankind.

For a long time I held in my mind the title, *Toil of the Brave*, but I could think of no book to fit it. I was well into my book about the Revolution before it occurred to me that *Toil of the Brave* was a perfect title for it, and so it was named.

There have come many letters from readers about this title. One man, a minister, wrote that he had taken it as the text of a sermon and had received many favorable comments. Others, who believe that nothing that has lived is ever lost, wrote to commend me for using that belief as the basis of a book. I feel that I have old Pindar to thank for his beautiful words, which hold an essential truth: "The long toil of the brave is not quenched in darkness."

This book was my sixth novel and the fourth of the Carolina Series. It was published in October, 1946. The special North Carolina edition was called Kings Mountain Edition. It was published also in an Armed Services Edition, Fiction Book Club, and in a story strip of thirty installments by Frank Godwin of King Features. Again, the book was published in England, Norway, Sweden, Denmark, France, Spain, and Czechoslovakia.

The book had its real beginning when I visited Kings Mountain battleground on the dividing line between North and South Carolina. I had already chosen the period, the Revolution when the war was moving south. I had already visited the battleground at Guilford Courthouse, and was intrigued by several facts that I gained through the government display there.

Two things stood out: First, in Cornwallis' Army there was a contingent of the Black Watch from Scotland. Second, natural causes had helped to defeat Lord Cornwallis; constant rain and high water delayed his army time after time.

But the real inspiration came when I saw Major Ferguson's grave on Kings Mountain. Something about that lonely grave on the mountainside stirred my imagination. I was told that it had been moved from the summit of the mountain, where the battle was fought, and placed down a hillside, away from all relics of fighting. When they dug up Major Ferguson, they found a woman's body close by. No one knew who the woman was or why her body was there. This in itself was dramatic.

Major Ferguson himself was a man of importance, an excellent soldier who had invented a repeating rifle. He had been alone in command on the mountaintop and had placed his men in order on the high places, in the best tradition of the British. But he was out-fought by a dozen American colonels and their men who followed Indian tactics of war. He died heroically, without assistance from the British forces not far away in South Carolina.

We scrambled through brush down the hillside. Visitors had built a cairn of rocks over his grave. I sat down on a rock, and for a long time looked at it. I pictured the day he had given up his life on Kings Mountain, to lie forever in a foreign land. Before I left, I said a little prayer for a lonely man. I was wearing a bright red camellia on my coat. I laid it on his grave thinking that the flower was as bright as the red coat he wore the day he died, and left him to his solitude—a sublime resting place that looked across the lovely hills and valleys of a pleasant, quiet countryside. Hail and farewell.

I remember when I was writing *Raleigh's Eden* I got into serious difficulties with the Battle of Guilford Courthouse. The available histories did not give me all I needed. I could not *see* the battle. Unless I can see people moving about, talking, in action, I take them out of the story. My theory is that if they are not real to the writer, they certainly are not going to be real to the reader.

I confided my troubles to General Fletcher Sharpe, a friend stationed at the Presidio, in San Francisco.

He responded at once, "I'll get you some material that will set you right." He sent to the Army libraries at Fort Leavenworth and Washington, and soon I had twenty or thirty pamphlets and books —tactics and strategy of both armies, the British under Cornwallis, the Americans under General Greene. When I had finished reading, I knew the plan of battle, how and why it was fought.

Cornwallis really won the battle, but he was obliged to retreat with his broken and disordered army across North Carolina to Wilmington.

Guilford Courthouse is considered one of the critical battles of the Revolution, for it pointed the way to Yorktown. I always liked Cornwallis. He was one of the men who stood up for America in Parliament. But he was a soldier and did his duty as a soldier, though often his heart was not in it.

As I have said, one of the reasons I am sometimes mistaken for a man, I have been told, is because of the way I write about battles. Van Wyck Mason included my Battle of Guilford Courthouse in his book *Fighting Americans, Battles of the Revolutionary War in Fiction*. The other authors were men.

When I think of the people who have helped me in my writing, I think of Fletcher Sharpe. He was in command on the Island of Cebu during the war with Japan. I believe he is the man who said he was "expendable," when MacArthur tried to persuade him to join in his move to Australia. He held out on Cebu until Wainwright ordered him to come to Manila to stop the reprisals of the Japs. He and Wainwright were together in prison camp on Taiwan (Formosa).

He must have been a thorn in the flesh of the Japanese because of his endurance. He stood six-feet-five and was magnificently proportioned. To the small Japanese he was surely a constant source of irritation.

If it had not been for General Fletcher Sharpe's interest in my problem, I could never have properly written the Battle of Guilford Courthouse.

We had been spending nearly half the year in North Carolina so that I could do research in the Edenton area, at the Hall of History in Raleigh and at North Carolina and Duke universities. We had made several trips by car between North Carolina and California. I grew so tired of motoring that I was reluctant to get into a car. Texas was the worst; it is so big that driving along one of the Southern routes one wonders if he will ever get out of Texas.

We had tried to buy a house in Edenton, or land in the country, but, like their Devon ancestors, Chowan County people do not sell land. Most of the land has been inherited, in some instances to the tenth generation.

I have mentioned the purchase of Bandon, Parson Daniel Earle's 1750 plantation. It was during the writing of *Toil of the Brave* that we moved from California and took up our residence in the long-neglected plantation house.

Eighteen years without occupancy had left the house in sad state, but we soon had a room arranged so that I had working quarters. We were back in the Colonial period in earnest; fireplaces for heat (there were eleven), candles for light, and a pitcher pump on the back gallery.

During the early stages of the writing, John Wood of Hayes suggested that I might find something of interest in the famous Hayes library. I found many things of great interest. The most absorbing items were the many letters from Penelope Dawson, daughter of Royal Governor Gabriel Johnston, to her cousin Samuel Johnston, owner of Hayes Plantation, Revolutionary hero, and the first U. S. Senator from North Carolina. These fascinating letters gave me a solid background of the thought of the people of eastern North Carolina and of Edenton.

It was through the letters of James Iredell, Collector of Customs and lawyer, later appointed to the Supreme Court by President Washington, that I had a complete picture of the village and its people during the years of the Revolution.

In the Library of Congress I found the journal of the Englishman, Captain Anthony Allison. He was a British agent, the opposite of my Captain Peter Huntley of Washington's Continental Army. The men are rivals for the hand of Angela of River Plantation (Bandon).

A reviewer has written of *Toil of the Brave:*

> Planters visit one another's mansions, have tea and sherry parties; there are duels on the Green, moonlight walks, drunken brawls, a roadside tavern and illicit love affairs; a

241

host of historical characters crowd the pages. Joseph Hewes, father of the American Navy, whose shipyard is on Albemarle Sound; Samuel Johnston, who sees the cause as one of strict legality and becomes a leader through the force of his cool conviction and logic; William Hooper, who shows his neighbors that this is not a war for the zealots of New England, to which North Carolina can afford to be indifferent. Anne and Cullen Pollock, Dr. Hugh Williamson, James Iredell, Penelope and Thomas Barker.

Then there was a favorite of mine, Cosimo de' Medici, a young Italian cadet of the famous Italian family, who as a captain of dragoons spent some time in Queen Anne's Town.

Into the story moved characters from earlier books; Adam Rutledge, Mary Warden and her husband William, Dr. Armitage, and Parson Daniel Earle. They stepped right out of *Raleigh's Eden.*

Indeed, Dr. Armitage is a character who caused me much trouble in several books. He had the habit of taking over and becoming much more important than I intended he should be. I finally had to count his scenes to see that he did not run away with the story. I had him living in the seventeenth-century Cupola House, where I discovered later that another doctor had really lived during the Revolution.

Another section of the book that interested me greatly as I wrote it was the introduction of Negro slaves into the stories. The Negro dialect presented a problem. I didn't want dialect of the Uncle Remus type. I wanted no more than an indication of dialect. I thought of the Negro in terms of the natives I had observed in Africa and the manner in which they spoke English. I patterned my dialect on that. The outcome was that I had a letter from a professor in a South Carolina college asking if I had made a study of the Gullah language as spoken in the country around Charleston. Since I had not made a study of Gullah, the inference was that the Gullahs spoke something similar to the native African's English. All African dialects come from the base language Bantu, which is spoken in all parts of Africa.

One critic, who was not interested in North Carolina history, said that I was one of the few writers who gave a true, dignified picture of Negroes and not something between Uncle Tom and a blackface minstrel Mister Bones; that I made them individuals.

In all my novels, I have endeavored to present a community of folk—rich and poor, planters of the Sound, tenant farmers, and the small yeomen who settled on the rivers and creeks.

Since waterways were the highways in the Colonial and Revolutionary period, it was necessary to obtain land that followed the water. Now the water is all but neglected, for highways belong to the land and motor vehicles. So far has this trend progressed that before many years have passed all houses and all living may be along the great transcontinental highways and those that bisect the country from north to south.

But in the early days of the Colony, sounds and rivers and creeks formed the basis of living. Rich bottom land was the settler's first objective. Sandy lands of the rivers and creeks were left to the yeomen.

Today, by their industry, descendants of the early yeomen of the West Counties of Devon and Cornwall have outstripped many of the descendants of the men who owned lands along Albemarle Sound. "Short crops" have been the answer—beans, peas, and melons, followed by corn, cotton, peanuts, and hogs.

The old "tar, pitch, and turpentine" has given way to tobacco and peanuts. A new life has developed that surpasses the old Colonial life of large plantations. Although timber remains a money crop, it must be developed by reforestation or it will be lost.

Toil of the Brave has in it something of the division of opinion concerning the Revolutionary War (which I consider a civil war, since it was Englishmen fighting Englishmen). Its main theme develops the idea that it is not enough to procure and develop land, but a man must be prepared to fight to preserve it in freedom.

Again we had a book that was on the bestseller lists. In the small town of Edenton, 385 copies were sold by the local drugstore on the first day it was published.

Bobbs-Merrill had again done a good production job. *Toil of the Brave* was nicely printed, had a fine dust jacket, and excellent promotion.

Most books cannot flourish without all of these attributes, but *Toil of the Brave* was launched with a degree of success the moment it reached the bookstores.

We made another publishers' tour to cities in the East and South. Once I protested these journeys, but my editor's answer was, "Wherever you appear in a city we sell books."

I am not sure that the same situation exists today as it did during the period of the earlier books. Speaking at book club meetings was a sure way to increase sales. I am thinking particularly of the clubs in California, over which Mrs. Jack Valleley presided. When a title was placed on her monthly list of recommended books, sales always jumped.

I remember a Book Fair in Atlanta organized by Luise Sims, of Davison, Paxon's book department. Many, many books by many, many authors who attended that meeting were sold on the spot. Authors, editors, critics, and publishers were present in great numbers, and it was a satisfactory enterprise for everyone.

"Book meetings," in Richmond, Virginia, with Peggy O'Neil as hostess were also very successful from the standpoint of both attendance and sales.

Rose Oller, of Marshall Field's, was one of the ablest of book people in arranging author parties. She had "the gift," as the Irish say, of organization and publicity. I've been told that more books were sold over the counter at the entrance to Marshall Field's book department than in any other store in America, with the possible exception of Macy's.

I remember particularly the oil painting that hung over the entrance to the book department at Field's at the time of publication of *Bennett's Welcome*, my sixth novel in the Carolina Series. It was a copy of the jacket, heroic in size. It overshadowed everything in the immense book department. After a time, it was taken down and sent to me. It is now in the old 1750 schoolhouse of Parson Daniel Earle at Bandon, and covers half of one wall. It is greatly admired by the hundreds of people who visit Bandon, and we enjoy it because it reminds us of pleasant times in Chicago, lunching and talking with book people.

My visits to Chicago (Illinois, as you know, is my native state) always stand out for that reason. Chicago reviewers have been kind. Fanny Butcher and Fred Babcock and Sterling North are friends whom I value highly.

It must be realized that when one writes an historical novel, one is not given the praise sometimes awarded to a contemporary novel, nor the fine criticism that a nonfiction book may enjoy. As I have often said, the historical novelist falls within the Western term of maverick. However, there are critics who really like "historicals" and review such books soundly.

Toil of the Brave was reviewed in the New York *Herald Tribune* by Jennings Rice:

> Skilled in manipulating plot and counterplot, equally adroit in handling dialogue or narrative, the author has prepared for her readers another beguiling tour into "the good old days." Mrs. Fletcher's powers of invention seem as fresh as ever. In short, if one may shift the metaphor, *Toil of the Brave* is a delectable cup compounded of romance and gallantry, shrewdly laced with derring-do.

Before I set aside remembrances of *Toil of the Brave*, I should like to tell you of another problem with which I was faced. I developed a case of shingles. The last third of the book was written sitting up in bed, while I tried to convince myself that shingles was a minor ailment, a slight nervous disorder that I could hold in check by forgetting about it. This idea was a delusion, but I had a deadline to meet, so propped up by my pillows and my doctor's kindly understanding, I managed to finish on time.

Jack always maintained that this book had the most appropriate title of any of my books—*Toil of the Brave*.

CHAPTER

2 1

The war was over, but the great devastation from persistent bombings was tragically evident when we arrived in London in May of 1948.

Two things brought us there: research in the British Museum and in the West Country of Devon and Cornwall, and a meeting in Zurich, Switzerland, of the International P.E.N. Club, of which I have been a member since my San Francisco days. It had been many years since I had been in England, and I looked forward to the visit with great anticipation. This time Jack was going with me.

But to go back to the events that led to the journey. As I have said, I always thoroughly enjoyed my research work, but it seemed that every time I researched a period in preparation for writing one book, I would run across incidents of an earlier period which aroused my curiosity and become deeply involved in that era.

This time I went a long way back, to the first attempted colonization of Roanoke Island. I felt that in order to understand the development of North Carolina, one must know about the very beginnings, and that meant the days of Elizabeth, the Virgin Queen, and her great sea captains who, adventuring in ships, made England queen of the seas.

I arrived at this decision, I think, after reading Richard Hakluyt's *Principall Navigations, Voiages, and Discoveries of the English Nation*. It was then that I realized Roanoke Island was the very beginning of English colonization in America, that this vast country had its birth on the little island off the coast of North Carolina. (In that far-off time of 1585, the land of the Carolinas was called Virginia.)

This was an exciting and thrilling thought for me. I was familiar with Paul Green's out-of-door symphonic drama, "The Lost Colony." In fact, I had been on the board of directors of The Roanoke Island Historical Association (which presents *The Lost Colony*) for some years, but had given no thought to the early attempts to colonize the island until I read Hakluyt.

I was fascinated by the fact that one hundred and eight young men from Devon and Cornwall were brought to this coast by one of the greatest of Elizabeth's sea captains, Sir Richard Grenville. I was carried away by the idea. I had a list of their names, but no more. Who were those men? Why did we not know something about them? Where did they come from, and why did they venture forth on the unfriendly seas to America?

Beside Hakluyt, I had several other sources of reading. Sir Walter Raleigh's book on the history of the world was one. I knew that Grenville was related to Sir Walter; that Sir Walter, the great courtier, was a cousin of the Grenville family of Stowe Barton in Cornwall and Bideford in Devon. Somehow all the publicity of this 1585 expedition centered around Raleigh, with small mention of Sir Richard Grenville. There was something wrong about this. I felt I must get to the source, and the source was not in the Library of Congress where I began working, but in England.

I received a great deal of advice as to why I should not attempt to go to England at that time; not much "tidying up" had been done, the English were still on austere rationing, we wouldn't get enough to eat, and a dozen other seemingly good reasons.

I weighed the matter. If the English hadn't starved, we wouldn't starve. We might be uncomfortable, but we would manage. One of the problems was hotels. There was some kind of ruling about a three- or four-day stay at hotels. This wouldn't do for us, for we wanted three months in London.

We enlisted the aid of Thos. Cook & Son, that marvelous agency that knows everything, and after some negotiations we were promised rooms at a small hotel in Knightsbridge for the three-month period we thought necessary for the work I had in mind.

Armed with letters (it is always well to have letters), we started off on our venture. We were going to fly! We had both flown often in America. In fact, we dated back to the period when Lieutenant Billy Mitchell commanded the North Island Army Post and its six little cockleshell flying ships, but we had never flown the Atlantic. All went well, with the exception of minor trouble with a couple of generators and an enforced stay of eight hours at Gander awaiting new ones from Boston. Gander, that lonely wind-swept outpost of flying, is a poor place for amusement on a cold, rainy day.

At the London airport, Cook's, true to tradition, had a courier meet our plane with a mass of information about rules and regulations; where we were to apply for ration cards and tickets and coupons and so forth.

The Normandie was a quaint little hotel, just recovering from bomb hits (several of which had fallen short of their target Knightsbridge Barracks, nearby). Workmen were about the place hammering and sawing, repairing damage. It made us feel that we were still under siege from the skies. We had even more of that feeling when we looked out our bathroom window and saw that many of the buildings that presented a decent façade to the street were like stage sets in Hollywood, completely demolished in the rear.

248

We had reserved a bedroom and bath. The bath was three doors down the hall, but it was considered as belonging to our bedroom and we had the only key.

We were ashamed to complain about anything, since everyone in the hotel from hall porter, doorman, and bellboy, to the maid who "did" for us, was happy and cheerful. The food was very bad, but we made no complaint. However, we found that it wasn't the war that was responsible but a poor cook, so we took to eating at the Hyde Park Hotel up the street or walking downtown past Buckingham Palace, along Green Park, to the Ritz, where we enjoyed very good food indeed. It was a matter of cooks. Good cook, good food. Of course, there was not a great variety, but what there was, was excellent.

In the morning we were awakened by the bugle call of reveille at Knightsbridge Barracks across the road. Not long after, we would hear the clatter of horses' hoofs on the pavement and rush to the window in time to see the red-coated guard, on beautiful horses, riding to their various stations; Buckingham Palace, St. James's Palace, and Whitehall.

After we obtained our ration books, we got into one of those delightful little London taxis and departed for the British Museum, where I was to do much research about the beginnings of the Roanoke adventure.

If I had time, I would write an essay on the London taxi and the taxi driver. I love those shiny little vehicles that can turn on a dime and carry one safely to one's destination. I could write an ode to London taxi drivers, their innate courtesy and profound knowledge of their beloved city.

I've learned to know London through these drivers; the peaceful London as well as the London of the war and the air blitz. It was a taxi driver who taught me the out-of-the-way spots where the working people go at noon, carrying their lunches in little paper bags—church steps and churchyards, small parks, and under the green trees along the Thames embankment.

Since I did incorporate some of this knowledge in my book

about the Elizabethans, perhaps the taxi drivers should belong to the list of people who helped me in my writing. I well remember their delight when one praised their city or the courage of their people, but they passed off the praise as though it were nothing to live month after month under the terror of sky siege.

The British Museum was well across town from our hotel; along Hyde Park, Park Lane, Oxford Street, and beyond. Curiously, the great glass-roofed rotunda was never damaged by bombs, though other parts of the building were. I had a letter to the Secretary of the Museum, Mr. Francis, from my friend David Chambers Mearns, nephew of my editor, who had assisted me earlier at the Library of Congress.

During the war, Mr. Francis had been in America, I was told, as guardian of the Magna Charta. (I believe there are three copies; no one knows which is the original.)

Somehow I like to think that in her time of great national peril, the Mother Country, England, turned to her largest former colony, the United States, to guard and preserve her greatest treasure, the paper that gave freedom to her people, the Magna Charta.

We found Mr. Francis delightful. He put the facilities of the British Museum at my disposal. I was welcome to work with its sacred and learned manuscripts. He was a little apologetic. "We are delighted to have you work here, Mrs. Fletcher, but I must tell you that our records are very meager before 1066."

To me, that is the apex of British understatement.

I was often reminded, when I went through the halls that held the beautiful and rare Elgin marbles, of our son Stuart saying that when he visited the British Museum on his midshipman cruise from the U. S. Naval Academy at Annapolis, he could never get beyond the Elgin marbles. Their cold, classic beauty caught his fancy and held him captive.

After we left Mr. Francis' office that first morning, we went into the rotunda under the great glass dome. Mr. Francis had warned me that I would find their method of cataloging and handling books very old-fashioned after working with the modern card index system of American libraries. On the contrary, I found their system more to my liking, for one was at once in the stacks. One could look in the great volumes that held their catalogs, turn to Devon, for instance, and find out exactly where books on Devon were located. In this way, a searcher would come on hundreds of books he had never heard of. Material beyond one's dreams was at hand without the time-consuming catalog search which usually revealed that the books one wanted were not available. Here they were, a plethora of books and information.

But before I had discovered all this richness, I had looked about the great rotunda. There were books upon books on shelves that ran from floor to ceiling. The very sight of so many books appalled me. Weakly, I asked one of the many librarians who sat behind the huge circular desk how many books there were on the shelves. As I recall, he said either thirteen million or twenty-three million, I forget which.

A sinking feeling hit me. I grasped Jack's arm. "Let's go home. I can't bear to think of writing the twenty-three millionth and one." It took two days before I could get up courage to go back to the Museum and begin on the books on Devon and Cornwall.

I have spoken of the list of names of the gentleman adventurers who came to Roanoke Island with Sir Richard Grenville. I felt sure that most of them came from the maritime counties of Devon and Cornwall, for Devon was the home of Raleigh and the Grenville houses were in both Cornwall and Bideford, Devon. An early Grenville had helped to build the bridge of Bideford-East-the-Water.

I thought, too, that most of the names were either Devon or Cornish, and that many were those of the great County families of the West Country. This proved to be true.

It seemed to me to be a strange thing that no one among all the historians who had written about the beginnings of America had troubled to find out who these people were who formed the first expedition (really the second, since Amadas and Barlow had preceded them) and who had lived on Roanoke Island for a full year.

One hundred and eight men, and we knew nothing about them.

I often thought that if Roanoke Island had been in New England those searching New Englanders would not only have listed the names, but they would have discovered who each man was, where he came from, and why he came to America in the first place, and it would all have been recorded in the history of New England.

It was different in the Roanoke Colony. We had only the names. We did know, however, that they came under the leadership of Sir Richard Grenville, the Elizabethan sea captain who died so heroically sailing his ship against fifty-three Spanish galleons. "Right into the mass of ships sailed Sir Richard in his little ship *Revenge*, to his heroic death," as it is so vividly told by Lord Alfred Tennyson, in his poem, "The 'Revenge': A Ballad of the Fleet."

But to trace the names, that was my objective at the British Museum. I did not find all of the one hundred and eight names, but I did find that over seventy had come from the County families of Devon and Cornwall. This confirmed Hakluyt and my thinking. Sir Richard Grenville and Sir Walter Raleigh were cousins; the ships companies had been made up of relatives and neighbors of the two leaders (Raleigh never came to America). The others could have been London men who accompanied Governor Ralph Lane, or servants to the Gentlemen Adventurers.

After I had satisfied myself that the first English colonists in America were from the West Country, I was ready to go to Bideford, in Devon, to search for the history of these men and the reasons for their going to America.

Before he left home Jack had obtained letters from one of the Standard Oil officials, an old friend, to the London office of British-American. He knew that gasoline would be in short supply, and we would have to get permission to motor to various places in the counties in order to visit the former homes of the men of the Roanoke adventure. The letters to British-American produced a cordial reception and arrangements were made immediately for a car and chauffeur and unlimited supplies of petrol.

We had called again on our friend Cook's. After some searching they got rooms for us at Portledge at a new inn to be opened about the time we arrived in Devon. We found Portledge Inn to be an ancient Norman castle that had been in the hands of one family since 1207. It was in the transition stage of installing bathrooms and preparing for a houseful of guests. We drove through massive entrance gates along a driveway which led through a tunnel of rhododendrons all in full bloom. We were among the first half-dozen arrivals on opening day and our reception was heartwarming.

The nearby village was Fairy Cross, about four miles west of Bideford in the heart of the most beautiful countryside we had ever seen.

We had come down from London on the Devon Belle, a deluxe train operated by the Pullman Company, and while it is a day train with no sleeping cars, it is beautiful and luxurious. We were off on our great adventure!

It was an adventure indeed. Things worked out in a wonderful way. The difficulties I had envisaged disappeared like magic. It was almost as though it "was to be," according to the doctrine of predestination or the Arabic kismet.

Arrangements were made for a large Austin car, with a chauffeur who knew every highway and byway in Devon and Cornwall, and every estate, mansion, and farm cottage along them.

Living at Portledge was delightful. The Inn was being operated on a seventy-five-year lease from the Pynne-Coffyn family (pronounced Pine-Coffin). The manager owned several other hotels so he had a well-organized staff and a clientele who appreciated the charm and comfort of the Inn. Everyone was very cordial and friendly. In fact, after we had been there several days, one English lady could not refrain from asking how we managed to do so much motoring; they were allowed only enough petrol to come to Portledge and return home, none for touring, she told me.

When we explained, her reaction was: "Well, thank goodness there is someone in this austere government who knows enough to be gracious to our guests!" There was no envy, no criticism of our special privileges.

At one end of Portledge, there was a long pergola built of black wood columns with gilded trimmings that had been recovered from the wreckage of galleons of the Spanish Armada, cast up on the shore of Bristol Channel. The outer walls were stone, four feet thick, and the inner walls were three to four feet of brick, which was discovered in the course of installing the bathrooms. In the former family dining room, where the wall had been cut through to the drawing room, they had taken out twelve tons of stone.

The ceilings in all public rooms were ornamented in plaster with the coats of arms of the two families and their various branches. I often wondered whether some of the beautiful carving in the house did not come from the hands of Grinling Gibbons who had lived at the nearby village of Kilkhampton. The church at Kilkhampton is a Grenville church, and the rood screen, pew ends, and other carvings are accredited to Grinling Gibbons.

A curious thing happened while we were researching in Cornwall. We were driving slowly across the central square of a small village when I saw a stone church. Without reason, I called to the chauffeur, "Stop! stop! I must go into that church."

When we went inside I saw that the windows bore the early Grenville names, among them Sir Richard who was lost at sea. Here was my man, the great sea captain of the days of Elizabeth. I knelt down in a pew that bore the three clarions, the coat of arms of the Grenville family, who had come to England with William the Conqueror in 1066. I said a little prayer for the great navigator who had safely carried the first settlers to America and landed them on Roanoke Island. I felt close to him there in his little church at Kilkhampton. In truth I felt close to him everywhere in Devon and Cornwall.

We drove slowly down the narrow lanes, cut deep into the earth through centuries of travel; so deep were they at times, that we had to get out of the car and scramble up several feet to get a view of the beautiful rolling country or a great stone house snuggled down in a valley amid a grove of trees.

I saw an England that I had never seen in my earlier visits. It is said that the Midlands are the heart of England. If so, Devon and Cornwall are its soul.

Day after day we drove out through the rhododendron drive at Portledge into the crossroad where Hubba the Dane fought the Saxons and along the tree-lined roadway to Buckland Brewer, where I found my family ancestors.

"Glorious Devon" the advertisements say, and glorious are the softly rolling hills and the gentle valleys where square old stone Norman towers marked a day's journey during the days of knights on horseback and pilgrims on foot. This is Kingsley country; the writer's statue is in Bideford and the words "Westward Ho!" are seen everywhere. But it is also the country of Kipling's *Stalky and Co.*, at Appledore. (That is where my ancestor, Richard Chapman, had his shipyard in the time of Elizabeth.)

At least thirty or forty writers have used Devon as the background of novels and poetry: Blackmore's *Lorna Doone* country not far away; Whyte-Melville, who wrote of horses and hunts; the romances of Marie Corelli; playwright and novelist Justin Huntly M'Carthy; Charles Dickens' *A Message from the Sea*; the two Williamsons, C. and A. M. And names known in the world of scholars: S. Baring-Gould's *The Vicar of Morwentstow*; Prince's *Northern Devon*; *The Portledge Family Papers: Sir Richard Grenville of the Revenge* by A. L. Rowse; Tennyson's "Revenge;" *The Cruise of the Nona* by Hilaire Belloc.

This was the country described by these authors and many more. One felt that the spirit of these writers was in the earth of the bracken-covered moors and the rugged seacoast of Cornwall. This wild coast, so different from the gentle hills of Devon, attracted one with its terrible beauty. Here, at Hartland Point, the British had trained their Rangers to scale high cliffs in preparation for Norway's release.

Our first real journey was to the country home of Sir Richard Grenville at Stowe Barton. I felt I must see it, so I could understand the man who was, to my mind, the greatest of Elizabeth's sea captains, not excepting Sir Francis Drake. I had found, from my reading in the Bideford Library, that the journey around the world accomplished by Drake had been Sir Richard Grenville's original plan. (The Queen refused to allow him to leave the country, as the Spanish were threatening.)

At Stowe, the seat of the Grenvilles, we found that the two earlier homes had been pulled down and only a farm cottage, of twenty or so rooms, remained. We were shown about that delightful Elizabethan house by Farmer Allin, whose family had been tenants on Grenville lands since before Elizabeth's time. In fact, one of the early Allins had been with Drake on his journey around the world. We enjoyed the hospitality of Mr. Allin (Yeoman Allin) and his gracious wife. The house still had the original immense stone slabs for floors and some of the original furniture.

I went out to the orchard to view the broad vista that had been gazed upon by all the Grenvilles since 1066. The place is described in *The Domesday Book*, as are all the lands and holdings in Devon.

I used that visit as the opening of *Roanoke Hundred*.

Some time after we had returned home, we had a letter from Mr. Allin. He told us that Colonel Thynne, heir to the Grenville lands, had retired from the army and gone to live in Europe. He offered to sell the land to the tenants, and Yeoman Allin bought the land his ancestors had farmed since before the days of Queen Elizabeth. I suppose, becoming a landowner, he is now Squire Allin instead of Yeoman Allin. But in Devon, yeoman is a title that a man wears with pride.

Besides Stowe Barton, we visited every property that Sir Richard Grenville had owned, including his town house in Bideford and his estate at Buckland in south Devon.

It was there that I learned of the bitter rivalry between Drake and Grenville, which I emphasized, giving the reasons, in *Roanoke Hundred*. I also discovered that almost all of the great Elizabethan captains had visited Roanoke Island: Grenville, Drake, Sir John Hawkins, Thomas Cavendish (who spent a year on the Island when he circumnavigated the globe), Carlisle (kin of Queen Elizabeth's great minister Walsingham), Thomas Harriot (historian of the expedition and one of the most famous mathematicians of his time), Ralph Lane the governor (who had been equerry to the queen), and John White (the artist who gave us the magnificent paintings of the Indians, birds, and fish of the New World). Together with the young cadets of the County families of Devon and Cornwall, this was one of the greatest representations of English gentlemen ever to come to America.

Before we left Devon, we had not only unearthed stories from the highways and byways of the county, but I had found at Sidney Harper's Sons, in Bideford, hundreds of books on the history of the counties. We sent home nearly thirty important histories, including the rare *Worthies of Devon* by Prince, Lyson's *Magna Britannica*, and Vivian's *Visitations of Cornwall*.

I might add that we found many pieces of old plate and silver at Bideford, at prices far less than at the London dealers.

I could write a book on Devon alone and our adventures as we researched for *Roanoke Hundred*, but I must write about research for books that followed.

I had been named delegate from California to the P.E.N. International Congress in Zurich, and we had just time to fly there from London, the day we returned from Portledge.

At the Congress, we met many famous writers who came from all parts of the world. There were meetings and luncheons and banquets and visits to nearby cities. I did not join in the trips for I had to sit in meetings, but Jack enjoyed Bern, Lausanne, and Basel, and the company of all the pleasant women who did not have to sit in committee rooms and discuss writing problems.

My first visit to the London P.E.N. had taken place some years before I became a member. I was the guest of John Galsworthy, through his nephew, Rudolph Sauter. Mr. Galsworthy had given his Nobel Prize Award money to the club, the interest to be applied toward the expenses of running the London organization.

I now had an opportunity in Zurich to renew old acquaintances: Prince William of Sweden; Storm Jameson, the English novelist; Desmond MacCarthy, the famous critic, who was president of the English P.E.N.

Jack and I experienced an amusing incident on our arrival at our hotel. We had engaged a room and bath at the fine, big Dolder Grand Hotel, high on the mountain just outside of Zurich. When the elegantly attired receptionist showed us our rooms, I looked about and asked, "Where is the bath?" The receptionist shook his head. "We are very sorry. We have no rooms with bath; but look, Madam!"

He led me to the double glass doors that opened on to a little balcony. "Behold!" he said with a sweeping gesture of his arm. "Behold the view before your eyes. When you are seated here, enjoying your coffee and croissants and the view of the Alps; you will never give a thought to the bath." Then he told us to summon a maid to prepare our baths and gave us a pile of tickets to the swimming pool.

He was quite right, for displayed before us was the whole panorama of the snow-capped Alps, from Mount Blanc on. I think we have never enjoyed our rolls and coffee as we did on those divine mornings on the Dolder Grand balcony.

We had made arrangements to visit my publishers in the Scandinavian countries. When the P.E.N. Congress had adjourned, we flew to Sweden. We had reservations, through Cook's, at the Grand Hotel in Stockholm. I wanted to go to that famous hotel because during the war it was supposed to have harbored spies of every country. I hoped that some of them would have lingered.

When we reached Stockholm, a Cook's courier met us at the airport. We could not go to the Grand Hotel because of an international convention of physicians and surgeons. Nor was there space in any other hotel in Stockholm. The place was overrun with doctors.

They had a "nice place" for us at Krohn Pensionat, the courier told us, "very nice indeed," with sitting room and bath. I said that I didn't want to go to any pension. I didn't like them. But the courier shook his head. There wasn't another place in Stockholm. We went to the *pensionat*.

It turned out to be not too bad. Our rooms were over some stores, but they were large and airy and spotlessly clean. (Everything *is* spotlessly clean in the Scandinavian countries.) They were made homelike and cheerful by great bouquets of roses and other flowers sent by Mr. Wickstrom and Stig Arbman, directors of Ljus, my publishing house.

There were newspaper interviews and plans for trips to nearby castles, out-of-door dinners, and a luncheon with Count Bernadotte and his wife, who was an American, Miss Manville. In fact, it was to have been a delightful week for us. It would have been, too, only I got sick and Jack had to take my place in all the trips and entertainment, while I lay in a nice bed in Karolinska Schukhuset (Carolina Hospital).

From this distance I can see how amusing it was. At the time, there was no amusement for me. I had awakened in the middle of the night with a nosebleed that we could not stop. I had never had such a thing happen before and was somewhat alarmed. We both grew alarmed as it continued.

Being housed in the far end of the *pensionat*, we didn't even know where the office was or whom to call. The telephone was in the hall, so Jack went out to call a hospital. Apparently no one in the telephone office spoke English. His Swedish was non-existent. His German was not equal to the occasion. The less the telephone girl understood, the louder he talked until he was shouting.

I heard someone speak to him. "Can I be of service, sir?" and presently Jack came back into the room with a young man who said he was Bulgarian. He spoke perfect English. He told us he was in the export-import business. I was not to worry. He had contacted a hospital. The men would soon be there.

Jack got dressed, put a few toilet articles in my overnight case, and by the time the intern from the hospital arrived, we were ready.

It really is a peculiar feeling to be carried out of a building on a main street on a stretcher. Crowds upon crowds of people were milling about, looking down on me curiously, chattering in strange languages. I thought vaguely of a cartoon I had seen called a "Worm's-Eye View." That was the view I had, looking up into strange faces from a prone position.

The shoved me into something that looked like a "Black Maria." Jack and our Bulgarian rescuer followed the stretcher. The Bulgarian held my hand and kept repeating, "Don't worry. You will be all right. Don't worry." Jack sat opposite, clasping my little case in his hands. He was as white as a sheet. I had never seen him look so alarmed.

Beside all this attention, the two stretcher-bearers were holding towel after towel to my nose, for the bleeding had not decreased any. Finally, the Black Maria stopped and we went through a long hall into a great room crowded with men. They sat on chairs and lay on the floor. I thought, where have they brought me? These men look like drunks. I was now very weak, but I heard a man whom I thought was a doctor say, "You shouldn't bring her here. This is an emergency hospital. Take her to Karolinska."

I heard Jack ask, "What is that?"

"Eye, ear, nose, and throat. Get her there quick."

The men picked up the litter and away we went. I heard a clock strike one as we rushed through the streets, bells clanging. I must have fainted (something I had never done before). I remember nothing of the arrival at the hospital.

When I opened my eyes, Leslie Howard was bending over me. I seemed to sense that he had died. I'm in heaven, I thought. How nice of Leslie Howard to be here to greet me.

I drifted off again. When I came to, I realized that it was only a doctor who looked like Leslie Howard. He was grumbling to the nurse, something about being awakened at two o'clock in the morning. All the time he was working away, packing my nose with gauze. He saw that I was awake and smiled and said, "Mrs. Fletcher, I did not think to see you first time, this way. I have read all of your books, every one of them."

"How nice," I said. Before I drifted off, I felt a needle being jabbed into my arm. I thought, I am not going to die or they would not have given me a dose of morphine.

When I woke in the morning, I found myself in a fresh clean room; a little round-faced nurse was bending over me, ready to wash my face. She greeted me brightly, but I could not understand. Presently she brought in another nurse, with a morning paper in her hand. She pointed to a picture of me, with a long piece under it, the result of the interview of the day before.

"Read it," I said. I saw her lips move, but I couldn't hear her words because of the great rumbling in my ears. It was like a train rushing by at tremendous speed.

I was alarmed then. I had lost my hearing overnight. I put my face in the pillow. I didn't weep, but I wanted to.

Jack came in at the same time breakfast arrived. I didn't eat anything. He ate the breakfast, which he indicated was delightful. All food is wonderful in Scandinavian countries.

Presently the young house doctor came. With him was the chief surgeon, Dr. Holmgren, who was to take care of me. He spoke perfect English, I found out later. He was one of the finest specialists in the world. He came to America every two or three years to study new techniques.

I was still annoyed because we hadn't been able to get into the Grand Hotel and said crossly, "If I had been at the Grand instead of the *pensionat*, I'd have had four hundred doctors to look after me, instead of being sent to the drunks."

Both doctors laughed, and my doctor said, "Don't worry. I'm going to take as good care of you as four hundred doctors would."

They had to shout to me. I saw that Jack was worried, but somehow I went off to the operating room to be examined, without a care in the world. I was in the hands of two competent men. Delightful, too.

261

For three days I remained in the hospital while Jack rushed from party to party with the charming girls from the publisher's office.

I had some pleasure too, in spite of the steady rumbling in my head. My little gray-frocked nurses came to see me, armed with pocket dictionaries. We translated the newspaper stories with much laughter, so much that the head nurse came to my room to find out what was going on. She stayed to read the articles to me, for she spoke excellent English.

The doctor told me that the cause of my trouble was that I had flown with a head cold. He said that aviators were not allowed to fly when they had head colds. I was soon completely recovered except for some dizziness. That did not pass entirely for several months.

Our next visit was to Denmark, to meet my publisher, Arnold Busck of Nat Nordisk Forlag. Copenhagen is certainly one of the most delightful cities in the world, and Mr. Busck and his charming wife were most gracious hosts during our stay.

Before flying back to London, we stopped in Oslo to visit my publishers, O/B Nasjoral Forlaget. We were met at the station by Dagfin Magnus-Andressen, the young son of my publisher.

It was Midsummer Night and the whole city of Oslo was celebrating the Midnight Sun. People were everywhere; on the streets, in the parks, and up the mountain sides. It was a gay, happy city. The children wore little bright red berets to celebrate their holiday and as a symbol of their joy to be free again from Nazi domination.

I shall never forget our evening in the Andressen home, or the stories they told of their experiences during the Nazi rule. The very home where we were sitting was taken by the Germans and used as an officers' club. The handsome young son, Dagfin, was one of the underground who performed miraculous deeds of courage and daring, both in Norway and in England. We heard later in London that he had been decorated by the British government for his part in raids by the Rangers. Since then, he has married an American. He stayed overnight with us at Bandon on his way to join his wife in Florida, where they planned to live.

We flew from Oslo to London, passing over East Anglia in the twilight, a reminder of the old invasion routes and the Viking ships. Back in London, I again visited my publisher.

Hutchinson Ltd. had been my London publisher since my second African book, in 1933, when it published *Red Jasmine*. When I visited, I talked with Katherine Webb, editor, and suggested that the firm arrange with Hodder & Stoughton, who first published *The White Leopard*, to take over rights and re-issue the book. She agreed and brought it out under the title, *The Young Commissioner*.

My relations with this company have always been most cordial through the years, although all business arrangements had been made through Bobbs-Merrill's agents, Curtis Brown, Ltd.

Hutchinson had been burned out during the war, and at the time of my visit had temporary quarters not far from the American Embassy.

I remember well lunching with Mrs. Webb at the Grosvenor. I had brought her some nylon hose. Nylons were in short supply in England, and I had brought gifts to each of my English friends. During the luncheon I asked if it was one of her tasks to lunch visiting authors.

She said, "Good Heavens, no! We have a thousand writers."

Jack and I went back to work at the British Museum. Since we were nearing the end of our visit, I took time out to visit my friends of years standing, the Rt. Honorable Leo Amery and his wife, in Eaton Square. Colonel Amery, who had helped me on my African trip in 1928, when he was secretary of the Colonies and Dominions, was now Secretary of State for India. He was a life-long close friend of Sir Winston Churchill and I think he was one of the most knowledgeable men in England, politically.

We also saw our old and dear friends, the Rudolf Sauters. He is a very fine artist, of rare intelligence and sensitiveness. He also writes fine poetry. His wife, Violet, is a beautiful and charming woman. Their war story was one of intense anxiety and fear, for they were living in Kent (where he was engaged in war work) with German buzz bombs flying overhead daily. Not only were the Germans flying over but the RAF was flying out to meet them, and many dogfights took place over their heads. Violet commented that when she kissed her husband good-by in the morning she never knew whether he would come home at night.

Rudolf Sauter was a double-nephew of John Galsworthy, the great English novelist. We knew the Galsworthys, had visited them at their home in Sussex, and later they stayed with us in San Francisco.

Again it was time to return home and settle down to work writing a book. The pleasure of research was over. At home I would find great stacks of blank paper which had to be filled with words, my words, to be hammered into a credible story of the most important event in our history, the first English Colony to settle in America.

After it was published, I had one of the most satisfying letters I ever received about one of my books. It was from Randolph G. Adams, Director of the William Clements Library at the University of Michigan. He wrote:

> *Roanoke Hundred* ought to be required reading in every high school in North Carolina. If I only had dictatorial powers, it would be required reading in every New England high school.

Roanoke Hundred is my most important book, historically, for it deals with the folk who came as Gentlemen Adventurers from the West Country of England to the land of America, in an attempt to found a new empire. The attempt failed, but it lighted the way to the permanent colony in Jamestown.

In 1949, a year after the publication of *Roanoke Hundred*, I was back in England working on a book of the Cromwellian period in Virginia. Like most people outside of Virginia, I did not know that men of Cromwell ever ruled there. I thought all Virginia governors were Cavaliers. I was indeed surprised to find that there were three followers of Oliver Cromwell who became governors of the land of Virginia.

I went up to Williamsburg and began an intensive study of valuable records, followed by a search through books and papers in the library of William and Mary College. From there, I went to Washington for a further look at Virginia. I found a great deal of interesting history, so interesting that I knew I must see the source material in the British Museum.

I had discovered a man named Richard Bennett, a Cromwellian governor who had lived across the James River on a plantation called "Bennett's Welcome." The name of his plantation delighted me. "What a title for a book!" I said to Jack.

"Why not use it?" was his reply. So I had my title before I had begun my research. This reversed my usual plan of finding a title as I progressed with my story. The more I read about Richard Bennett, the better I liked him. For one thing, he allowed the former Cavalier, Governor Berkeley, to stay on at his plantation, Green Springs, through his whole administration. Usually, in such cases, the retiring governor was sent back to England. But Bennett had been a man of broad vision, a humanitarian, which Berkeley was not.

So off I went again by air to London. Perhaps the fact that the P.E.N. National Congress was meeting that year in Venice had something to do with my decision to work in the British Museum. At any rate, there I was in my old haunts in the greatest of all research centers. I did not find the wealth of material that I had found on Devon and Cornwall, but it was enough to keep me busy. As time went on, working day after day without much to show for it, I grew discouraged. Besides, it was still difficult to get hotel space, and Cook's had set me down in a hotel I didn't like.

One morning, the receptionist told me that I could have the room only four days longer, because the Motor Show would open then and all the rooms had been engaged since the preceding year. Not an international doctors' convention, but a wretched Motor Show!

I at once moved down to the Savoy, where they told me they could keep me for three days. That was not long enough to meet the date set for the Congress in Venice.

The Commissionaire helped me. "If you talk to Mr. Blank, I think he will allow you to stay on."

I waited until Mr. Blank was on duty and approached him with a request for three extra days. He at once told me it was impossible. I was about to turn away, disconsolate, when I had a brainstorm. I looked Mr. Blank firmly in the eye. "You leave me nothing but a bench in Hyde Park. How will it sound in the newspapers, "American woman, refused hotel room, spends three days sleeping on bench in Hyde Park?"

The dignified gentleman looked at me a moment, then laughed.

266

"You win," he said, sounding almost like an American. "You can stay another three days, but no more, mind you, no more."

"That's all I need," I said joyously. "I leave for Venice early morning of the third day, but please save a room for me when I return."

Venice was a thousand times more beautiful than I had expected. Mr. Herman Ould, permanent secretary of the London P.E.N., had arranged for me to stay at the Hotel Donelli on the Grand Canal. Members whom I had met in London and Zurich were staying there, which made it very pleasant. I had a wonderful single room. From its little iron balcony I looked down on the Bridge of Sighs. Beyond that was the Doge's palace, St. Marks, and the Campanile. Below was a narrow lane which the Italians call a *via*, which led out to the broad flagged space that bordered the canal. At the foot of the *via* there was a boat landing for gondolas and larger boats coming to and from the Lido and the Church of St. Giorg Maggiore.

When we arrived, the film festival had just ended, but a festival participated in by all the various provinces of Italy was in progress. I used to walk down to the great paved piazza in front of the cathedral to watch the merrymakers in the costumes of their provinces dance and sing. It was a colorful sight. I was enchanted to see Italians walking along the canal, or sitting at the little sidewalk cafes, wearing medieval costumes.

Venice is medieval. I think it is one of the few cities in the world which cannot be changed. Its canals protect it from the inroads of modern living. Industrial Venice is out of sight, hidden away from the visitor. That is as it should be.

One wants to think of Venice as it was in the great days of the Doges, Marco Polo, the d'Estes, or the Borgias; to take part in the ceremonies of the marriage of Venice to the Sea; or to see the great paintings.

Palazzi Guistinian, a fifteenth-century Gothic building, was headquarters for the P.E.N. meetings. Dinners and evening gatherings were held in the Doge's Palace or at the Rezzonico, a magnificent building with ancient furniture and walls draped in brocaded satins.

There were trips to the city of Vicenza to see the beautiful buildings designed by the famous architect Palladio, to the nearby Villa of Balmerana to see the frescoes of Tiepolo, and later to a performance of *The Coronation of Poppea*. There was an excursion to Padua where we saw fragments of Mantegna's frescoes and the ancient University founded in 1222. A journey to the island of Torcello ended with a magnificent ball at the Rezzonico, after a reception by the Lord Mayor.

All this sounds like a tourist circuit, but there were P.E.N. Club meetings every morning and afternoon, which were always exciting to me. "Criticism" was the subject of the whole congress, and there were sometimes very heated arguments about the place of the critic in the literary world.

The English delegates were honoring their poets who were present: Winston H. Auden, Stephen Spender, Cecil Day Lewis, and the critic, Cyril Connolly.

I remarked to an English author, E. Warrington Smith, that the English seemed to honor poets more than we did in America. I think the order in America would be dramatists, novelists, essayists, poets. She was horrified. "Poetry is the genius of England, from the days of Shakespeare to today." And that settled that.

The British had a large delegation. I believe that many from the rationed countries came to Italy to get a square meal. The Italian food was superb, plentiful, and in great variety. The Italians are naturally a gay people, friendly and hospitable. I think I like them better than any of the Continental peoples I have met.

I knew many of the members from former visits to P.E.N. meetings in London and Zurich in '47. It was pleasant to renew old acquaintances and profitable, too, to learn of the problems of other writers.

All the great Italian writers were present. The best known was Ignazio Silone, president of the Italian P.E.N. He had been my partner at a dinner during the Zurich Congress. He spoke no

English, I spoke no Italian, but his wife sat on the other side of the great man and translated and we had a very pleasant evening.

I belong to several writing groups, but I think these international meetings are the most instructive and pleasant.

While in Venice, I put all work out of mind, but the thought of it began to weigh me down after I had crossed the English Channel and was on the London train. There was that ever-present business of hotels to plague me. The Savoy, as I suspected, would not extend my stay, no matter what story I put up. Suddenly it came to me that I would go to the American Embassy and ask the Navy Department to help me. I told the Savoy receptionist that, after all, my son was a commander in the Navy and they should want to do something for his mother.

I had traveled half the world alone without knowing a single foreign language, and I had never before called at an American Consulate or Embassy to ask for help. But having proper lodging was necessary if I were to continue my research at the British Museum and Somerset House.

The Savoy would house me for three days and gladly feed me at the prescribed-by-law price (with extras). The morning after my arrival, I was at the Embassy, a beautiful building, by the way, and well staffed. I was sent to the adjoining building where the Navy offices were. It was Labor Day and every office was closed, I was told by two snappy Marines who guarded the portals. Could they help?

I told them my woeful story about hotels. They agreed solemnly that it was really an emergency, an American woman moving from hotel to hotel every three days for three months. They tried not to laugh but I saw they were amused. One of them said to the other, "Admiral Carney is in his office. Perhaps she might watch for him."

That was hint enough for me. A short time later, the admiral entered the hall. I approached him. I said, "Admiral Carney, I may be out of line, but I want some help from the Navy."

He listened while I told my story. He was not stern but a

little remote until I repeated what I had told the receptionist at the Savoy. Then he laughed.

"I see that you must be helped. We can't have you sleeping on a bench in Hyde Park when you have a son in the Navy; that would be a reflection on the whole service." His eyes were twinkling as he spoke. I knew right then that I had no further worries. The Navy and the Marines were on the job.

"The boys upstairs will help. They are always finding quarters for stranded Americans. But there is no one here today; it's Labor Day. We always celebrate American holidays, or did you know?"

I told the Admiral I would come back tomorrow and was about to leave when he said, "Wait. Have you tried the Embassy? They have some young ladies whose business it is to settle traveling Americans in hotels. Go to see that department in the morning."

After telling me good-by, he walked jauntily away. I shall always place Admiral Carney in a particular niche, along with other naval favorites of mine; Admiral Callahan, Admiral Crawford, and Admiral Hart. He is an officer with a great reputation, I know, but even his war record could be no higher than my esteem for him for the rescue of a forlorn female who didn't have a place to lay her head in all the great city of London.

In the morning I was again at the door of the Embassy. I found a beautiful and charming woman from Kentucky, whose business it was to find lodging for junketing congressmen and stranded females.

"What hotel would you like?" she asked me.

My father, who had owned hotels, had often told me always to go to the best. "It is better to have the poorest room in the best hotel than to have the best room in a second-class one," he would say.

So I told her, "I want to go to the Dorchester."

Miss Bland raised her eyebrows and shrugged her shoulders. "I won't say that is impossible, but nearly impossible. That is certainly the finest hotel in London."

"That's why I want to go there."

She laughed. "We can always try, but you must know that the chances are slim. How long do you want to stay?"

"Two months." That really floored her.

"It's impossible. Simply impossible."

I said, "But you'll try. I'm sure with that beguiling smile of yours you can soften the heart of the manager."

She laughed. "I'm just now trying to get nine congressmen in the Dorchester."

I said, "I don't want to wish anyone bad luck, but I hope one of the nine doesn't come."

And that's the way it happened. One congressman on the European junket went home, and three days later I was in the Dorchester, to my mind, one of the finest hotels in the world. Not only was I in, but I was there for the full time of my stay in England.

That was one piece of luck. The second came through my friends, the Rudolph Sauters. They called me by telephone from their country place in Herefordshire. I suppose I sounded discouraged when they asked me about progress.

I said, "I am getting along with research, but I haven't any story."

They insisted that I come up to them for a long weekend. The next day I was on the train, traveling north to Herefordshire. I had never been in that part of England. I was delighted with what I saw from the car window. From my map, I discovered that the country where the Sauters lived was close to Wales, very near the border. My friends met me at the station with their car. I felt guilty for I knew there was still strict control over petrol and that it had taken some of their precious ration even for the short trip from Coddington Manor.

I was happy to be with the Sauters again and to see their charming home. They had moved to this remote spot to be away from the aftermath of bombings that had played such havoc near their home in Kent.

Coddington Manor was built in the twenty-sixth year of the

reign of Henry VIII. The stone building and dependencies are fine examples of the period. Some of the tenant houses and the buildings of the nearby village and farms were the beautiful half-timbered variety, which the English call "black and white."

We talked at dinner about the history of the county and looked at many books in the library that told of it. But it remained for the old gardener to give me the clue that I needed. He was a grizzled old fellow, dressed in a smock.

"If the American lady is looking for something about Crummel (Cromwell) she has come to the right spot. Over there, at yon church, which you see is where he tore down the cross and told the country folk to worship God and not images. . . . 'Twas the bell in the tower that he ordered to be torn down, and it was in Worcester where Old Noll's army set Prince Charley on the run."

He left the room and went out to his work in the garden, leaving me to rejoice in what he had disclosed concerning the Cromwellian period. I went to my room and crawled into the great oaken bed, but I could not sleep. I got up and went to the window and sat on the seat.

It was a night of the full of the moon and the grounds were bright as day. I saw the lip-shaped pool, like a "kiss of the gods," reflecting the moon on its quiet water; the breeze stirred it into silvery ripples. Marsh hens moved across the greensward; a few ducks dropped out of the sky to rest on the pond. The garden lay quiet and still. The "lady's-bower," enclosed in its high yew hedge, was filled with shadows, black and eerie; the square stone tower of the old church cut upward into the sky, massive and dark.

I thought of the people who had strolled the paths, outlined with yew and may (as the English call hawthorne). Presently I saw shadows moving along the paths; the tall figure of a man entered the lady's-bower. I do not know whether or not I fell asleep and dreamed, but the folk who stood at the pool and walked the garden paths were as real as you and I.

In the morning I went downstairs, exalted by my experience.

"I have my story!" I exclaimed. "I have the folk who lived here at the time of Cromwell! I know everything about them, all but their names."

Rudi said, "I think I can help you there." He brought out old documents and maps. "Here is the first deed to Richard Monington, Lord of Coddington Manor." As Rudi read the dozen names signed to the deed, I again saw people rising from the past, each one bending over the table to affix his signature. These were real people, flesh and blood people; not only did I see them, I heard them speak, I knew what was in their minds.

I have never had an experience to equal this one at Coddington Manor. I not only saw the past, I was a part of it, even when the hero escaped from England, after the capture of the king, and sought safety in the young Colony of Virginia.

I wrote the whole book under the inspiration of my experience at Coddington Manor. I have never written any other book in which I have not had breaks in the story line or trouble with the characters, trying to fit them into history.

I had no trouble with *Bennett's Welcome.*

I went back to London, still in a state of excitement, and began rereading history. There was a wealth of material available. For the Quaker section, I visited the Euston Street Meeting Society of Friends; for details on furnishings, I went to the Victoria and Albert Museum.

In Washington, I finished off with material at the Library of Congress and the Folger-Shakespeare Memorial Library.

I used King Charles' own journal for the flight and Thomas Blount's *Boscobel* for the true tale of the King's escape from Cromwell's men. This included the King's hiding in Pollard Oak. His enemies camped beneath the tree while he lay concealed under the thick leafy crown of the oak.

I was able, in *Bennett's Welcome,* to follow through the discovery I had made in research for *Roanoke Hundred*—that many of the names of the folk who were in the First Colony on Roanoke

Island appeared again in the Jamestown Colony. This proves, I believe, that Jamestown was really a continuation of Roanoke, the colonies that failed.

Many reviewers wrote that *Bennett's Welcome* was my finest book. As I have said, many of my readers have favorites, at least so they write me.

Bennett's Welcome was published in October, 1950. It was one of the Permabook series and was translated into a number of foreign tongues.

My editor, Laurence Chambers, wrote:

Her work began in an exigent present and she has written of an exigent past. From the first she was aware of the inescapable relation between the critical periods of American history, and this awareness has informed all her writing. . . . She has devoted her skill as a novelist in chronicling a significant part of the American adventure for freedom in the New World.

23

The seventh novel of the Carolina Series was published in October, 1952. According to one reviewer it was the keystone volume in the large design to encompass the story of two hundred years' history of North Carolina from the first attempted settlement of Roanoke Island to the ratification of the Constitution.

In time it is nearer to *Raleigh's Eden*, my first historical novel, and to *Toil of the Brave*, the novel of the Revolution. Many of the characters of those earlier novels appear again in this book.

The scene is again Edenton, the town on Queen Anne's Creek. The year is 1788, and the folk who were united in war are divided in peace through political beliefs that plague the newly organized (or shall I say, loosely organized) Thirteen Colonies.

Adam and Mary Rutledge appear again, as principal characters. Mary believes that the new Constitution will safeguard the liberty and freedom so dearly won. Her husband, Adam Rutledge, believes that the new Constitution ignores the rights of the ordinary people. North Carolina as a whole is divided on the issue.

Two conventions, one at Fayetteville, one at Hillsborough, show the deep division between political leaders.

The same problem was faced by the makers of the Constitution. They struggled to safeguard the peoples' rights; to provide checks and balances which would hold the three divisions of the government in line; to assign to the Executive, the Legislative, and the Judiciary departments complementary functions which would assure perfect balance.

In a measure the fight is no different from the fight of today in which the Judiciary appears to be making, rather than interpreting, laws. Our Founding Fathers feared this overlapping judicial-legislative function and today, one hundred and seventy years later, many Americans share the fears of their ancestors of 1788.

North Carolina was the last Colony but one to sign the Constitution. Along with Rhode Island, North Carolina waited to sign until she was sure that George Mason's Bill of Rights, which would protect the common people, would be included. For this reason, North Carolina was not represented at General Washington's inauguration.

The doubts of artisans, craftsmen, laborers, and farmers were expressed with violence and deep-seated fear that their rights would be swallowed up in the fine phrases and generalities of politicians. There were secret meetings, angry speeches, and a riot on the Green in Edenton. It looked for a time as though the new confederation would fall apart, as the leaders in Philadelphia wrangled and bickered and fought, each for his own beliefs.

All this was exceedingly confusing to follow. The more I read the more confused I became. Who believed what? Where did the writers of the Constitution stand on various issues? Where did the North Carolina political leaders stand on the important division on the Constitution?

When I write about real people, particularly political figures, I use their speeches or writings as background, then I am sure that I have them in their proper place and that I express their own opinions in all political matters. But the Constitution squabble defeated me.

I finally hit on a plan, which I now follow on all of my books—I went up to Chapel Hill, to the University of North Carolina, and audited Dr. Hugh Lefler's class in North Carolina Colonial History.

I could have saved myself a great deal of reading and searching for facts if I had thought of that idea earlier. Not only did I get the political story straightened out, but I had a complete bibliography of the period presented to me through Dr. Lefler's informative classes.

At the end of the term I was asked to address his graduate students on the period about which I was writing. I said that I had gone from a freshman to a class instructor in two weeks, probably a record in educational progress.

Queen's Gift, the new book, turned out well, from the standpoint of reviews and sales. It was reprinted in Europe and South America. It was reprinted by Permabook and that edition, too, had an excellent sale.

One reviewer wrote:

Inglis Fletcher is at once a master of realism and romance. *Queen's Gift*, the most ambitious and successful of her novels, reveals the foundation and distinction of our National Character, while it absorbs us with its constant entertainment.

In *Queen's Gift*, as in my other books, I followed my editor's constant admonition: "Never forget your story. You may be carried away with all the history you have absorbed, but the story is the thing, and remember also that the love story is what your reader is looking for; not your knowledge of history."

I am sure that he is right, so I endeavor to hide my history in the lives of a group of people. After all, history does not make events. It is people who make the events which become history.

In *Queen's Gift*, I carried my characters along the years of their great trial, when they were new at governing and at guiding the young ship of states through troubled waters. We may give thanks to God that we had dedicated men at the helm, dedicated and patriotic, whose one thought was the country. Perhaps never again will we have at one time such a galaxy of men of great stature. But they were there in their youthful enthusiasm and the years of their struggle gave us America. Those early years were indeed our days of greatness, and great men lent their efforts toward building the new country. Washington, Jefferson, Alexander Hamilton, the Adamses, and Madison came at the hour when we needed them. So did Patrick Henry and other orators, to influence men of action. For wisdom, we had Franklin and John Jay and a host of legal minds to guide us through the mazes of building a government.

In North Carolina we had great men whose voices were heard. In Edenton, a small town of six hundred people, we had Joseph Hewes, signer of the Declaration of Independence and first Secretary of Maritime Affairs; Dr. Hugh Williamson, Chief Surgeon of Green's Southern Army and signer of the Constitution. Across the sound in Bertie lived John Blount, another signer of the Constitution. James Iredell, of Edenton, one of the great legal minds of the State, was appointed by President Washington to the Supreme Court; Samuel Johnston of Hayes Plantation, Edenton, was the first Senator from North Carolina; and his cousin, Charles Johnson of Bandon Plantation, was the second Senator.

I am reminded of the Arabic proverb: "A star never rises or falls, save in its own time."

Old wills always intrigue me. I found many in the 1764 courthouse in Edenton. Others, in Raleigh, disclosed the likes and dislikes of Tyrell County, among them one made by a member of my own Chapman family. I have that will before me now. It was written in the early 1700's.

Miss Patty D., spinster, disposed of her property, and the wording of the will portrays her character as vividly as though she were before me. The land, her plantation, she leaves to her brothers.

To her sisters, she leaves her clothes: to one, two heavy riding habits; to another, two dark riding habits; to a third, a light and a dark riding habit. To a niece, she gives, "My Madeira shawl, which I have never worn." To an aunt, "My Queen Anne silver teapot which she has always coveted. To my beloved niece Cecelia, I bequeath my crimson cloth coat."

It always seemed to me that there was a story here. Can you not see a young, sparkling-eyed Cecelia, her aunt's favorite, wrapped in a crimson cloth coat? It might have been lined with fur, although the will does not mention that. Fur was too plentiful to deserve comment. The pocosin behind the plantation abounded in squirrel, otter, and mink. Trappers, white and Indian, were almost as plentiful as the little fur-bearing animals. But crimson cloth, that was different! It must have come from London in one of the plantation shallops, or it could have been brought over by Richard Chapman, who built ships on the shore of Albemarle Sound near the mouth of the Scuppernong River where Miss Patty's plantation was located.

Another thought came to me; perhaps the "crimson" really was hunter's pink and the coat an elegant hunting jacket made in London.

It is easy to imagine Miss Patty. She was an inveterate hunter; did she not will six habits to her sisters? She probably ran the plantation (with the help of a white overseer) and fought with her sisters. The aunt who got the Queen Anne silver teapot had long coveted it. Perhaps there had been a family quarrel over it. Miss Patty was surely one of those hard-riding, independent spinsters who wanted her tea when she came in from the hunt. Maybe she owned twenty or thirty Pitchley foxhounds.

The only soft spot in her heart was for little Cecelia, so she left her the treasured crimson cloth coat.

One's imagination leaps off from that springboard. Two women many years in their graves come to life and push their way into a story, "The Crimson Coat." What a title for a book! I have thought of it from time to time, but it's yet to be written. And so

I find another answer to the question asked so frequently, "Where do you get your characters?" For me, many of them, like the above, come out of wills.

Always, in any book, I am careful of my background. The big, dramatic effects are good and often necessary, but the body of the book is made up of small events, the actions of people and what they eat, wear, and talk about, the books and papers they read. Through these small things you re-create a period of time and the events that give substance to the story.

Consider again Sir Walter Scott and the historical novel; Anthony Trollope, Dickens, if you will. What do you remember? The little things, the small events. I enjoy Proust and Stendhal, Dostoevski and Gogol. I like the gradual leading up to a dramatic climax.

Often, if you have carefully paved the way, you find that your climax can be written in a page, or even a paragraph.

I faced many problems in writing *Queen's Gift*. I had a number of characters to keep going. (I always manage to have too many characters to handle without working out some genealogical charts.) They were people of widely divergent views. The period was almost like a time of war, with the exception of the shooting and battle lines. But somehow I carried them through to the end.

Queen's Gift, also, made the best-seller lists, and the publishers were pleased with its reception.

Again, I made some public appearances. I like best to speak at colleges. It pleases me to think that I have influenced some young people along the fascinating path of history. One young girl said, "I wish our history could be taught as interestingly as you tell it."

I answered her as I have answered many such comments, "If you remember that history is made by people, not a date or a name on a page, you are on the right track. Think of the people who made the history and it will come alive for you."

So many young writers come to consult me, as they do all writers. I always talk with them, but I am obliged to say, "I can't teach you anything. Writing is something you must do alone. It comes out of you, out of your own experience. Even if it reflects another's, it must still go through your mind before it comes out as a story."

A writer needs to be alone, with time to think. Many days I sit at my desk and cannot put down a word. On others, I write furiously, so fast that I skip through words, even sentences.

I do not plot my story. I become thoroughly familiar with my background, then I place upon it a group of people living at a certain time, in a certain place. After that they are on their own. They do their own talking, they live their own lives, otherwise I have to get rid of them.

I remember one character in *Raleigh's Eden*, Lady Caroline. She was patterned after a real woman who came to America before the Revolution. She said she was a cousin of the Queen and that she had great influence at court. She was a fascinating person, in the grand manner, and she turned the heads of several political gentlemen of the Colony by letting them think that she could obtain for them various positions at court (for a price). I used her effectively in the book, or so I thought.

When the book was in galleys, my editor telegraphed that I must do something about Lady Caroline. Now, I'd had her come into the story mysteriously in a storm, and I'd let her go out of the story the same way, mysteriously into the night. She was an unwholesome character and deserved her "comeuppance."

This was really a problem. I thought the finish of Lady Caroline as I had written it was just right, but an order from an editor must be obeyed. I told my troubles to Mrs. McMullan, librarian and curator of Cupola House Museum.

She said quickly, "Well, you can't kill her in Cupola House. I won't have it."

I couldn't kill her on the courthouse steps. I had already had duels on the courthouse Green, so that was out.

For a whole day, I made Jack drive me about Edenton and the countryside, looking for a suitable place to commit a murder and get rid of Lady Caroline. Finally, just at sunset, we were driving toward the bridge across the Chowan River. My eyes fell on Johns Island, the great swamp.

I said, "Stop! Stop the car! I'll have her killed over on Johns Island. No one will ever find her there. Not even her body or the jewels she stole from the Queen." (The prototype for my Lady Caroline had turned out to be a lady's maid in the palace, who had stolen jewelry.) So Lady Caroline rests in the deep cypress swamp near the Chowan River, and the Greek verities have been fulfilled by her obscure and lonely death.

When I finished *Queen's Gift*, I decided that I would end my Carolina Series on that period of history, the signing of the Constitution by North Carolina.

That does not mean that I have finished writing about North Carolina, far from it. There are many periods in the long and vital history of this democratic state that need telling. I can think of several that are known only to historians. I could write a number of books without going beyond the period of the Constitution.

The North Carolina Bill of Rights contained twenty-five articles. It reaffirmed the English Magna Charta of 1215 and the English Bill of Rights and some other English laws that the colonials had asked for and had never been granted. It contained, almost verbatim, items from the Virginia Bill of Rights and that of Maryland. Other sections had evolved from North Carolina's Colonial experiences. It guaranteed, among other things, freedom of elections, freedom from arbitrary taxation, supremacy of civil power over the military, and the right of assembly and elections. Personal liberties also were guaranteed: individual rights in criminal trials, trial by jury, immunity from excessive bail, immunity from cruel or unusual punishment and from search warrant. That great bulwark, freedom of the press was joined with freedom of expression, conscience, and religion. On these fundamentals, our present freedom and liberty rest.

All these things I tried to bring into *Queen's Gift*, implicit in the lives of the individuals.

I do not know what position *Queen's Gift* holds among my books, not the best, nor the poorest. Somewhere in the middle, I think, but it assuredly was the most difficult to write.

When people ask which is my favorite of all the books I have written, I answer, "If I had a dozen children, could I have a favorite child?"

Queen's Gift had a good sale. Garden City brought out an edition, Permabooks reprinted it, and the Dollar Book Club distributed it to its members.

I am not sure when I conceived the idea of writing a book on the Scots who settled in North Carolina on upper Cape Fear River.

At one time I had thought that I would write about each of the European groups who came to North Carolina in the early days of the Colony—the Moravians at Salem, the Huguenots who came up from South Carolina, and the Scots.

I wrote the story of the Scots first. They came to the Cape Fear district of North Carolina before the Revolution and have been an integral part of the state ever since. The historical story was fascinating in itself, for it revolved around the Scottish national heroine, Flora Macdonald.

My dedication to *The Scotswoman*, reads: "To the Highlanders bold and valiant, whose inherent love of freedom, courage, and integrity have contributed much to the strong character of this country."

Perhaps I wrote this thinking of my grandmother, Elizabeth Moray, descendant of the Morays of Scotland, or perhaps it was because I have been long married to a Scotsman, two generations removed, who has every characteristic of his Highlander ancestors.

Again I returned to the Revolutionary period of North Carolina history that embodied the first conflicts and regional disagreements. I wrote about the people who remained loyal to the Crown, as most of the Scots along Cape Fear did; but I was dealing with one of the truly romantic bits of our history.

This is the American story of Flora Macdonald, who is beloved to this day in Scotland for her compassion and fearless courage in the rescue of Bonny Prince Charlie during the days of his hiding in the rocky Hebrides and on the Isle of Skye. I saw in this story of Flora, romance, adventure, and fearlessness. She was a woman of strong will, even in her youth when she rescued the Prince and carried him to safety through stormy seas to his refuge at Skye. It took even greater courage to leave her homeland, and, with her husband and several children, undertake the dangerous journey to far-off America. The more I read about Flora Macdonald, the more interesting material I found in her long career, both in Scotland and in America.

Several things disturbed me. In none of my books heretofore had I taken an historical figure as a hero or heroine. My principal characters had always been fictional. Then I could do as I pleased with them, without criticism from my readers or letters telling me that I had been unkind to someone's ancestors.

(An exception to this: I had a letter from the husband of a descendant of Sir Richard Grenville about an extra-curricular love affair I had given him—author's license—asking where I got my authority. Aside from that, fiction is fiction and I keep my historical characters within the bounds prescribed by their journals and speeches.)

I realized that using Flora as the heroine would be difficult, but how could one put Flora Macdonald into a book without having her take the principal role? It couldn't be done. So I made up my mind that I wouldn't try. She would be the leading lady.

I read many books about Flora; there are dozens, with divergent opinions about Prince Charlie and Flora. Were they lovers or were they not? What was the significance of the fact that she kept the linen sheets that he slept on when he was hidden in Kingsborough House and was buried in them when she was an old woman?

Rumor had it that Flora never heard from Prince Charlie after he left Scotland forever and ran away to France. But the Stuarts were never noted for their loyalty. "They took, but never gave," was the old Scotch saying.

One thing was certain: I could not write a credible book about Flora Macdonald unless I went to Scotland and the Isle of Skye.

This was the dead of winter. People told me that I could not go to England in February. It was too, too dismal; all the dampness, the unheated houses. (There is no central heating in Bandon. We have a fireplace in every room, including the kitchen, and a man to chop wood and keep fires going.) But I was determined, so I wrote to the manager of my favorite hotel, the Dorchester in London, and to my guide, philosopher, and friend, Cook's, and made my arrangements.

The only stipulation Jack made (he was staying at Bandon to keep the fires burning) was that I go by ship so I could have a few days' rest while crossing. I agreed, if I could get passage on the *United States*. I did, and in February, 1953, I sailed. I enjoyed every minute of the journey on that gorgeous ship. I don't think I rested much, for there were a great many people aboard and entertainment every minute of the day, and night, too, if one wanted it.

Although all the passengers were going to England or the Continent, with one accord they tried to discourage me. "Scotland!" they said. "How can you think of going to Scotland in winter?"

Before leaving Bandon, I had talked with a friend who had lived in Scotland. "It is all right. Of course, not many houses have central heating. But do buy some fur-lined boots to slip over your shoes; take plenty of sweaters, and a woolly to wear in bed, for you'll have cold beds."

Of course I had no trouble about heat at the Dorchester. It was not raining in London; cool, brisk, but not damp.

The first thing I did the morning after I arrived was take a taxi and go to Harrods to buy fur-lined boots, a sweater, and the woolly.

Friends in London were horrified when I told them I was going to Scotland. "My dear, you can't! Why this is February! No one goes to Scotland in February; in the autumn for the shooting, but not in winter."

I was not to be diverted. I went around to Cook's to get my mail. The woman who handed out letters remembered me, which was very complimentary.

Being remembered, reminds me that coming up on the boat train the night before, several Canadians sat opposite me. Suddenly I heard one of the women say, "You must read this book that Helen gave me, *Queen's Gift*. It is quite wonderful. I could not lay it down once I started it."

What heartwarming words! I resisted for a moment, but the impulse was too strong. I leaned forward and said, "Thank you so much. I am Inglis Fletcher and I wrote *Queen's Gift*."

The Canadians were really astonished and delighted. They insisted that I come over and join them for a drink. We had a merry time and the journey up to London, usually so slow and uninteresting, was far too short. When I told them I was going to Scotland, they, too, protested. "It is all right for Canadians, we are used to cold weather, but since you live in North Carolina you won't be able to stand the cold and damp."

I didn't say that I had lived in Spokane where we had plenty of snow and cold, twenty-five below zero. It was no use. Everyone was determined to keep me from going to Scotland.

But they didn't know that Flora Macdonald was my objective, and she could be found only on Skye.

The following day I was aboard that famous train The Royal Scotsman (or is it The Flying Scotsman?) warmly dressed with an extra sweater under my Vicuna coat and wearing my fur-lined boots. (This was the only time I ever wore those boots and later I gave them to Vi Sauter to wear about the country.)

I was truly astonished when I reached Edinburgh to find it such a bewilderingly lovely city. Some say it is second only to Paris, others that it outshines Paris. The great ravine that divides it into two parts is beautifully landscaped. The castle rising high above it gives the city a princely medieval splendor, unequalled by any city I have seen.

My hotel, the Caledonia, was a great rambling structure over the railway terminal at one end of the street, and Register House, where I would work, was at the other end, more than a mile away. I used to walk it four times a day with great zest. The air was crisp and cool and one could see the snow on the far hills.

I found great hospitality and cordiality everywhere. My friends, the A. J. J. Ratcliffs, whom I had known from the Zurich and Venice P.E.N. meetings, were expecting me and they, together with my letters to the directors of various museums and college libraries, were a great help.

While I was at the Caledonia, the famous horse, Trigger, arrived with his entourage. He created an enormous sensation, not only with the children but grown-ups as well. Roy Rogers and Dale, his wife, were dressed in complete theatrical cowboy regalia, and they also attracted considerable attention.

While in Edinburgh, I attended a meeting of the Scottish P.E.N. I believe Compton MacKenzie was president. I saw a number of members whom I had met in Venice.

Here more people advised me against going to the Isle of Skye. "In the wintertime? We never heard of anyone going to Skye except during the summer tourist season."

Again I visited Cook's and made my reservation at the hotel where Prince Charlie was supposed to have spent his last night in Scotland. I was never certain whether Flora Macdonald went with him to Portree or not, but for the sake of romance, I felt that she must have gone. I could fancy her standing at the boat landing watching the little boat that carried him to the mainland and out of her life forever.

The trip to Skye was broken by a stop overnight in Glasgow to attend a dinner given by the Glasgow P.E.N. for the English historical novelist, Margaret Irwin. Some years ago I had read her fascinating book *The Gay Galliard, The Life Story of Mary, Queen of Scots*. Now, I was intensely interested in her trilogy of the life of Elizabeth: *Young Bess, Elizabeth, Captive Princess*, and *Elizabeth and the Prince of Spain*.

I had the good fortune to sit next to her and found her as delightful as her books. We made plans to meet in London on my return there. And we did. She and her sister lunched with me at the Dorchester, and I had a long afternoon with her at her flat. I hope she soon writes other novels of the Elizabethan period which she knows so intimately.

Even in Glasgow I was warned against the weather on Skye but not so vigorously as in London.

The journey to Skye was wonderful; the farther north we progressed the more snow I saw on the mountains. How beautiful were the pines, firs, and cedars rising from the snowy earth, and the herds of deer coming down close to farms and habitations, to graze almost on the railway tracks.

I was amused by the sight of droves of sheep in the snow with their buttocks painted bright orange, blue, or yellow. A passenger on the train told me the reason. Several farmers turned their sheep into common pastures; by painting those bright colors on their rears, each owner could readily claim his sheep without trouble.

The trip by steamer from Oban to Skye was as beautiful as the Norwegian fjords. The Cuillins, those craggy mountains, stood out in icy splendor against the blue sky. There was no snow on the lowlands, only on the hills. The whole island had the beauty of the north—a hard bold beauty in contrast with the soft, gently rolling countryside of England.

I have an affinity with mountain country. I prefer the stern reality of a land that one must fight to conquer, the mountains and the wild gorse-covered moors. There is a satisfaction in fighting a hostile land; it makes for a stern, bold people.

When I saw Skye and the deserted rock huts of the herders, I knew why so many Scots of the Highlands had come to America, to the green, fertile country along Cape Fear. From my first look at the Isle, I began to know the truth about Flora.

The seventeenth-century hotel was delightful. I had a room that looked eastward to the water and the mountainous mainland, an inspiring sight. I felt that I could write a dozen books if only I could remain on Skye. I liked the island and its people. There was something self-contained and strength-giving in the life there. I would like to see the island in summer as well as in winter.

There wasn't a clock in sight in the hotel. I asked about it and with a shrug of his shoulders the manager said, "Why have clocks? One can tell time by the steamer whistle; it goes out at seven in the morning and returns at five in the evening."

His reply delighted me, for I, too, do not like the limitation of time.

I telephoned to the man I had been told had a car for hire. He was a delightful person with a strong, broad burr to his speech. He knew every inch of the island. He would take me to every spot connected with Flora Macdonald, and every house where she had lived.

She was from the outer island of Uist, but her married life had been spent on Skye. I would visit all the seats of the Clan Macdonald.

Before I knew it, I was involved in the clan system, something I have never quite understood, although I have three Scottish lines in my family, the Morays, the Spruills, and the Clarks.

I was lost in the maze of Macdonalds, MacLeods, Mackinnons, and MacQueens; all folk of the Isle of Skye. The various intermarriages defeated me, for there would be several of the same name and it would have taken an expert genealogist to sort out those folk and put them in their right place.

Later, I was fortunate to meet in Edinburgh such an expert in the history of Skye and its hereditary families, the Reverend Donald Mackinnon who is the best living authority on Flora Macdonald. He had been a pastor on Skye for many years, and had prepared *The Truth About Flora Macdonald* by Allan Macdonald, edited by Rev. Donald Mackinnon. He was not only interested in my endeavor but generous with his time and patience. He had none of the contempt that many historians exhibit toward a writer of historical fiction. He pointed out inaccuracies in several of the books about Flora, the savior of Prince Charles Edward Stuart. He taught me the ballad, so dear to the Islanders:

Farewell, lovely Skye, lake, mountain and corrie,
Brown Isle of the valiant, the brave and the free.

He always spoke of Flora Macdonald as though she were living and might at any moment enter the room in which we were sitting. I had found that same attitude in Skye. She remains in Scottish hearts, alive and ever-present, along with Bonny Prince Charlie. Scotland has many heroes and heroines who bring color and life to its history, but none, I think, so beloved as Flora.

The gentleman who drove me all about the island had been as deeply interested as the Reverend Mr. Mackinnon. We went from one end of the island to the other, looking at the homes where Flora had lived. We visited the spot where the boat had landed with Prince Charlie dressed as Flora's serving maid; Monkstaat, where Lady Margaret had hidden him during his escape; Kingsborough House, where Flora had lived with her husband's family after her marriage to Allan Macdonald; her burial place at Kilmuir. Here, in a lonely spot at the north end of the island, she rests in peace after her long and turbulent life.

On the west side of the island, at Dunvegan Castle, I lunched with Dame Flora MacLeod, whom I had met, with her twin grandsons, in Aberdeen, North Carolina. This remarkable, energetic woman, now chieftain of Clan MacLeod, lives alone in the ancient castle, the history of which goes back to medieval times. It sits on a high, basaltic rock that projects out from the shore over a creek near Loch Dunvegan. I was told that there were ten building stages of the castle through the twenty-eight generations of the clan who had lived there since the time of the Norse invaders. One of them, Sir Rory Mor', was a great hero of ancient times. He gave mighty feasts at Dunvegan, which lasted six days. A poem by one of the bards of Clanranald gives a vivid picture of the lusty eaters and drinkers of those days:

> We were twenty times drunk every day
> To which we had no more objection than he had.
> Our mead was in abundance, which consisted of
> Four, three, seven along with six varieties
> Six nights.

I have seen and visited in a number of old castles in England, but there was never anything to equal Dunvegan. The centuries roll out before one's eyes as one walks from room to room amid the rich relics handed down over the centuries. And what centuries they were! Of war and bloodshed, sword and dagger. Such killing in close combat seems cruel, but perhaps it was no less humane than our mass destruction by bombs dropped from miles away.

Sometimes I think if we could go back to medieval hand-to-hand fighting it would be better. In those times, the chieftains led their men into battle. They did not sit in a safe place miles away and direct the conflict of others, often untried youths. Perhaps a return to the skean dhu and the claymore would change that.

I could not help thinking of these things as I sat at luncheon in the great dining hall of the castle, only Dame Flora and myself, at the end of a long table. The walls held portraits of the MacLeod chiefs down through the centuries, and their beautiful ladies, the last space filled by a newly-painted portrait of the present twenty-eighth chief, Flora of MacLeod, Dame of the British Empire. She wore the clan colors and in her hand the bonnet with the three long eagle feathers, the badge of the chief.

Dame Flora talked with enthusiasm of her correspondence with MacLeods scattered over the world. She takes very seriously her obligation to the far-flung members of her clan. I left Dunvegan with real regret and a new understanding of the clan spirit which holds Scots together.

I had by now visited all of Flora Macdonald's homes, walked the paths she had walked from her home to the water's edge and looked across loch and sound as she had, to the rocky out-islands, rising bare and stark out of the sea. I think I saw on the Isle of Skye the spirit of Scotland; strong, sturdy, and valiant with all its fundamental integrity.

Back in Edinburgh I did some intensive work at Register House. At the Lord Lyon office, I traced my ancestors, the Spruills, and found them an ancient and honorable family. The Morays, I already knew, came from the clan of the Earl of Moray.

One last little remembrance is about the room maid who looked after me with such interest at the Caledonia Hotel. She was a Cruikshank character in appearance, very large, but she moved swiftly. She was pleased that I spent so much time at my window which looked directly up the hill toward the Castle, an unforgettable view of beauty and strength. I liked to listen to the bugles in the early morning as the regiment moved out on parade, and at night, the taps.

When I was packing to leave, I thought of that pink woolly bed jacket which I had never worn, and gave it to her.

Tears came to her eyes as she thanked me. "Madam, I have good use for it, for my house is damp and cold. Madam, thank you." She lingered at her work and before she left, came up to me at the window. "Madam, may I say something to you? Every day since you have been here, you have reminded me of the Duchess of Beauclough. She always has this room when she comes to the hotel. You are like her. I notice when you walk down the halls, you speak to everyone—the maids on the floor, the hall men, and the bellboys, always a cheerful word to them. The Duchess is the same. She is pleasant to everyone, Madam."

I was extraordinarily pleased. What a very nice compliment to have received for giving away a woolly bed jacket.

When I was in Edinburgh the second time, I wrote a line to Ian, The Fletcher, who lived in Argyllshire at the seat of the Fletchers, Dunans Castle. He came in to visit me. I found him much like his kin, Sir Angus Fletcher, who now lives at Fireplace Landing, Long Island, with his wife, Lady Fletcher, born Helen Stuart. I saw Ian several times and was sorry that I was not able to accept his invitation to visit Dunans. I should have liked to bring back to Jack a report of his family, but my time was getting short and I still had more research to do in London before I sailed for home.

I went to tea at the English Speaking Union in Edinburgh, saw my friends the Ratcliffs, and was off for London and my "home in England," the Dorchester. By now, after several visits, I knew many of the staff, as well as the management; they all endeavored to make me feel at home.

I telephoned to the Sauters and they came down from the country to visit me at the hotel. I took time out to have lunch or dinner with other friends.

At Southampton I boarded the S.S. *United States*, for home. I had been writing the book whenever I could snatch time on Skye, in Edinburgh, in London. I worked furiously to finish it. This I did at Bandon, by the May deadline.

But the great excitement came when Ross Baker, of the New York office of Bobbs-Merrill, wired me that *The Scotswoman* had been selected by the Literary Guild. This was the ultimate for me. Thirteen years had passed since the Junior Literary Guild had put *The White Leopard* on its list. I was so happy that the very next day I took my pen in hand and began a novel I had long had in mind. The scene was again North Carolina, in the days just before the Revolution.

It would tell of the great controversy between Governor William Tryon and the Regulators, from the standpoint of the western men who revolted against corrupt government and unjust taxes. I had already selected the title, *The Wind in the Forest*, the rising wind of the American Revolution.

25

Publication of *The Wind in the Forest,* in 1956, broke the rhythm of a book every two years. For a number of complicated reasons, publishing was held up more than seven months. My "book-for-the-Christmas-trade" record was disturbed and I have never managed to get into the swing again.

For a long time, I had wanted to write about this period, when the first rumors of the coming Revolution were heard in the land. I believe that the historian Lossing considers the Battle of Alamance, which was fought on May 16, 1771, to be the first battle of the war. But as another historian has said, it couldn't really be the first because there were no redcoats engaged in it.

That is true. It was the western trappers, farmers, and back country mountain men against the militia led by Royal Governor William Tryon. But Alamance showed the way the wind was blowing. The high flame of revolution came not long after.

Against the Royal Governor was the Quaker, Hermon Husbands, a quiet man opposed to violence and war, yet one who inflamed men to violence by his writings. He was not one of the leaders of the western men, called Regulators, who fought the Royal Governor's troops at Alamance. He was a pamphleteer, a friend (some say a relative) of Benjamin Franklin. He wielded a powerful pen and put on paper the thoughts of those less articulate. He fought tyranny, unequal taxes, unequal representation, and most of all, he fought the group of court officials who were victimizing the people.

I thought of my own North Carolina forebears. They had been in the struggle. I would start with them. I had a rich family tradition to draw on. They must have lived and acted in the same way as other folk acted under the stress of this dissension.

So I started with the Caswells and Chapmans in Tyrrell County of eastern North Carolina. My ancestor was the uncle of Richard Caswell, the first governor of the state of North Carolina. He was deep in politics, so I included him to give political flavor as opposed to the planters' point of view.

Then there was the shipbuilder Chapman, another ancestor, whose ships, built in his own shipyard on Albemarle Sound, sailed up and down the coast between Boston and the West Indies. His point of view differed from both the politico Richard Caswell and the planter Matthew Caswell. Then I turned to records in Tyrrell County and came on some old wills of the family.

To write a book about that period entailed many problems. One could easily be swallowed up in the political struggle that followed the victory of Yorktown, but who wants a novel filled with political bickerings, or so my editor questioned.

I turned to the basic problem that was disturbing the people of North Carolina—the interests of the eastern planter as opposed to those of the western farmer, trapper, and mountain man.

Where was I to look for these folk who would carry a story dramatizing the ills that beset the country? I must have people who were a part of the struggle, both Whigs and Tories. Where was I to find them?

William Tryon preceded Josiah Martin, the last of the Royal Governors of North Carolina. Tryon was a man of substance and, through his wife, connected with important political families in England. Although Tryon and Husbands were wide apart in upbringing and thought, they are forever linked in history through the Battle of Alamance.

Tryon left North Carolina shortly after the battle, to become governor of New York. In truth, he had notice from London of this promotion before he led the militia against the Regulators. In the novel, I tried to portray each man as seen through the eyes of the other. Tryon was castigated in the press and in the Assembly. The division was wide between Tories and Whigs, those who upheld English sovereignty and the old order and pioneers in the growing new world of America. I tried also to show that the causes of the violent political dissension which divided North Carolinians between the years 1768 and 1771 were the same as those embodied in the larger issues of the American Revolution, soon to follow.

Many of the characters were drawn from real life. All of the conversation was based on pamphlets, letters, and records of the period. The title of the book was taken from a pamphlet written by Hermon Husbands, published in 1761: "Oh ye Daughters of Jerusalem! . . . *He* will come in the time when it shall please Him, and be as a wind in the forest among the trees."

Husbands was a mystic, and he foretold the second coming of the Lord. He retreated from North Carolina before Alamance and took refuge in the western forests of Pennsylvania, then a wilderness. This was to be the place he would prepare for the Lord.

Later, he was elected to Congress. He was one of the instigators of the Whisky Insurrection.

The contrast between Tryon and Husbands was vast, yet they were drawn together by fate, to be part of the great drama that moved on to revolution.

Wind in the Forest brought me recognition to which I had long aspired. The Boston *Herald* said:

When you get discouraged over some stuff that passes for historical romance nowadays and remember that Kenneth Roberts has passed on and Van Wyck Mason can't turn them out faster than once in two years, then along comes Inglis Fletcher and all is fine again. Most of her novels are set in the early days of America and all of them have been characterized by careful research, fine writing and a flair for the romantic.

There is a fine story running through it [*The Wind in the Forest*], but Mrs. Fletcher never lets it run away with her story. She is too great a historical novelist for that, and she has never been better than in this book.

I had often told my editor that I wished I could write like Kenneth Roberts and Van Wyck Mason, for these are my favorites among recent historical novelists.

Kenneth Roberts I never met, although I felt that he must have been pleased at my genuine admiration because he had used a review I had written of one of his novels on the back of his *Lydia Bailey*.

Van Wyck Mason I had met several times. At literary luncheons in California, we had often sat side by side. He used to look at the green peas and chicken patties and wish for a good mutton chop. (One of his ancestors had been a Pynne-Coffin, of Portledge.)

Wind in the Forest was beautifully printed and the illustrations (line drawings) were very interesting indeed. It was later sold to "Best in Books," Nelson Doubleday's condensation medium, but *The Wind* was included in its entirety.

This brings me to the end of my books that have been published. I have several others in the making, but publication dates have not yet been set.

I learn new things with each book I write, but in every instance I have felt that I could have done better if I had had more time. That eternal deadline looms up ahead to interfere with one's perspective. I think most authors will agree that if books could be written and laid aside for a year, we would return to them with more selectivity and deeper insight.

I believe I have had more personal letters about *The Wind in the Forest* than any other book in the series. They have come from all over the country, and I treasure the kindness and sincerity that prompted them.

A writer is alone so much. I sit in the River Room on the second floor of Bandon and look out on the lovely, quiet Chowan River. Sometimes, when I am weary, I think what is the use of working day after day, writing page after page which perhaps no one will ever read? Then come those kind letters and my spirit rises.

During World War II, I had hundreds of letters from servicemen. There was one from Italy, not long after Anzio Beach. It was a long letter written by an injured man lying in a hospital. At the end, he said: "Thank you, Mrs. Fletcher, for writing these wonderful books. I have so much pain, I read to forget. But your books are different. When I found yours, I thought to myself, now I know what I am fighting for."

I cannot think of this letter without tears. I wish everyone of us could have so clearly in mind the goals of life toward which we strive.

Epilogue

The season has advanced from the first spring dogwood blossoms that twinkled like candles in the pines to Indian summer. The sourwood leaves have turned glowing red and the sycamore and the alianthus gleam with gold. Bandon rests quietly under the bright blue skies of autumn, and the broad Chowan reflects the scene in its placid water.

I have set down old days, old experiences, and talked of old friends. But there is still much that remains untold. I have said little of my transplanted life to my adopted state, North Carolina, a matter now of fourteen years. Those years have been filled with varied interests, many of them concerned with the history of the state and the societies which cherish it. I try to participate in the activities of all of them. One is the North Carolina Society for the Preservation of Antiquities, which Mrs. Charles Cannon brought from a small group to a large state-wide organization and of which she was the enthusiastic president for many years. The current president, Mrs. Elizabeth Stephenson Ives, of Southern Pines and Bloomington, Illinois, shares her enthusiasm.

Another is the Elizabethan Garden on Roanoke Island, developed by the Garden Club of North Carolina as a memorial to those valiant English men and women who came to America to settle on the Island and bring to the New World something of the culture of the Old. We know these folk, who came with Governor White, as "The Lost Colony," one of the great mysteries of history.

I serve on the Board of the Roanoke Island Historical Association and on the governing board which presents Paul Green's symphonic drama, *The Lost Colony*. The play has been produced out of doors each summer on Roanoke Island for the past twenty years. It is inspiring to sit under the stars and see the story of those Devon folk played out before your eyes on the exact spot where their ships landed in the New World.

I am on the Richard Caswell Memorial Commission; a member of the Carolina Writers, which I helped to organize; and the Tryon Palace Commission, which is restoring the mansion that Royal Governor Tryon built to show the strength and solidarity of the British Government.

I am interested in the restoration of Judge James Iredell's home in Edenton, an undertaking of the Tea Party chapter of the D.A.R. Again locally, I participate in the activities of the Colonial Dames of America and the Colonial Dames of the Seventeenth Century.

Our grandson "Jock" lives with us. He was graduated last year from Valley Forge Military Academy at Wayne, Pennsylvania, and is now a sophomore at the University of North Carolina in Chapel Hill.

Our second grandson, David, is a freshman at East Carolina College, Greenville, North Carolina. Granddaughter Carolista is old enough to think of her forthcoming debut in Raleigh. Our youngest grandson, Jim, twelve, has his living all planned: twenty-two years in the Navy or Coast Guard, then retire, and build a fishing pier at Nags Head on the Outer Banks! He wants to take my Bessie to cook for him, and Bessie has promised to do so if she can still creep around.

Life here at Bandon is tranquil. We have a half-mile of river frontage and a sandy beach within our vision. I can see the river from my bed. The first event of my day is to look out on the river, as I drink my morning coffee. It is quiet now, only a few oil or pulp wood barges move upriver to Virginia. But in spring, when shad frogs croak in the ditches, the river is alive with activity; the herring run brings millions of fish upriver to spawn. Fishing nets are spread all along our shores, and boats of fishermen dot the river.

Besides the river, our view includes masses of trees—pine, cedar, and oak flowing with Spanish moss. There are advantages to living in a Colonial house, and some disadvantages, as, for instance, when heavy old plaster comes hurtling down and repairs have to be made.

We are about fifteen miles from Edenton and twelve from Belvedere where my sister, Jean Chenoweth, and her husband, Lloyd, live in their seventeenth-century house on Perquimans River.

I stay here quietly on the plantation, working every day from nine until four, for, as every writer knows, writing a book is a full-time job.

Many people come to Bandon, hundreds, in fact, stop to see the house and the author. They come from all over the states, and Europe, too. These visits are arranged by the D.A.R., and the small fee they charge is used for the Iredell House furnishings.

We have many visitors of our own who come for weekends or longer. Our son, Stuart (Commander, U.S.N.), and his wife, Gladys, frequently motor down from the Brooklyn Navy Yard.

We love having guests. It is a break in our even life. But Bessie, our cook, likes it even more than we do. She loves company and she loves to cook. She remembers not only *all* the guests we have had but also the dishes she cooked for them. On those occasions, John, Bessie's brother, who is woodman in winter and gardener in summer, puts on a white coat and becomes our butler.

Both Bessie and John were born on the place, also their father and his father! In Senator Charles Johnson's time there were five hundred slaves on his large acreage at Bandon, then a thousand or more acres. (We have only sixty-three acres now.)

We have entertained many large groups of people—fifty or a hundred—it "makes no mind" to Bessie. She gathers in her sisters and her cousins and quickly we have a staff.

One of our friends, Nicol Smith, who lectures about far places in the world, said to me, "It is fantastic; you have thirty people for dinner, yet you don't do any work. I looked out in the kitchen and saw six in help. Do you know what that would cost you in New York? A fortune."

Bessie is famous for her hams from our smokehouse, her little biscuits, and her herring roe—the food of our region.

I love country living. I have lived too much in cities. I like the quiet. I like to see things growing. At present we have three dogs and six cats, all friendly playmates. The number varies from time to time, for they came to us out of nowhere. They hang about the fringes of the woods for awhile, then gradually come closer and closer. In no time they have joined the senior members of the little circle and are eating out of the same dish. We now have two Irish setters and a terrier. They greet everyone who gets out of a car and all but say, "Welcome to Bandon."

I opened this book with mention of a P.E.N. luncheon in San Francisco and the horror of my friends there when I announced that we were moving to Edenton, North Carolina, where, they said, "You will be out of the world." But no such dreadful thing happened to us. We come and we go, and sometimes the world comes to us. Under the influence of the authentic setting, my writing progressed, and now, fourteen years later, we are more than ever delighted with the "little town on Queen Anne's Creek."

That our pleasure is shared by others in the world of books was evident at a recent reading club meeting. Thirty ladies motored down from Virginia to visit Edenton's ancient buildings and joined us at Bandon. One of the ladies told me that she lived at "Bennett's Welcome," the home of the Cromwellian governor. I had visited there when I was writing the book of the same name.

Many other groups come to Bandon: book clubs, the D.A.R., Colonial Dames, the State Literary and Historical Society, State

Press Association, Boy Scouts, and classes from various schools.

The one I like best of all is a little club from the Edenton grade school, which comes every year. Their members change but they are always young and overflowing with energy. They romp in Parson Earle's old schoolhouse, play badminton and croquet, and swing. They drink "cokes" and eat quantities of cookies and then they "make their manners" and say: "Good-by, we have had a very nice time." They call themselves the Inglis Fletcher History Club, and I am flattered.

The days of "Pay, Pack, and Follow" are over, but I think of that far-off time with nostalgia. I am glad for the experience of having lived in many states in those mining camp days, for it led to a better understanding of America and our people.

We are settled at Bandon now. We have our Chowan River and our quiet days. We have the close companionship of our friends from nearby Edenton and visits from friends all over the world.

We have our garden, our peach orchard, and our smokehouse with Chowan County hams. We have Bessie Sessom to cook her good Southern cooking and John Sessom to keep our fireplaces bright.

We are not overly troubled by outside conflicts, for from this pleasant background of serene living, we know that, given time, the world will right itself and move forward, as the world has always done. It will be a good life for our children and our children's children, for the land remains, vital and ever-giving of its richness to those who cherish it.

Bibliography

BOOKS*

The White Leopard: A Tale of the African Bush. 304 pp. Indianapolis-New York, Bobbs-Merrill, 1931. Reissued 1948.
First American publication: August 25, 1931.
Length: 70,001 words.
Selection of Junior Literary Guild.
Published in British Empire, 1932. Reissued in England as *The Young Commissioner*, 1951.
Translation: Norway, 1950.

Red Jasmine: A Novel of Africa. 350 pp. Indianapolis-New York, Bobbs-Merrill, 1932.
First American publication: April 20, 1932.
Length: 95,000 words.
Published in England, 1933.
Translations: Sweden, 1942; Denmark, 1943; Norway, 1949.

Raleigh's Eden. 662 pp. Indianapolis-New York, Bobbs-Merrill, 1940.
First American publication: September 23, 1940.
Length: 257,320 words.

* For complete detail of this listing we are grateful to Richard Walser, author of *Inglis Fletcher of Bandon Plantation*, Chapel Hill, 1952.

Manuscript: First draft in storage in California; first galley at Cupola House, Edenton.

Special editions: North Carolina Edition, numbered 1-500 and signed by Governor Clyde R. Hoey of North Carolina and author; Albemarle Edition, numbered and signed by author; Old North State Edition, numbered and signed by author.

Selection of Book League of America; Dollar Book Club.

Popular edition: Sun Dial.

Published in England, 1941.

Translations: Sweden, 1942; Denmark, 1942; Belgium (French), 1947; Czechoslovakia, 1948; Norway, 1948.

Men of Albemarle. 566 pp. Indianapolis-New York, Bobbs-Merrill, 1942.

First American publication: October 19, 1942.

Length: 233,600 words.

Special edition: Albemarle Edition, numbered and signed by author.

Popular editions: Garden City, Doubleday.

Published in England, 1943.

Translations: Sweden, 1943; Denmark, 1944; Norway, 1946; Czechoslovakia, 1948.

Lusty Wind for Carolina. 509 pp. Indianapolis-New York, Bobbs-Merrill, 1944.

First American publication: October 16, 1944.

Length: 239,000 words.

Manuscript: Wilmington Public Library.

Special edition: Clarendon Edition, signed by author.

Selection of Dollar Book Club; Book League of America; Literary Guild.

Popular editions: Sun Dial; Blakiston.

Published in England, 1943.

Translations: Sweden, 1943; Denmark, 1946; Brazil (Portuguese), 1946; Spain, 1947; Norway, 1948; Czechoslovakia, 1948.

Toil of the Brave. 547 pp. Indianapolis-New York, Bobbs-Merrill, 1946.

First American publication: October 29, 1946.

Length: 204,970 words.

Manuscript: Publisher's typing at University of North Carolina Library.

Special editions: Kings Mountain Edition, signed by author; Projected Books, Inc. (for use of physically handicapped).
Selection of Fiction Book Club.
Popular edition: Armed Services Edition.
Story strip in 30 installments with illustrations by Frank Godwin, syndicated in newspapers by King Features, 1947. (Serial picture panels with condensed text.)
Published in England, 1948.
Translation: Sweden, 1948; Denmark, 1948; France, 1948; Czechoslovakia, 1948; Norway, 1948; Spain, 1950.

Roanoke Hundred. 492 pp. Indianapolis-New York, Bobbs-Merrill, 1948.
First American publication: October 18, 1948.
Length: 185,640 words.
Manuscript: First typescript at University of North Carolina Library.
Special editions: Carolina Edition, signed by author; 600 special book plates for use only for sales by Leggett & Davis Drug Store, Edenton.
Selection of Dollar Book Club.
Published in England, 1949.
Translations: Norway, 1948; Denmark, 1948; Sweden, 1950.

Bennett's Welcome. 451 pp. Indianapolis-New York, Bobbs-Merrill, 1950.
First American publication: October 6, 1950.
Length: 183,522 words.
Manuscript: Author's longhand of chapters 1, 2, and 5 at University of North Carolina Library.
Special edition: Cavalier Edition, signed by author.

Queen's Gift. 446 pp. Indianapolis-New York, Bobbs-Merrill, 1952.
First American publication: October 17, 1952.
Length: 182,336 words.
Special edition: Constitution Edition, signed by author.
Selection of Dollar Book Club.
Published in England, 1953.

The Scotswoman. 480 pp. Indianapolis-New York, Bobbs-Merrill, 1954.
First American publication: April 7, 1955.

Length: 195,360 words.
Selection of the Literary Guild.
Special edition: Flora Macdonald Edition, signed by author.
Published in England, 1955.

The Wind in the Forest. 448 pp. Indianapolis-New York, Bobbs-Merrill, 1957.
First American publication: October 31, 1956.
Length: 182,336 words.
Special edition: Alamance Edition, signed by author.
Published in England, 1958.
Best in Books. (Complete Book) Nelson Doubleday Inc.

Cormorants' Brood. In press.